SIX of SWORDS

ADVENTURES IN THE WORLD OF ALDEA

WRITING: Jaym Gates (*Storm Over Kamala*), Steven Jones (*The Night Market*), Kira Magrann (*A Wanton Curse*), Alejandro Melchor (*A Harvest of Masks*), Malcolm Sheppard (*The Sixth Beast*), Rebecca Wise (*Mistress of Gloamhale Manor*)

EDITING: Lynne Hardy   **DEVELOPMENT:** Steve Kenson   **PROOFREADING:** Steve Kenson & Evan Sass

ART DIRECTION AND GRAPHIC DESIGN: Hal Mangold

COVER ART: Nen Chang   **CARTOGRAPHY:** Phillip Lienau

INTERIOR ART: Olga Drebas, Claudia Ianniciello, David Keen, Priscilla Kim, Stephanie Pui-Mun Law, Johnny Morrow, Mirco Paganessi

PUBLISHER: Chris Pramas

GREEN RONIN STAFF: Joe Carriker, Crystal Frasier, Jaym Gates, Steve Kenson, Nicole Lindroos, Hal Mangold, Jack Norris, Chris Pramas, Donna Prior, Evan Sass, Marc Schmalz, Malcolm Sheppard, Owen K.C. Stephens, Dylan Templar, and Barry Wilson

GREEN RONIN PUBLISHING

GREEN RONIN PUBLISHING, LLC
3815 S. OTHELLO ST. SUITE 100,
#311 SEATTLE, WA 98118
WWW.GREENRONIN.COM
CUSTSERV@GREENRONIN.COM

age
adventure game engine

TABLE OF CONTENTS

INTRODUCTION

Welcome to the world of *Blue Rose Romantic Fantasy Roleplaying* and the stories of adventure you and your friends can tell here!

Six of Swords presents a set of six such adventures for *Blue Rose* heroes, starting from the beginning levels of the game and progressing to some high-level challenges. Each adventure spotlights a different area, different supporting cast, and different adversaries, but all are suitable for a group of Aldin envoys in service to the Sovereign and the Kingdom of the Blue Rose. The adventures also have notes on adapting them to different groups, as suits your own series.

The adventures in this book include ruined mansions, masquerade balls, vampiric curses, mysterious masks, sorcerous secrets, ghostly hauntings, lost loves, looming threats, and tragic quests where heroes are called upon to make the right choices.

THE ADVENTURES

The following is a short summary of the adventures found in this book.

THE MISTRESS OF GLOAMHALE MANOR

Levels 1–4. The envoys are summoned to a town on the outskirts of a newly drained lake, where conflict with the local swamp-dwellers has escalated, but the mysterious disappearances happening near the lake have more to do with the ruins of the ancient manor house uncovered by the receding waters, and the restless spirits dwelling therein. The envoys must investigate the mysteries of Gloamhale Manor and put to rest what dwells there.

THE SIXTH BEAST

Levels 1–4. A bandit army is preying upon villages belonging to an isolationist religious sect in Aldis. The envoys must investigate the mysterious bandits and their beast-masked leaders, and learn more about the sorcerous forces driving them, while navigating the challenges of feuding factions within a culture that wants little to do with outsiders. If they fail, a small scale war could be the result!

THE NIGHT MARKET

Levels 3–5. A coded message falls into the hands of the crown, offering the Sovereign's Finest the opportunity to infiltrate a secret "night market" trading in illicit—and often dangerous—goods and artifacts. The heroes venture into the murky depths of the Veran Marsh to find this criminal haven, posing as interested buyers, and looking to prevent the most dangerous wares from falling into the wrong hands.

A HARVEST OF MASKS

Levels 5–8. A chance encounter with a merry band of Roamers and strange happenings in a border village of Aldis plunge the heroes into a tales of secrets, truth—and consequences. Strange enchanted masks are taking over people in the area and transforming them into the darkest reflections of their heart's desire. Where are the masks coming from, and what is their true, sinister purpose?

STORMS OVER KAMALA

Levels 9–12. A witch from the Plains of Rezea is looking for a stalwart group of heroes to help free her clan's ancient ancestral wintering grounds from a curse. The heroes take a sea journey to Rezea and travel overland to reach the Kamala lands, confronting sea-serpents and mad elementals along the way, to eventually battle the evil that holds the wintering ground in its grip, and experiencing the sacrifice needed to clean the land.

A WANTON CURSE

Levels 12–15. The heroes are invited to a lavish masked ball on Gravihain Eve, but a pack of vampires crash the party, revealing a strange love tangle between the nobles of the neighboring castles, and the lost love who is now a thrall of a vampire lord! Who is telling the truth about the vampire's predations on the region, and can the heroes learn the necessary lore to find the blood-drinker's lair and end his threat once and for all while saving the vicitms of his wanton curse?

The first four adventures can be played as a series, progressing the heroes through several levels, possibly with some side adventures interspersed, while the last two are intended for fairly high-level *Blue Rose* heroes but offer options to scale them for lower levels.

SIX OF SWORDS

THE MISTRESS OF GLOAMHALE MANOR

The plains of Zea have never been particularly welcoming, but civilization requires space, and just over a year ago, it finally claimed the valley of Husqan. Shapers diverted a river and drained Lake Husqan, creating a crescent of fertile farmland arcing around a bog that was formerly the deepest part of the lake.

Intending to create a breadbasket in the barrens, Zea officials offered anyone willing to settle in the Husqan Valley free land and the hope of a better life. The settlers received the promised land and founded the town of Lakesheart, but continue to wait for the better life to manifest. The birth rate in the area is abnormally low and, to make matters worse, the community's precious few children are disappearing. Two days ago, Eric, the son of the town's most successful farmer, vanished. Several of the townsfolk have taken the matter into their own hands, but they are in need of aid.

INTRODUCTION

THE MANOR BECKONS

The Mistress of Gloamhale Manor is a *Blue Rose* adventure for a group of 4–6 heroes, levels 1–4, and can be adapted for higher level parties. It is advantageous for the group to have one or more characters with psychic arcana, but not essential. The adventure description presumes the characters are altruistic heroes in the service of Aldis and

its people (that is, members of the Sovereign's Finest), but the Narrator can modify the descriptions and events to suit mixed or other types of groups.

At its heart, the adventure revolves around a trek through a decrepit house deeply haunted by the evils of its past.

The adventurers first encounter a town plagued by kidnappings, as well as an obvious culprit: a mysterious swamp-dwelling people who live nearby. However, as the Sovereign's Finest investigate, they uncover the secretive tribe has suffered the same bizarre disappearances. The assumption of the text is that the characters come across the town and its troubles during their travels, making the adventure suitable for inserting in-between other stories, but characters can just as easily be assigned to investigate the recent goings-on in Lakesheart, if preferred.

Strange voices and clues lure the adventurers deeper and deeper into the swamp, where they discover the rotting remains of an ancient manor house. Upon entering, the heroes shrink into the bodies of children. The longer they spend within the manor's confines, the more their adult strengths drain away, and the more their childhood fears rise up to haunt them. They must uncover the dark secrets buried within the house, as well as determine which of the trapped spirits they should trust, aid, or destroy…

Each room holds a clue providing more information about the manor's history and the horrors committed there, leading up to a final encounter with the spirit of the manor's former owner. The Finest may attempt to battle their way to victory, or opt for a series of no-less-harrowing noncombat tests. The consequences of their actions may provide fodder for further stories if players enjoy the setting, or may simply give them something to think about once the adventure is over.

Note: As written, this adventure involves investigating and uncovering evidence of the non-sexual abuse and murder of a number of children. Narrators should consider issuing a trigger warning—or altering the story—for players who may be especially sensitive toward this kind of subject matter.

PART 1

THE VILLAGE

These scenes are designed to introduce characters to the basic plot elements and entice them to become involved in the mystery.

SCENE 1

A FOILED TRAP

ROLEPLAYING ENCOUNTER

To begin, read or paraphrase the following aloud to the players:

The rocky, uneven landscape around you lacks the majesty of some of the vistas you've discovered in your journeys. The boulder-strewn hills look like they're covered in the chipped and rotting teeth of a great beast, and spots of green are hard to find amid the overwhelming brown: brown rocks, brown dirt, brown weeds.

Several long days of travel have not brought any change in scenery. However, you all know monotony is no reason to let your guard down.

You spot an overturned wagon blocking the way ahead and immediately identify clumsily-hidden tripwires strung across the road in front of it.

If the heroes investigate, they notice six humans waiting in ambush. These aren't trained warriors, or even local guards. They're townsfolk and farmers, armed with farming implements and kitchen knives. They have abilities of 0, no significant focuses, and 15 Health each. All are more frightened by the heroes than anything else, though they try to hide it with a bluff of bravery.

Amos, the youngest of the group, has visibly shaking knees. His knuckles are white from clutching his shovel, and his voice cracks with youth when he speaks. He doesn't, however, back down.

The heroes may try to talk to him, or may question the leader of the group: a burly woman wielding the only real weapon—an antique sword. Her name is Griseld—"like the bear," as she introduces herself—and grizzled would,

indeed, be a fitting description for her. Her hair has faded to a tarnished copper streaked with gray, and her face is taut with worry. The sunlight catches a faint sheen of gray peach fuzz on her upper lip. Her authoritative bearing encourages respect.

Speaking with the townsfolk, the characters quickly discover the nature of their concerns: a number of children have disappeared without a trace from the nearby town of Lakesheart. The villagers have decided to take matters into their own hands. They created this trap, and others like it, in an attempt to stop travelers for questioning and identify any suspicious folk. A TN 9 Perception (Empathy) test determines if the would-be ambushers are being honest. If the test is successful, not only are the heroes convinced the townsfolk are telling the truth, but Amos also breaks down in sobs and begs the party for help: his sister was one of the first children to vanish, nearly a year ago.

If the heroes are reluctant to help, Griseld offers to pay them a reward for any information they can dig up. She makes a decent living as the town smith and amateur tattoo artist. Amos and the others offer to contribute as much as they can, though Amos expresses concern about hiring mercenaries, saying, "They don't care about us. If they're only doing it for money, how do we know we can trust them?" Griseld reminds him they have no other options and nothing, really, to lose.

If the characters attack their would-be ambushers immediately, the townsfolk drop their weapons and surrender at the first signs of real violence, throwing themselves upon the heroes' mercy and explaining the situation to them.

SCENE 2

ATTACK BY THE FEN

COMBAT ENCOUNTER

Griseld, Amos, and two other villagers escort you down the road to Lakesheart; the other two remain behind to keep watch at the ambush point. Griseld tries to arrange your escort in military formation, but they don't have the training to pull it off and end up just walking beside you in a clump.

The road descends, and the parched landscape to its right gives way to a swamp; always present around the water's margins, it became much larger with the draining of the lake. The ground there is hidden beneath the choking grasp of ferns and vines. However, while you can't see the earth beneath them, you can certainly smell it: mud and rot and stagnant water.

Clouds of midges swarm towards the moist caverns of your mouth and nose. The buzzing and clicking of larger and less-harmless insects creates a constant, numbing drone in the distance.

The Narrator should secretly roll a TN 13 Perception test for each of the characters at this point; the Hearing, Seeing, or Smelling focuses all apply. Success means they notice they're being followed by a number of **Fen warriors** in the swamp, and are not surprised when these warriors attack. A test result of 15 or more allows the character to estimate the number of warriors, catch sight or sound of weapons, and grants a +2 bonus when they roll for initiative. Failing the Perception test means they are not alerted to the presence of the attackers until the first spear is flung and the Fen warriors surprise them.

There is one Fen warrior for each hero, plus four additional warriors. Additionally, there is a **Fen shaman** with the assailants. (See the **Adversaries** section of this adventure for further details on both the Fen warriors and their shaman.)

Painted with mud and clothed in fronds, what rushes toward you out of the swamp at first looks more plant than person. However, their battle cries are decidedly humanoid…and bloodcurdling. Their yells waver and yodel at an uncomfortably high pitch. When one warrior pauses for breath, another has already taken up the cry, creating a constant barrage of sound.

The Fen warriors' cries have a distracting effect: players must succeed at a TN 11 Willpower (Self-Discipline) test each round or suffer a –1 penalty to all tests that round. If the sound is stopped or blocked out, the cries have no effect.

When half the Fen warriors have been defeated, the rest retreat into the swamp. Griseld insists the heroes should not pursue the attackers, but rather help get her people home safely. If the characters do not acquiesce, Amos mentions it will be night soon, and the heroes are likely to be sucked into the drowning mud should they stumble through the swamp in darkness.

The surviving townsfolk complain about the attack, and debate the fen dwellers having been responsible for the kidnappings all along. Some claim the tribe has always hated Lakesheart's proximity to the swamp, and theorize the kidnappings and attacks are an attempt to drive the town away.

If the adventurers refuse to go with Griseld and venture into the swamp regardless, proceed to **Part 2, Scene 1: The Fens Beckon.**

SCENE 3

LAKESHEART

EXPLORATION ENCOUNTER

The road angles away from the swamp, and you reach Lakesheart without further incident. It's small, but clearly growing: some of the buildings are so new, you can still smell the fresh paint. Fields sparsely dotted with farmhouses sweep out from the town's main street, soft lights shining through their open windows. Metal clangs against metal as several villagers work to repair an oddly-mangled plough outside the tavern.

Darkness hasn't yet fallen, but everything besides the tavern seems to be already shuttering up for the night. The few townsfolk on the street are either hurrying home or to the tavern. There's not a child to be seen anywhere.

If all four townsfolk make it back safely, Amos offers to let the heroes stay at the tavern for the night, free of charge. If any of them were at death's door and not revived, the characters must make their own arrangements.

Players may roll a general Perception test when their characters arrive in Lakesheart. Consult the accompanying table for what each roll reveals:

LAKESHEART	
TN	**OBSERVATIONS**
7	People seem nervous. No one really seems to smile or laugh.
9	Dozens of crows roost on the town's buildings. People curse at them and even throw things as they pass.
11	The iron arms of the plough the townsfolk are repairing have been deliberately bent into the shape of an odd symbol.
13	The symbol is unfamiliar, but looks tribal in nature.
15	The symbol looks like a protective ward or blessing of some kind.
17	You think you briefly hear the sound of a child crying.

Players who roll a test result of 17 or more may make an additional TN 13 Perception (Hearing) test. Success tells them the crying sound came from back down the road, towards the swamp; failure means the sound cannot be traced. Characters with a Communication score of 4 or greater automatically succeed at the test.

If the heroes investigate the sound further, they disturb a nest of sparrows, which quickly flutter away in the wind. Perhaps the sound was nothing more than a muted bird call.

The following information can be obtained freely if the adventurers ask around:

- The disappearances have occurred both at night and during the day, but the residents feel most vulnerable after dark—people are asleep and unaware when something strange happens.

- Crows and other birds eat the town's freshly-planted seeds before they can sprout. The soil is good, but because of this, harvests are poor.

- Townsfolk frequently find a variety of strange artifacts and fetishes hidden around the town and the surrounding fields; the plough is the latest example. The other charms have all been burned or destroyed. These discoveries do not seem to correspond with the disappearances.

- Younger settlers blame the fen dwellers for both the artifacts and the disappearances.

- Even before the lake was drained, local legends claimed its depths hid lost treasure. Older townsfolk believe draining the lake has upset whatever spirit was guarding the treasure, which is now seeking vengeance by stealing the children.

SCENE 4

LATE-NIGHT ENCOUNTER

ROLEPLAYING ENCOUNTER

This encounter occurs wherever the adventurers choose to spend the night. It may be in the tavern, at a campsite, or while they patrol the town. If they are asleep, the sound wakes them up.

You hear the muffled jingle of a bell or rattle. It sounds like someone is cupping a hand over the noisemaker in an attempt to keep it quiet.

No test is required to reveal the source of the noise—a ten year old girl hiding and giggling nearby: Chantria, or "Chant," as she prefers to be called. She heard the heroes were in town and wanted to see them for herself. She thinks she'll be an adventurer someday, because it seems like one of the only jobs where you get to throw things at people. She's really good at throwing things at people, especially her brother. She can almost always hit him, even if he's far away.

Chant wears a string of bells and rattles tied around her wrist. She usually wears such noisemakers around both wrists and both ankles, but couldn't get the knot undone on this one. Whenever they're not in school, all the town's children have the important job of scaring birds out of the fields by running around and being as noisy as possible. Lately, though, a lot of families haven't wanted to let their children wander the fields unsupervised. Chant's lucky; her aunt still lets her, but she has to check in with her a lot.

She is not afraid of being kidnapped and volunteers this information whether asked or not. The only thing she's afraid of is heights because she fell out of a hayloft once and broke her arm. She really hopes this fear won't stop her from becoming an adventurer—that would be the worst thing ever, if it did.

Chant asks each hero what they were most afraid of as children. Heroes should try to share a brief vignette of a time they faced a fear as a child. The vignette must take place when the adventurer was between the ages of seven and fifteen. The scene can be as short as a sentence, or may

WHAT ARE YOU AFRAID OF?

To make a random selection, roll 1d6 to select the column (1 or 2 for Column 1, 3 or 4 for Column 2, 5 or 6 for Column 3). Roll another 1d6 to select a result from that column.

CHILDHOOD FEARS

ROLL	COLUMN 1	COLUMN 2	COLUMN 3
1	Spiders/insects	Darkness	Being buried alive
2	Fire	Water	Knives/sharp objects
3	Heights	Flying/floating	Cramped spaces
4	Wild/loud animals*	Loud noises	Thunderstorms
5	Strangers	Death	Separation**
6	Masks	Blood	Snakes

*Can apply to a specific species, such as dogs or bears, or more generally to any particularly loud or uncontrolled animal.

**Separation from a loved one or specific object, such as special blanket or doll.

take a few minutes to tell. These stories become important once the group reaches Gloamhale Manor (**Part 3**), as the heroes may well have to face these fears once again as they explore the manor.

If players need help coming up with a childhood fear their character experienced, they may choose one from from the **Childhood Fears** table, above. This is also presented as a handout that can be found on page 132. Alternately, they may roll for a random fear.

DEALING WITH FEARS

Some characters may be reluctant to participate or refuse to share details of their past. Players can be given the option of simply describing their characters' thoughts as an internal flashback if they feel their characters would not share such information with the group. Alternately, playing the role of Chant, the Narrator can make up and relate a story of their choosing for characters that refuse to participate at all. Pick a young age, between six and eight, and have Chant lightly tease the adventurer about the fear. For example, "When you were seven, I bet you were so terrified of the dark that it made you wet your pants!" or "When you were eight, I bet your sister stuck a tarantula down your shirt and you've run away from spiders ever since!"

When the last story wraps up, Chant scampers off. If the heroes wish, they can accompany her to a nearby farmhouse and help her sneak back in through her bedroom window.

OPTIONAL SCENE

THE DAWNING DARK

COMBAT/EXPLORATION ENCOUNTER

This scene can help further establish the atmosphere of the town, and provide characters with a more concrete lead to pursue when investigating the disappearances. It can easily be removed if the players have already developed a plan on how to proceed, or if the adventure seems to be dragging. Read or paraphrase the following:

Morning dawns in a gray drizzle. Tendrils of mist hang above the ground like tattered curtains. The Lakesheart farmers have gathered in one field and begun tilling it together, their movements sluggish beneath warm layers of clothing. The other fields stand waiting.

The heroes should make a TN 10 Perception (Seeing) test to see if they can make out a Fen shaman in a distant field. If successful, they spot a figure in the middle of the field; it looks small—perhaps a child, or an adult crouching and skulking. The figure then takes off towards the swamp. A test result of 15 or more definitively reveals the figure as an adult sneaking through the fields, struggling to hide among the low crops.

The retreating figure is too far away for the heroes to catch up. The group can only follow, closing in as the person vanishes into the swamp. If the adventurers reach the edge of the swamp, they are met with a hail of blow darts. Two **Fen dartsmen** per hero hide at the swamp's margins, providing cover for the escaping shaman (see **Adversaries** in this adventure for the dartsmen's stats). The dartsmen do not retreat, but fight to the last to cover the shaman's flight.

If, rather than immediately giving chase, the heroes investigate the field, they find a strange charm partially surrounded by a ring of pebbles, as if the shaman wasn't finished with the arrangement when they noticed them. The symbol painted on the hide charm looks similar to the one twisted into the plough. With a successful TN 15 Intelligence (Religious Lore) test, characters realize it looks much more like a blessing than a curse. A failed test only reveals the materials the charm is made out of: ferns, vines, mud, and dried toad skin, all of which could be easily found in any swamp.

OPTIONAL SCENE

LOSING CHANT

ROLEPLAYING ENCOUNTER

If the adventurers seem uninterested in pursing the mysteries of the town, this scene can be an excellent motivator. It can also provide additional emotional "heft" to the adventure, or can be used if the heroes seem to particularly enjoy Chant's company. It's recommended to skip the scene if the players already assume Chant will disappear as soon as they meet her. Read or paraphrase the following:

A shrill scream pierces the morning chill. A woman staggers out onto a farmhouse porch. It is Chant's house, and the woman is screaming Chant's name.

The woman turns out to be Chant's aunt, Enit, who has looked after Chant and her brother since their parents died. Chant has vanished.

A successful TN 11 Perception (Seeing) test reveals Chant-sized footprints leading from her bedroom. Rhydan can make a TN 7 Perception (Smelling or Tracking) test to find and follow the tracks. The footprints lead back along the road the heroes came in on yesterday—toward the swamp.

Enit offers the heroes a reward if they can return the girl safely. It's a small hope chest of jewelry and embroidered linens—likely her life savings.

PART 2

THE SWAMP

In this portion of the adventure, the characters set out into the unknown… hopefully towards the missing children.

SCENE 1

THE FENS BECKON

ROLEPLAYING/COMBAT ENCOUNTER

The trek into the swamp isn't easy. The mud squelches as your boots sink into it with every step, then sucks at your feet when you pull them out. Vines curl toward you as you brush past them. Sometimes they manage to wrap around a finger or weapon handle, but snap when you pull away.

Fen charms dangle high in the trees, well-camouflaged at first, but obvious once you know what you're looking for. Each depicts two triangles: one with a stick figure crouched inside, like a tent, and one shaped like an arrow, pointing toward the next charm.

Players should make a TN 15 Perception (Seeing) test for their heroes. A success means they notice figures moving through the shadows in the brush. A test result of 17 or more reveals the fen dwellers moving to surround them do not have their weapons readied. Failure means the heroes continue squelching forward and are surprised when the Fen reveal themselves. Read or paraphrase the following:

A number of fen dwellers step out from the underbrush, completely surrounding your group. All click their tongues in an unsettling form of communication.

A particularly large warrior steps forward. Their gender is indeterminate, but they are heavily decorated in jewelry and wearing particularly ornate wooden armor.

"We do not wish to fight you," they say. "But you're near our camp. Let us escort you there so you may speak to the Mud Mother."

At a signal from the warrior, the Fen show you their empty hands, demonstrating they have their weapons stowed.

"We will not strike first."

The Fen are true to the warrior's word and do not attack first. If permitted, they peacefully escort the heroes to their camp. See **Scene 2: The Mud Mother**.

If attacked, the Fen do not fight back for one round, instead begging the adventurers to reconsider their use of violence. If any of the Fen are killed, the adventurers later discover only an empty encampment in the swamp (see **Optional Scene: The Fen Vanish**). They also discover a grisly tableau next time they return to Lakesheart (see **Optional Scene: Murder**).

Contrary to the rest of the swamp, the Fen encampment smells pleasantly of jasmine and smoked meat. Hammocks and tents dangle from the trees like cocoons. There is only one real structure: a rough-hewn hut on a platform between a grouping of four trees.

The largest warrior halts you at the door, then smears a thick arc of black mud across their forehead.

If the group has a leader, the warrior moves to anoint their forehead in a similar way, telling them "It is tradition," if asked or challenged. If the group has no leader, the warrior approaches the hero with the highest Communication score first. Any adventurers who do not submit to being anointed must remain outside the hut and are not offered any food. No Fen speak to these taboo-breakers except to hiss softly. Read or paraphrase the following:

Inside the hut, a small feast waits on a low table. The dishes are mostly unidentifiable, but smell appetizing.

The Mud Mother lounges on a cushion made of rotting plants. She is a thin, wiry woman, well past middle-age, but obviously heavily pregnant. Her skin is thunder-black, and it is impossible to tell where her hair ends and ropey lichen "extensions" begin.

"Greetings and merry meetings," she says. "We do not usually have the pleasure of receiving visitors. Of course, we do not usually consider visitors a pleasure, but the Sovereign's Finest are a different matter. You honor the Fen by visiting our central village and bathing your heads in the blood-mud. Now, allow me to honor you. Help yourselves to our delicacies. Let us share a table, and our hearts."

The Mud Mother speaks in an impeccably dignified manner. If adventurers comment on this, she grins widely, and says, *"Two hundred moons ago, one of my lovers taught me your tongue. I taught him a few tongues in return."*

She shares the following information, depending on how long the heroes speak with her:

- The Fen are not kidnapping Lakesheart's children.

- Fen children are disappearing as well.

- The charms her shamans have left around town are protective wards. They are simply trying to share their swamp arcana to spare the lives of Lakesheart's children.

- She apologizes for the attack on the party on the road. It was executed by a rogue band of Fen who are angry at the townsfolk for their suspicions and raids.

- The Fen have always lived around the swamp, and around the lake before that. Their legends indicate the lake did not always exist and was created to drown a cursed treasure.

The Mud Mother opens a covered bowl and offers some additional food to the adventurers: moist, gelatinous balls, each about the size of a pearl, which reek of fish and mucus. Any hero who tries to eat one must succeed at a TN 13 Constitution (Stamina) test or vomit. Succeed or fail, the Mud Mother laughs uproariously. "Pickled bodrougille eggs are an acquired taste," she says.

If any adventurer at least attempts to eat an egg, the Mud Mother explains no one "steals" the missing children. The swamp sings to them at night, and they wander towards the song. Sometimes, even adults can hear it, if they know to listen. It's said bodrougille eggs help, but only if they have been pickled for longer than six months. The batch the heroes just ate from has only been pickled for four.

If our protagonists ask for six-month pickled bodrougille eggs, the Mud Mother gladly provides some. In exchange, she requests a precious object. It does not have to have monetary value, but must have personal value to one of the adventurers. She does not share her eggs for free.

If given an item, the Mud Mother cradles it against her breast and says, *"A gift from the heart contains true power."*

If the characters decide to return to town before investigating any further, proceed to **Optional Scene: Preparing for Harvest**. If the group sets out for the depths of the swamp directly from the Fen encampment, see **Scene 3: A Child's Rhyme**.

OPTIONAL SCENE

THE FEN VANISH

EXPLORATION ENCOUNTER

This encounter is designed to be used only if the adventurers kill any of the Fen in **Scene 1** (after the Fen request peace). The party can attempt to track any Fen survivors through the swamp, in which case they will be led to this abandoned encampment. The protagonists may also continue to follow the Fen charms through the swamp; these, too, lead them to the abandoned encampment. Read or paraphrase the following:

The encampment is silent; even the usually raucous birds and insects appear to be holding their tongues. Wood crackles, but it's only a charred log in a still-smoldering fire pit.

Hammocks and tents dangle from the trees like discarded cocoons, and a few personal artifacts lay scattered and trampled into the mud, as if the tribe beat a hasty retreat. There is only one real structure: a rough-hewn hut on a platform between a grouping of four trees. It stands empty.

Those who succeed at a TN 14 Perception (Tracking) test can tell a group of Fen hiked off in the direction of Lakesheart. The rest seem to have headed deeper into the swamp. Heroes who fail this test realize the Fen seem to be deliberately hiding any signs of their passage.

Should the party continue exploring the swamp, proceed to **Scene 3: A Child's Rhyme**. If they return to Lakesheart, consider running one of the optional scenes: **Murder** or **Preparing for Harvest**.

OPTIONAL SCENE

MURDER

ROLEPLAYING ENCOUNTER

This encounter is designed to be used only if the characters kill any of the Fen in **Scene 1** (after the Fen request peace) and is intended to create a sense of consequence for the party's actions.

After **Scene 1**, the heroes may head deeper into the swamp before returning to town, or may head back to civilization immediately. If they return to town immediately after **Scene 1**, considering having them arrive in time to catch the tail end of the violence and perhaps even help chase the Fen attackers away. They should not, however, arrive in time to save the town from all loss of life. Read or paraphrase the following:

From a distance, the town looks still. This isn't necessarily odd, however; it's a farming community, and the villagers are often at work in the fields. But the fields look still, too.

As you get closer, you notice a mound in the road. Bodies. A half-dozen dead bodies. Their blood is cold and hardening. Some have obviously been dragged here from the fields or from inside houses. They are meant to be seen. The corpses are on display. Each has a Fen charm pinned to its chest with a crude dagger.

A message painted in mud on the side of the meeting hall reads: "Our score is settled."

The surviving villagers have locked themselves in their homes, grieving. A few have gathered at Griseld's shop and are debating what to do.

OPTIONAL SCENE

PREPARING FOR HARVEST

ROLEPLAYING ENCOUNTER

Should the adventurers decide to return to town at any time after meeting the Mud Mother (even after discovering the manor in **Part 3**), they find the anger, confusion, and suspicion brewing there finally boiling over. The villagers have had enough with being victimized; they believe the Fen are responsible for the kidnappings and intend to put a stop to it. Read or paraphrase the following:

> Shouts fill the air and dust fills the main street. Metal rasps as it's sharpened. A mob of armed villagers gathers outside the town meeting hall. They have the pitchforks; all they're missing are the torches.

The Sovereign's Finest return to Lakesheart and discover the townsfolk have decided to declare war on the Fen. If they have played the scene where Chant disappeared, the ringleader can be recognized as Chant's aunt, Enit. The villagers intend to march into the swamp tomorrow at sunrise.

The heroes may convince the mob not to attack the fen dwellers with a TN 17 Communication (Persuasion) test. A test result of 15 or 16 convinces the villagers to delay their attack for another week. Anything less simply sows additional confusion within the ranks, but does not prevent the attack from proceeding.

SCENE 3

A CHILD'S RHYME

EXPLORATION/COMBAT ENCOUNTER

Feel free to proceed directly to **Part 3, Scene 1: The Barren Plantation** to speed the adventure along, if required. If not, then read or paraphrase the following:

> Night falls in the swamp with the buzzing of a thousand mosquitoes. A colony of bats erupts from a tree just beyond the Fen encampment and flaps erratically into the darkening sky. As if on cue, fireflies illuminate and drift out from under ferns and bushes, bobbing through the humid air.

The heroes can make a TN 14 Perception (Hearing) test to see if they hear a child singing, thus giving the group some direction. Any adventurous souls who have eaten a six-month pickled bodrougille egg gain a +5 bonus on the test. Success leads the Sovereign's Finest through the swamp without incident, the singing waxing and waning mysteriously throughout the trek.

If they fail the test, however, the adventurers wander through the swamp and stumble into a strix nest (see **Strix Swarm** in *Blue Rose* **Chapter 12: Adversaries**), one for each hero. When the strix are defeated, the character with the highest Communication ability hears the child singing and guides the group in the right direction.

PART 3

THE MANOR

These scenes form the true meat of the adventure: the places where some degree of truth can finally be discovered, and where some actions can be taken to protect Lakesheart and the Fen—both from further kidnappings, and from each other.

SCENE 1

THE BARREN PLANTATION

EXPLORATION/ROLEPLAYING ENCOUNTER

> There's a road beneath your feet. An old one to be sure, almost hidden in the swampy tangle, but the ruts made by wagon wheels years and years ago are unmistakable. They are so deep, they even survived being underwater.
>
> The road descends steeply, then evens out. The weeping, skeletal trees before you open up into a clearing. A hulking, rotted manor stands in the center of the depression. It seems almost to glow—but surely that's just the moonlight. Vast, verdant lawns must have once surrounded the manor, but now the land is barren. Even the swamp plants avoid the place.
>
> The road splits and curves around a large fountain, long dry, then continues to the manor's front entrance. The broken fountain seems to have once depicted young children, frolicking in the spray. Now, the rusted remains of a wheelchair curl around one of its toppled statues like a cage. A few cracked marbles lie scattered among the pieces, their colors still bright and beautiful despite the damage.

The players should roll a TN 11 Willpower (Meditative or Self Discipline) test for their heroes. A success means they block out all other distractions and briefly hear the child crying one last time. A test result of 13 or more means they can pinpoint the mansion as the direction the cries are coming from. Failing the test means the adventurer is briefly overcome by the negative energies swirling around this place. They see a nightmarish woman's visage exploding from the manor's front doors and rushing towards them. It opens a fang-lined maw and howls. A test result of 7 or less makes the protagonist *positive* the ghostly face is about to consume them.

Of course, it doesn't. It was all in their mind. No one who succeeds on the test sees or even senses the apparition.

BLUE ROSE

SIX OF SWORDS

When possible, the Narrator should incorporate elements of the fear the hero described to Chant into their description of the snarling face. If they were terrified of spiders as a child, perhaps the face has spiders crawling out of its eyes and mouth. If they mentioned being afraid of the dark, perhaps the face seems to be the physical embodiment of darkness itself. The connection can be as obvious or as symbolic as the Narrator wishes.

The group may wish to investigate the rest of the manor's grounds. If they do, they find the area mostly as described above: barren except for occasional hunks of broken statuary. They also find the **Grotto** (see **Outside Grounds: Grotto**).

SCENE 2

HEROES REBORN

COMBAT/EXPLORATION ENCOUNTER

The manor's front door opens easily, revealing what was once a grand foyer. Water damage has buckled and rippled the parquet floor; some areas have rotted away entirely to reveal the rough-hewn subfloor beneath.

The smashed remains of a crystal chandelier lie in the center of the floor, partially blocking a sweeping staircase missing most of its center steps. The foyer is framed by five more doors—two on the left wall, three on the right—which stand closed. Mold and mildew have eaten into the wallpaper around them, weaving dark, lacy patterns on its surface.

When all the characters have entered, the front door swings shut behind them.

Thunder crashes outside, and lightning flickers wildly beyond the windows. The flashes seem to last longer than they should. When they finally end, everything seems somehow bigger.

You have all become children.

In fact, each of you seems to be the age you described while talking to Chant: between seven and fifteen years old.

If the adventurers leave the manor, they remain children even outside its doors. They can only reclaim their adult forms by: destroying the manor in some way, leaving the entire lakebed area, or seeking arcane aid from the Mud Mother. Refer to **Resolutions** for more details and consequences.

Every 1d3 hours spent within the manor's grounds alters the adventurer's ability scores (see the accompanying table). These scores return to their original state when the characters return to their normal ages (unless otherwise specified).

EXAMPLE

When the heroes first enter the manor, the Narrator rolls 1d3 and gets a 2. When two hours of in-game narrative time have passed, the Narrator announces the group feels weaker and explains how their stats have changed. The Narrator then rolls another 1d3 to find out when the next stat change will occur.

GLOAMHALE MANOR

THE BASEMENT

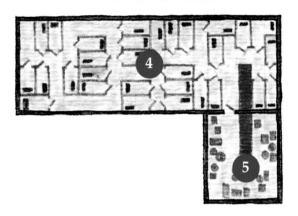

THE SECOND FLOOR

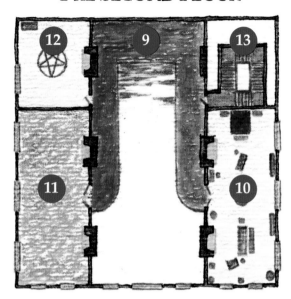

THE GROUND FLOOR

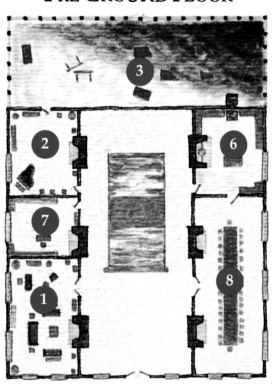

THE ATTIC

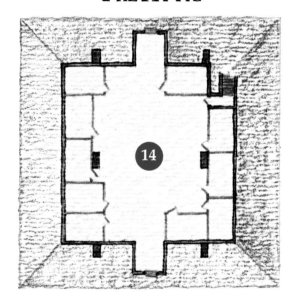

MAP KEY

1. Parlor
2. The Drawing Room
3. Conservatory
4. Cellar
5. Wine Cellar
6. Kitchen
7. Study
8. Dining Room
9. Upstairs Hallway
10. Mistress Bedroom
11. Master Bedroom
12. Playroom
13. Attic Stairway
14. Attic

The Mistress of Gloamhale Manor

About the Manor

The tragedies at Gloamhale left it a haunted place, deeply scarred on a psychic level. The furniture is always changing its arrangement, as if trying to find a way to fit together to make the place whole again.

No such arrangement exists.

If the heroes reenter a room they have been in before, the details should always be slightly different; there may be an extra window, the furniture has shifted positions, a closet suddenly exists, etc.

Characters that die in the mansion do not actually perish. Their bodies vanish, reappearing outside the mansion in the **Grotto**, with 1 Health (see **Outside Grounds: Grotto**).

Each 1d3 hours spent in the manor has the following effects:

Manor Effects		
Stat Change	**Bane**	**Boon**
First change	-1 all stats except Com, Dex	None
Second change	-1 all stats except Com, Dex	+1 Com
Third change	-1 all stats except Com	+1 Com
Fourth change	-1 all stats except Com	+1 Com
All subsequent	No change	No change

The five doors in the foyer lead to the **Parlor**, the **Drawing Room**, the **Dining Room**, the **Kitchen**, and the **Study**. Opening one of the four doors in the upstairs hallway leads to either: the **Master Bedroom**, the **Mistress Bedroom**, the **Playroom**, or the **Attic Stairs**. Detailed descriptions of each room can be found on the following pages.

Parlor

The overstuffed leather furniture here held up remarkably well underwater. Though stained and discolored, the chairs and couches mostly retain their shape. However, the taxidermy heads ringing the room were not so lucky.

Inexplicably, they seem to have rotted from the inside, leaving dark smudges and dripped stains on the walls beneath them. Most have decayed beyond recognition, though a few bear recognizable features such as antlers or tusks.

A roll-top desk hulks in front of a bank of windows, eerily silhouetted in the half-light from the storm outside. Words scrawled on the wall in mud read: "The innocent summon an evil fellow."

The hero with the lowest Communication score must make a TN 13 Willpower (Purity or Self Discipline) test. Failing the test forces the adventurer to attack the nearest female character for 1d3 rounds, aiming to kill her by any means necessary. After that time, or once the target is reduced to 0 Health, the rage ends.

If there are no female characters in the group, the child brutally smashes and stomps the porcelain bust of a woman on a side table with an all-encompassing rage.

The phrase scrawled on the wall, "The innocent summon an evil fellow," is the second line of the rhyme needed to begin the ritual in the **Playroom**.

This room has one door, which leads into the **Foyer**.

Drawing Room

The room is decrepit and dusty. Velvet curtains hang in tatters, and animals seem to have nested in the rotting silk upholstery. A grand piano stands in one corner. A multi-paned door, its glass long shattered, sags from its hinges. The pungent tang of animal urine bites at the stale air.

Heroes may make a TN 11 Perception (Smelling) test. A success means they detect the faint odor of a woman's perfume. A test result of 13 or more allows them to track the scent to the piano, while a result of 15 or more reveals specific notes in the perfume: dahlia, black cherry, and coriander. Failing the roll means they have just filled their lungs with the overpowering stench of acrid ammonia for nothing.

Investigating the piano shows it remains in working order, though horrifically out of tune. There are books strewn on the seat, practically dissolved by mud, but identifiable as early childhood primers. The book in the best condition has a name scrawled on the inside cover: "Heath." The corner of one page has been folded back. The marked page seems to show a poem of some kind, though the passage is heavily water-damaged and most of the words are missing. The poem reads as follows:

> By   rs   and   ow
>   in   on an   fe .
>   trap   , y hope   h,
> he   r of good   ab .
>   mar s   bove my   ,
>   May   wa me   bed.

The handout of the poem can be found on page 132. Pressing any of the piano keys triggers an illusion that lasts as long as the mournful note lingers in the air. The illusion shows the room in its original state, lushly decorated in deep blues and calming greens, with all its fabrics intact: velvets, silks, cloud-like cottons—anything pleasant to the touch.

17

If the piano lid is opened, a hag-like **shrieking specter** erupts out of it (see **Adversaries**). It is hideously obese, with groping, stick-like fingers. Two empty pink voids gape where its eyes should be, the muscles twitching inside as the creature casts about blankly. A successful TN 11 Intelligence (Arcane Lore) test reveals shrieking specters are difficult to kill, but easy to escape from. A test result of 13 or more reminds the heroes that light, especially sunlight, causes shrieking specters physical pain.

If the specter is not defeated, it continues to track the adventurers through the manor. Each time they enter a new room, roll 2d6. A total of 9 or more means the specter breaks into the room and attacks.

This room has two doors: one to the **Foyer**, and one to the **Conservatory**.

CONSERVATORY

Rain beats at the remains of the glass roof. An immense mound of mud left by the receding lake slopes from the far wall to the door to create a steeply slanted floor. The splintered remains of potting tables protrude from the mud like tombstones, oddly shadowless in the filtered light. All the windows are reinforced with close-set iron bars. They make the room look more like a prison than an elegant greenhouse.

Words scrawled on one wall in mud read: "The trap is laid, my hope is high."

A successful TN 9 Perception (Seeing) test reveals a beautiful, perfect grapefruit sitting half-buried in the mud. Its dimpled skin seems almost to glow. Characters with the Second Sight arcanum immediately notice the grapefruit is enchanted. Rhydan heroes may make a TN 9 Perception (Smelling) test; success determines the fruit doesn't smell right. A test result of 11 or more tells them it's made of wax.

If the grapefruit is touched or moved, a trap is triggered. A man's voice booms out from everywhere at once: *"We do not steal food!"* Whoever touched the fruit notices their palm turns bright red. It remains dyed this way for one hour. If it has not already been discovered, they also realize the fruit is made of wax.

The phrase scrawled on the wall, "The trap is laid, my hope is high," is the third line of the rhyme needed to begin the ritual in the **Playroom**.

This room has two doors: one to the **Drawing Room** and a trapdoor to the **Cellar**. A door to the outside is buried in the mud on the far wall and is, therefore, inaccessible.

CELLAR

A chorus of otherworldly voices cries and pleads and sings. The sounds are not loud, but take on an almost physical presence in your head, like a maggot burrowing through meat. The voices emanate from several petite, translucent creatures drifting around the room. Most do not possess anything resembling a mouth, and even those with mouths do not move their lips when they speak.

The entire cellar seems to have been divided into several dozen small closets with corridors in between. Rain leaks into the space from several broken windows high on the walls, each guarded by an iron grate. Odd pockets of shadow completely unrelated to the lighting or the windows hang throughout the room.

The Narrator should roll an opposed test of 3d6+1 vs. the Willpower (Psychic) ability of any characters with the Psychic Shield arcanum as soon as the heroes open the cellar door. Characters who win the test cannot hear the ghostly cries or voices, and do not need to make the following ability tests. Heroes who described a childhood fear relating to darkness, insects, being buried alive, or similar must succeed at a TN 11 Willpower (Courage) test each round they remain in the cellar. A failure means they flee to the top of the stairs and remain there until their next turn, when they can roll again. They must succeed at the roll to venture back down.

Each "closet" is more like a prison cell, containing a rusty bed frame and the remains of a bucket, as well as other odds and ends. Some contain bones; others contain makeshift toys. A successful TN 7 Intelligence (Healing) test shows the bones to be small and delicate. A test result of 9 or more reveals the bones have not fully fused and belong to children.

A total of two **haints** per hero haunt this space. Half of them are cloaked in pockets of arcane darkness. See the **Adversaries** section in this adventure for more about haints.

One haint seems to be having a tea party with several sticks clad in scraps of fabric, using shards of glass and porcelain as plates and cups. It wears an old teapot as a head and can be dispelled with a gift of a doll or a teacup. Several others are clad in newer-looking rags, reminiscent of the clothes worn in Lakesheart.

Narrators can populate the cellar with haints from the accompanying tables or can make up their own, which could be tied to the childhood fears described by the heroes. For example, a haint clutching a broken lantern that can be dispelled by the gift of a real lantern could represent a fear of the dark.

To choose random haints, roll 1d6. On an even-numbered roll, proceed to **Table 1**; on an odd-numbered roll, proceed to **Table 2**. Roll another 1d6 to select a haint from the table.

At the Narrator's discretion, haints can be dispelled by other gifts, especially handmade ones. If an adventurer takes off a sock and draws a face on it, it would work very well as a puppet, for example.

The haints follow the adventurers out of the room. Most of the haints keep their distance, but some try to hug any protagonist they perceive as doing or saying something particularly kind. They do not attack unless they are attacked. (Haints cannot "turn off" their passive effects, however. These should not be considered "attacks.") The haints flee back to the cellar if the heroes lead them near the shrieking specter.

		HAINT TABLE 1	
d6 Roll	**Head**	**Holding**	**Desired Gift**
1	Porcelain doll arm	A broken or makeshift doll	Porcelain doll
2	Animal skull	Decaying squirrel corpse	Stuffed animal
3	Wad of rags	A few squares from a quilt	A quilt, blanket, or cloak
4	Wooden spoon	A broken plate with mud patties	Actual or toy cookware
5	Doll or puppet's head	A scrap of a cloth like a puppet	A puppet
6	Battered helmet	A stick sharpened like a sword	Tin soldiers

		HAINT TABLE 2	
d6 Roll	**Head**	**Holding**	**Desired Gift**
1	Rotting ball of paper	The cover of a book with no pages	A book
2	Hobby horse head	A stick it pretends to ride	Rocking horse or hobby horse
3	Wad of rags	Makeshift handkerchief doll	A ragdoll
4	Small painting	A stick it draws in the mud with	A paint set or drawing set
5	Dried gourd	A human skull it kicks around	A ball
6	Animal skull	A leash dragging a dead rat	Stuffed animal or wheeled toy

This room has a trapdoor up to the **Conservatory** and a door to the **Wine Cellar**.

Wine Cellar

As soon as you open the door, the whispers are impossible to ignore. They alternately sound like quiet sobs, distant laughter, and plaintive voices.

A sickly sweet scent overpowers the claustrophobic space. The low ceilings hang over a few decaying kegs, as well as several cage-like structures, half-sunken into the dirt floor. One corner of the room is shrouded entirely in darkness. No light penetrates it.

Words scrawled in mud on one wall read: "When nightmares circle 'bove my head."

Investigating the cages reveals bones half-buried in the dirt. A successful TN 7 Intelligence (Healing) test shows the bones to be small and delicate. Characters who score 9 or more discover the bones have not fully fused and belong to children.

A marble rolls out of the darkness toward the hero with the highest Constitution. The marble is non-arcane. If anyone rolls the marble back into the darkness, the darkness grows marginally brighter, and the marble rolls back out. Rolling the marble back into the darkness a total of four times causes the darkness to disappear completely, revealing a haint: the marble haint. (The darkness can also be dispelled by Light Shaping.) See **Adversaries** for more details on haints.

If any adventurer picks up the marble and holds it for more than a few seconds, the darkness rushes forward and envelops them. The darkness has a five-foot radius centered on the haint inside, which attempts to bite them. It attacks only until the marble is dropped; it then retrieves its toy and hurries away with it back to its corner.

Characters may also ignore the marble and attempt to enter the darkness. In this case, the darkness darts away from them, towards the marble. The haint hiding in the darkness rolls the marble back at the heroes again, trying to get them to play with it.

The haint attacks only if it feels its marble is being threatened or stolen. Otherwise, it simply tries to play, and continues following the group with this purpose in mind once it spots them. The haint flees if the heroes lead it near the shrieking specter.

The marble haint wears a rotting taxidermy trophy as a head, with gleaming glass eyes. It requires a gift of a marble or makeshift ball in order to be dispelled.

The phrase scrawled on the wall, "When nightmares circle 'bove my head," is the fifth line of the rhyme needed to begin the ritual in the **Playroom**.

This room has two doors: one to the **Cellar** and a trapdoor up to the **Kitchen** via a rickety set of stairs.

Kitchen

The reek of rotten food hangs thick in the air, though surely the last food here would have decayed long ago. Rust and dead coral cling to the remains of the oven and cooking pots. A wasteland of broken crockery covers the floor and crunches beneath your boots. A bulky knife block stands on the counter, prickling with moldy handles.

Heroes who described a childhood fear relating to fire, knives or other sharp objects, or the like must succeed at a TN 11 Willpower (Courage) test each round they remain in the kitchen. A failure means they flee to the door and remain pressed against it until their next turn, when they can roll again. They must succeed at the test to venture away from the door.

A successful TN 13 Perception (Seeing) test alerts the heroes to various objects in the kitchen moving on their own. Some are sliding slowly across the counter, while others are simply shuddering in place. A test result of 15 or more shows the objects are moving *towards* the adventurers. Failure on this test means the character is surprised when the objects attack. See **Poltergeist Whirlwind** in the **Adversaries** section of the adventure for further details.

If any cupboards are opened, a **rat swarm** hiding within attacks, surprising the group (see *Blue Rose* **Chapter 12: Adversaries**).

This room has three doors: one to the **Foyer,** one to the **Dining Room,** and a trapdoor down to the **Wine Cellar**.

Study

The room looks sumptuous and perfect, undamaged by water or time. Packed bookshelves line the walls; the wood-paneled ceiling hangs low, giving the room a cozy, dark feel. Papers and folders lie in neat piles on the desk, some stacked a foot high.

The room offers a wealth of information with a Perception (Searching) test:

THE STUDY	
TN	**FACTS**
7	Despite their outward organization, many of the papers seem to contain the ravings of a madman and are near-indecipherable. Some are stamped "Gloamhale Sanatorium."
9	One folder contains a treatise entitled "Treatment of Infected Children." Another contains a paper on "Infections of Childhood." The author of each is listed as Jaymes E. R. Gloamhale.
11	The books on the shelves have titles such as *Cure Through Control: The Curative Effects of Fasting; Solitary Salvation: Hermetical Healing;* and *The Isolated Fast: New Ideas on Curing Disease.*
13	Cream-colored envelopes contain beautiful, effusive love letters from Jaymes to someone named Erila.
15	Medical files list patients' ages from infancy to mid-teens. They describe symptoms such as dysentery, boils, pox, excessive melancholy, hysteria, and wild arcana. The diagnosis is always "an imbalance of humors," "a coagulation of toxins," or similar non-scholarly rubbish.
17	Treatment journals seem almost exclusively focused on curing a range of diseases and conditions through isolation and fasting. See the "Sample Diet" described in **Handout: Meal Diary,** which can be found on page 132. (Narrators should consider printing a copy of this handout for the players to read.)

This room has one door, out to the **Foyer**.

Dining Room

The room is opulent and pristine—a perfect recreation of what it was before being flooded. The gleaming oak table can seat several dozen people, and is laden with enough fine food for a small army. A hundred scents tempt your nostrils: roast venison, honey-oat biscuits, spicy duck sausage, garlic roasted potatoes, elderberry jam…and, somehow, your very favorite childhood dish.

Each player should state what their character's favorite childhood food was. Even if it was a delicacy only found in a certain region, or only prepared from a grandmother's secret recipe, it is there, on the table, begging to be eaten. Each food looks and smells exactly the way they remember.

The heroes should make a TN 12 Willpower (Self-Discipline) test to see whether or not they can resist eating the food. Success means they sense something is wrong and do not indulge. A test result of 15 or more means they briefly see through the illusion, perceiving the room in its ancient, water-damaged state, the table covered in spiders' webs, rotting lake weeds, and wooly mildew.

Any adventurer who fails the test dives into the food, stuffing themselves with great handfuls. The more they manage to eat, the hungrier they become. Their stomachs growl ferociously, and yet they cannot stop. Surely if they just consume one more bite, they will start to feel satiated…

Other characters may try to pull them away, but they are determined to get back to the food. After an initial bite, they are willing to do anything to get another. (Note that, as-written, nothing is actually intended to be consumed. The food is imaginary, and the characters eat only air. However, Narrators wishing to play up the disgust factor may choose to have them actually consume the spiders' webs, lake weeds, and/or mildew.)

Adventurers who succeeded on the Willpower test may make a TN 10 Perception (Seeing) test. A success means they spot a small, silver bell at the head of the table. If they ring it, the illusion ends immediately. Otherwise, the illusion ends only when each hero has consumed the entire plate of his favorite childhood food. (The characters hear the bell ring when the illusion ends even if no one in their party has rung it.)

A small bell rings, sharp and piercing. Immediately, the illusion falls away and you see the room for what it truly is: damaged and rotting, everything covered in dusty mold and cobwebs. Only two places seem to be set, at opposite ends of the table.

All characters who "ate" any of the food on the table must subtract one from all further Willpower tests while inside the manor.

If the heroes look down, they see ghostly hands reaching up through the floor, pawing and clawing desperately toward the table. Each can only stretch a few inches, and none can reach.

The Dining Room has two doors, one to the **Foyer** and one to the **Kitchen**.

If the adventurers return to this room later on in their "stay" in the manor, anyone who ate the food hears their stomachs growl. However, all the heroes view the room the second time in its actual state; they do not see the illusion of the feast again.

Upstairs Hallway

Plush, burgundy carpet lines the hall, which is lit warmly by a copious number of ornate, glowing sconces. Paintings depict pastoral picnics and still lifes of fruit and flowers. It looks beautiful, except for directly in front of one of its four doors.

The illusion of grandeur seems to have worn away in this area. The wood here is gray and buckled, and the wallpaper around the doorframe peels away like a snake's skin. A jumble of broken furniture barricades the door, which has had a word scrawled on its surface in a dark red that might be paint, mud, or blood: "TRAITOR."

The furniture is heavy and difficult to move. In all, it takes the heroes about ten minutes to clear a path to the door. Opening the door reveals the **Mistress Bedroom**.

The three other doors lead to the **Master Bedroom**, **Playroom**, and **Attic Stairs**.

Mistress Bedroom

The room is breathtakingly beautiful, with sumptuous, velvet wallpaper, gilded furniture, and gleaming crown molding. A silk canopy drapes the bed like a tent fit for a princess. Vases of dahlias perfume the air, and more flowers lie heaped in the center of the bed.

A vanity table beside the door sports countless tiny vials and pots of cosmetics and beauty products. The mirror above it is the only area where the illusion of perfection is broken: the surface is dusty and cobwebbed.

Looking in the mirror reveals the room in its true state: destroyed, decaying, and water-damaged, with a long-abandoned rat's nest in a pile of dried lake weeds in the center of the bed. Looking into the mirror makes the room smell like rot and animal dung. The mirror reveals a phrase scrawled in mud on the wall (and readable in the reflection): "The power of good may yet abide."

The female character in the group with the least ability with arcana feels a psychic presence probing her mind. If there are no female characters, or if they all have the Psychic Shield arcanum, this occurs to a male party member lacking Psychic Shield.

The affected hero can sense the presence trying to possess their mind. A cacophony of sobbing, shrieking, and whispers echoes between their ears. A successful TN 7 Perception (Psychic) test allows the hero to pick out certain words and desperate phrases from the whispers: "Please," "I can help," "Listen," "Lend me your will," "I

21

Erila Qinrel

Erila met Jaymes Gloamhale when she was a Jarzoni orphan and he a young healer who visited the orphanage where she lived. When she was old enough to leave, he offered her a job at his sanatorium. She helped tend the sick children there, acting as nurse and teacher. Grieving families brought more sick children to their door, desperate for help.

Despite their best efforts, tombstones bloomed like flowers in the backyard. Erila gradually realized Jaymes was not healing, but hurting. Sick children arrived, then only got worse. She snuck them food and medicine; Gloamhale didn't know. He fell in love with her; she didn't know. Cradling another dying child, she decided to leave. Jaymes didn't want her to go; he wanted to marry her, but she was engaged to a Jarzoni man in the village.

Gloamhale flew into a rage. He lost all control. He lost physical form. It was as though he became a being made of pure fury and possessiveness. He melted into the very floor. Erila tried to flee. Doors flew shut in front of her, and furniture moved to block her path. The house itself turned against her. He had become the house.

He imagined her to have transformed into some kind of beast. He tracked her down like one of the animals in the parlor. He slaughtered her. He slaughtered the remaining children. The house was discovered. There was horror. The house was flooded. It lay dormant, but not dead.

The water receded. The ghosts grew restless. They cried out. They cried out for love, for companionship. They cried out to be remembered. They cried out, and other children came. They wasted away among the dead. The cycle continues, and there is no peace.

Other facts:

- Erila despises being a ghost and being trapped in this house. The casual use of something as dangerous as arcana goes against everything she believes in as a Jarzoni, and it is torturous to feel condemned to spending an eternity trapped in a house so full of wild, unrestrained forces. She hates even having to use it for the purpose of this communication.

- Whenever a party member uses arcana, Erila forces the possessed hero to say something to the effect of, "May Leonoth have mercy on our souls," "Leonoth forgive me/him/her," "May Leonoth smite the Shadow lurking in our hearts," or similar.

- When alive, Erila possessed some natural arcane talent, although she tried to hide it and stifle it. She (incorrectly) blames her lack of control as a child for the accident that led to the death of her parents.

- If the possessed hero enters the playroom, Erila can explain Jaymes' thoughts on playtime. It was considered dangerously stimulating for sick children (though useful as a motivator) and severely restricted. Toys were kept under lock and key most of the time for the children's safety. Erila may admit she saw logic in this at first and regrets being so blinded by Jaymes' authority and charm.

- Erila knows the haints are responsible for the symbol on the floor of the playroom. It was created in a time when the haints retained more of their former selves. Some of the children at the sanatorium were "corrupted" by "sorcery" and had hoped to accomplish something by creating the symbol. She does not know what their intent was and tried to distance herself from this activity.

- She does not know how her spirit can be freed from this place.

am not the monster," "The pain is too great." A test result of 13 or more indicates the source of the whispers has pure motives and is not attempting to deceive.

The character must choose to either accept the possession or resist it. Accepting the possession allows the spirit to volunteer information as well as answer questions, but the possessed hero must subtract 2 from all Intelligence tests and 3 from Intelligence (Arcane Lore) tests. Resistance requires a successful TN 15 Willpower (Self-Discipline) test. Failing to resist the possession only allows the spirit to answer direct questions and provide limited information each time it speaks, but only requires the character to subtract 1 from all Intelligence tests. Successfully resisting the possession causes all the bottles on the vanity table to explode in a harmless shower of shards and triggers a heart-wrenching shriek of "Nooooooo!"

which reverberates throughout the room (audible to all present).

If the possession is successful, the spirit of a Jarzoni woman named Erila Qinrel now inhabits the adventurer's mind. She is able to share any of the facts listed in the **Erila Qinrel** sidebar presented above. This information is also presented in handout form on page 133. (The Narrator should consider printing this out ahead of time to hand to the possessed player, allowing the player to speak for Erila whenever possible.) Erila cannot force the character to take any action other than speaking.

In addition:

- A successful TN 11 Intelligence (Cultural, Historical, or Religious Lore) test leads adventurers to conclude freeing Erila's spirit requires dispelling the spirits of all the haints and destroying the house.

- Gloamhale—both the house itself and the spirit of Jaymes—remain furious with Erila for spurning him. She never appreciated him the way she should. She never appreciated all he did for her, a lowly orphan. Whenever the possessed protagonist enters a room in the manor, furniture flings itself at them. It requires a successful TN 7 Dexterity (Acrobatics) test or a successful TN 9 Strength (Jumping or Might) test to avoid taking 1 point of damage from this furniture.

- The shrieking specter is the embodiment of how Gloamhale has come to view Erila. However, as long as her spirit inhabits one of the characters, the specter can no longer track them.

- If the possessed hero is reduced to 0 Health and transported outside of the manor to the Grotto, the possession ends. Erila's spirit cannot leave the confines of the manor.

- The possessed hero can force Erila out of their mind with a successful TN 9 Willpower (Self-Discipline) or Psychic Shield test.

- The phrase scrawled in mud on the wall, "The power of good may yet abide," is the fourth line of the rhyme needed to begin the ritual in the **Playroom**.

This room has one door, which leads to the **Upstairs Hallway**.

Master Bedroom

No illusion of grandeur haunts this room. The place has been utterly destroyed. All the furniture is in splinters, and mud—or worse—seems to have been flung and smeared over every wall. Every page has been ripped out of the books.

However, despite the destruction, the room also seems to be some sort of focus of the manor's power. All of the slivered furniture and torn paper hang suspended in the air, drifting around the room. It looks like a floating ocean of debris, though there is no water present.

Words scrawled in mud on one wall read: "By the stars above and the star below."

A **poltergeist whirlwind** (see **Adversaries**) attacks the group. It focuses its initial attack on any character currently possessed by Erila.

If any haints are still following the group, they refuse to enter this room and remain in the hall outside, weeping.

A successful TN 9 Perception (Seeing) test reveals an ornate key whirling and twinkling amid the debris. It can be snatched out of mid-air with a successful TN 7 Dexterity (Legerdemain or Initiative) test. Once captured, it loses its animation and can no longer fly.

The phrase scrawled on the wall, *"By the stars above and the star below,"* is the first line of the rhyme needed to begin the ritual in the **Playroom**.

This room has one door, which leads to the **Upstairs Hallway**.

Playroom

Sunlight filters through the linen curtains and bathes the room in a warm, orange glow. It seems the rain has ceased. Cozy pastel hues adorn the walls, decorated with lovely paintings of ducks, puppies, kittens, and baby animals having picnics. There is no sign of rot or water damage anywhere, but the room is largely empty.

A large padlock dangles from a closet door in the corner. Similar padlocks hang from several toy chests. A ten-foot pentagram has been scrawled in the center of the empty floor, scratched into the wood in places and painted on with mud in others. Half-burned candles stand spaced around the perimeter.

The padlocks require the key from the **Master Bedroom** to open. They can also be opened with a successful TN 13 Dexterity (Lock Picking) test or broken open by inflicting a total of 18 damage to each lock. The closet contains larger toys, such as rocking horses, hobby horses, tricycles, a puppet theater with puppets, and wheeled wooden animals (some large enough to be ridden; smaller ones are pulled with string like a leash). The toy chests contain dolls, stuffed animals, tin soldiers, painting sets, balls, marbles, and toy cookware; virtually everything needed to appease the haints in the manor.

The pentagram on the floor is surrounded by five candles and looks like it was drawn by children…or child-like ghosts. The pentagram is obviously meant to be an arcane circle.

A successful TN 9 Intelligence (Arcane Lore) test reveals the symbol is used in summoning and banishment rites. A test result of 11 or more reveals details on starting the ritual (see **Scene 3: Playroom Ritual**). If no adventurers roll an 11 or better, anyone with an Intelligence focus in Arcane Lore, Cultural Lore, Historical Lore, Religious Lore, Research, Shaping, or Sorcery Lore may spend 1d3 hours piecing together the details. Proceed directly to **Scene 3: Playroom Ritual** if the group wishes to start the ritual.

This room has two doors: one to a closet and one to the **Upstairs Hallway**.

Attic Stairs

A narrow stairwell leads up to the **Attic**. Adventurers who described a childhood fear of heights, flying, cramped spaces, or similar must succeed at a TN 11 Willpower (Courage) test to climb the stairs, or they remain in the **Upstairs Hallway**. They may re-roll the test each round.

The stairs have two doors: one at the top which opens into the **Attic**, and one at the bottom which opens onto the **Upstairs Hallway**.

Attic

The soft sounds of crying and singing waft through the air, along with a number of dust motes, highlighted in beams of sunlight from the two windows. The space has been divided into a number of small closets, or cells.

Words scrawled in mud on one wall read: "May this song wake me in my bed."

Each "closet" is more like a prison cell, containing a rusty bed frame and the remains of a bucket, as well as other odds and ends. Some contain bones; others contain makeshift toys. An Intelligence (Healing) test, TN 7, shows the bones to be small and delicate. Characters that score 9 or more discover the bones have not fully fused and belong to children.

Two living children huddle in a corner, quaking with terror. Both are painfully thin and malnourished. One, Eric, is wearing a simple linen tunic and breeches. Bells dangle from a bracelet around his wrist. The other child, Bamala, is naked except for a loincloth woven of palm fronds. Her hair is elaborately beaded. Both obey any command given to them by the adventurers.

They are too weak to help in fights unless they are healed or given some food. In this case, Bamala can do 1d3 damage with her slingshot. Eric can deal 1d3 damage with a sharpened stick he uses like a spear.

The phrase scrawled on the wall, "May this song wake me in my bed," is the sixth line of the rhyme needed to begin the ritual in the **Playroom**.

This room has one door which leads to the **Attic Stairs**.

Outside Grounds

Grotto

If a hero is reduced to 0 Health inside the manor, their body immediately disappears, only to reappear in the **Grotto**. They awaken to find themselves still in child-form, but stabilized at 1 Health.

Rain mists down, softening the view of the back of the manor. The building looks less foreboding at this distance… or it would, if not for the tiny, crumbling tombstones dotting the view.

A shallow, manmade cave, each rock meticulously placed, shelters you from the weather. A statue once stood in the center, but the face has been gouged off and the arms removed. While the ground between here and the manor is just as barren as in front of the building, a thick cloak of ivy curls over the grotto. Lush strands of leaves and moss dangle over the opening.

The first character to appear in the grotto finds Chant kneeling inside. She wanted to be an adventurer and prove she's brave, so she snuck out at night to try and find the other children. She ended up at the manor, but hasn't yet worked up the nerve to go inside.

The hero may invite her to go with them into the manor, or instruct her to remain in the safety of the grotto. She obeys either way.

In combat, she throws rocks at enemies with a +0 bonus to the attack roll, doing 1d3 damage on a hit. She only helps with the ritual in the playroom if an adventurer falls unconscious, stepping in to take their place.

Protagonists who examine any of the tombstones find they do, indeed, belong to children, none older than teenagers, according to the birth and death dates.

Scene 3

Playroom Ritual

Roleplaying/Combat Encounter

The details of the ritual are as follows:

* The ritual summons the spirit of Jaymes Gloamhale and traps him in the center of the pentagram. Successfully completing the ritual exorcises this evil from the mansion and banishes him to another realm.

* The ritual is an advanced test with a success threshold of 12 + the number of characters in your group (see *Blue Rose* **Chapter 10, Advanced Tests**). For example, a four-person party has a success threshold of 16 (12+4) and a six-person party has a success threshold of 18 (12+6).

* The protagonists must perform three ritual tasks to generate Drama Dice toward the success threshold: keeping the candles lit (a TN 11 Constitution (Stamina) test), reciting the ritual poem (a TN 11 Willpower (Self-Discipline) test), and preventing Gloamhale from escaping (a TN 11 Intelligence (Shaping) test).

* Each of the three tasks must be performed at least once. For example, heroes cannot simply roll the TN 11 Constitution test over and over until the success threshold is reached; they must also roll the Willpower and Intelligence tests at least once each.

* Any party members who ate six-month pickled bodrougille eggs earlier can succeed on a 10 for any test. This ability can only be used once per adventurer.

* Gloamhale's spirit should be considered a hazard (see *Blue Rose* **Chapter 10, Handling Hazards**). Each time an adventurer rolls a test, Gloamhale attempts to inflict 2d6 psychic damage on them. If the test is successful, they take only half of this damage. If the test is a failure, they suffer the full damage.

If any haints have been dispelled (not defeated), they return during the ritual as translucent children made of golden light. A cloud-like portal opens in front of a window, and the spirits pour inside like sunshine. They don't seem to see Gloamhale, but focus exclusively on the adventurers, beaming up at them, waving cheerfully at them, and murmuring softly. They repeatedly say things like "Thank you," "Thanks for helping me," "I wanna try! Let me try!" and "Can I help you?" Each hero can ask the haints once for help. The haint can either negate half the damage the character is about to receive, or allow the character to succeed on a 10 for a test.

The ritual poem is as follows:

> By the stars above and the star below
> The innocent summon an evil fellow.
> The trap is laid, my hope is high,
> The power of good may yet abide.
> When nightmares circle 'bove my head,
> May this song wake me in my bed.

The poem is a round, so the chant can start with any line, repeating over and over. Once the success threshold is reached, the ritual ends.

Gloamhale begins to laugh. His ghostly image hardens into what looks like a glass statue. The statue fractures, then explodes into a dozen glowing wisps of pure energy. One brilliant, flickering orb floats up to each of you and hovers in front of your face.
They absolutely radiate power.

The Narrator should explain not all of the power in each orb is evil. Just as all beings have some balance of light and dark within them, so does the arcana here. The Narrator should then address each player individually, describing what is on offer.

If the character spreads their arms and takes a deep breath, the glowing wisp will enter their being and permanently imbue them with power. This should sound as tempting as possible: intelligence-based characters might be offered some of the wisdom of the ages, or a piece of lore they've been searching for their entire lives. Strength-based characters may be offered the might of a thousand ancestors. Fighters could be offered all the expertise of a legendary master in the weapon of their choice, etc. The Narrator should tailor a specific temptation for each character, trying to incorporate some element of the hero's personality, backstory, or desires. Mechanically, the character receives a permanent +1 bonus to the ability the Narrator has described.

No matter what players choose to roll in order to discover any potential consequences of accepting the orb into their characters' beings—or how high their test result is— they can't get any sense of what might be in store if they do. No *obvious* repercussions exist, though only a fool would ever believe there aren't any. Players must decide whether or not their character would believe the known benefit outweighs the unknown, and possibly not insignificant, risk.

Any characters who decide to welcome a wisp into their beings find later on that a minority of non-player characters (NPCs) they meet are less friendly, more hostile, and/or afraid of them. Some NPCs may refuse to speak to

the adventurer at all and physically avoid them when possible.

This is especially true of children. Chant, Eric, and Bamala do not voluntarily speak to any heroes who imbues themselves with Gloamhale's arcana and try to keep a reasonable physical distance from them. They cannot explain why they feel this way.

At the Narrator's discretion, the player must make a TN 15 Communication (Leadership or Persuasion) test if they want to improve certain NPCs' attitudes towards their character.

Any unabsorbed orbs simply dissolve away. The house itself no longer reeks of evil, and the air feels somehow lighter. Jaymes Gloamhale's twisted spirit has been entirely banished and can never return to this realm. The shrieking specter and any remaining poltergeists or rat swarms vanish without a trace. Erila and any undispelled haints remain.

Any players who let their characters absorb a wisp of Gloamhale's power may choose to alter their character's appearance in a subtle way. One or both eyes may slightly change color; a small wart may sprout on their face or neck; an odd birthmark or liver spot may appear on one of their hands; etc.

Note: The ritual can be stopped voluntarily at any time. Stopping the ritual immediately releases Gloamhale's spirit back into the mansion and prevents the party from suffering any further damage. Once the ritual has been stopped voluntarily, it cannot be attempted again.

In this case, the air in the house still feels heavy with evil. Jaymes Gloamhale has been weakened and forced to retreat, but given a few months or years in his sanctuary, his spirit will recover and return to full strength.

RESOLUTIONS

Ideally, the heroes should attempt to address each of the problems in the manor. It is then up to the Narrator to determine the consequences of their actions using the guidelines here.

HAINTS

If the adventurers manage to dispel all the haints in the manor, their souls return to the Wheel of Rebirth, and the birth rate in the area rises. No further disappearances occur.

If any haints are not dispelled, the disappearances in the area continue as the lonely ghosts continue to cry out for love and companionship, luring other children into the swamp. War erupts between Lakesheart and the Fen, each blaming the other for the kidnappings. The birth rate in the area remains low for unknown reasons.

ERILA

For Erila's soul to be freed, all haints must be dispelled and the manor itself must be destroyed. If these conditions are not met, Erila's soul remains tied to the manor, lost between

death and rebirth. Over time, legends grow of a ghostly woman in white who wanders the swamp, wailing hopelessly. It's said her cries can drive listeners to madness.

THE MANOR

The characters can destroy the manor by re-flooding it or setting it on fire. If they wish to flood it, a nearby dam can be damaged enough to serve this purpose. Careful direction and manipulation of the water can even preserve the town of Lakesheart and the Fen's encampment, flooding only the area around the manor. Burning the manor, on the other hand, is initially difficult in such a wet, swampy area, but not impossible. If the characters implement either of these solutions, they are successful.

The adventurers return to their adult forms when the manor is destroyed. If it is flooded, all disappearances and strange events cease immediately…unless the lake is ever drained again.

If the manor is burned, the shrieking specter and poltergeists are destroyed, but the ghosts of Jaymes Gloamhale, Erila, and the haints remain, unless otherwise dealt with.

ALLIES & ADVERSARIES

This section contains the stats and descriptions for the major NPCs encountered in this scenario.

HAINT

Haints rise when lonely or neglected children die. Most of the rest of the child's personality and spirit fades away, leaving only desperation for some sign of love or companionship. While they may dress themselves in the dead child's clothes out of convenience, they have forgotten what the child looked like and cannot form a likeness of the child's face. Most haints wander headless for some time, until they find a lost or forgotten object that strikes their fancy; they then wear it on their shoulders in place of a real head. They are sometimes known as "attic haints" because they so often find such objects in musty attics.

If haints sense a living child nearby, they will do all they can to tempt the child into being their playmate. They may cry sadly, sing nursery rhymes, whisper fairy tales, or even leave broken toys or mysterious objects lying around in the hope of piquing the child's curiosity and care.

"Killing" a haint weakens it to the point where it no longer has passive powers and cannot make attacks or wear clothes or a head. Its spirit and power temporarily dissolve, but always return. Neglect is not something that can be simply defeated. When the haint is strong enough again, it finds new rags in which to clothe itself and a new object to use as a head.

To rid an area of haints, they must be dispelled. This involves giving the haint a desired gift. Haints are simple creatures, and view gifts as a sign of compassion and

HAINT

ABILITIES (FOCUSES)	
2	ACCURACY (BRAWLING)
-1	COMMUNICATION
1	CONSTITUTION
4	DEXTERITY (STEALTH)
0	FIGHTING
-2	INTELLIGENCE
1	PERCEPTION
0	STRENGTH
0	WILLPOWER (MORALE)

SPEED	HEALTH	DEFENSE	ARMOR RATING
14 (FLYING)	25	14	0

WEAPON	ATTACK ROLL	DAMAGE
DRAINING TOUCH	+4	2D6

SPECIAL QUALITIES

FAVORED STUNTS: Pierce Armor, Stunned Silence

DARKNESS: Haints that feel particularly neglected live in an orb of arcane darkness with a five-foot radius. This darkness can only be dispelled through arcana (Light Shaping) or by giving the haint some sense of friendship. This may be as simple as singing it a nursery rhyme or telling it a story.

DRAINING TOUCH: The touch of a haint drains the life force from any living thing, causing 2d6 plus Willpower penetrating damage (usually 2d6+0). This attack uses Accuracy (Brawling) to hit. This is a passive effect the haint cannot control.

SHADOW MELD: Haints gain a +2 bonus to Dexterity (Stealth) tests at night or in areas of heavy shadow. This is in addition to any other bonuses such favorable conditions may give.

THREAT: MINOR

love. Once a haint receives a desired gift, they are enveloped in a brilliant column of light. Their rags dissolve, and whatever they are using for a head falls away, briefly revealing a ghostly image of what they looked like before they died. They ascend into the light with beatific smiles, then fade away, finally at peace.

Determining what will dispel a haint requires a successful TN 17 Perception (Empathy) test, though what a haint is wearing and/or holding can often provide enough information for an educated guess as to what it would consider a desired gift.

FEN WARRIORS & SHAMANS

The tribes of the Fen are defended by their warriors and dartsmen, who are skilled at the art of swamp combat.

Fen shamans are often the children or grandchildren of the tribe's sacred leader, the Mud Mother. Intimately familiar with the swamp's dangers and defenses, they are

Fen Warriors/Dartsmen

ABILITIES (FOCUSES)	
2	ACCURACY (SLING*, LIGHT BLADES)
1	COMMUNICATION
2	CONSTITUTION
1	DEXTERITY (STEALTH)
2	FIGHTING (HEAVY BLADES, POLEARMS)
0	INTELLIGENCE
2	PERCEPTION (SEARCHING)
1	STRENGTH (INTIMIDATION)
1	WILLPOWER (MORALE)

SPEED	HEALTH	DEFENSE	ARMOR RATING
11	15	11	3

WEAPON	ATTACK ROLL	DAMAGE
SPEAR	+4	1D6+4
MACHETE	+4	2D6+1
SLING*	+4	1D6+2

SPECIAL QUALITIES

FAVORED STUNTS: Skirmish, Knock Prone

POISON DART*: For 2 SP, a dartsman can poison his weapon, slowing and partially paralyzing his victim, who suffers a -2 penalty to Dexterity, Fighting, and Accuracy until the end of the encounter, or until they benefit from a healing arcanum.

TALENTS: Armor Training (Novice), Single Weapon Style (Novice)

WEAPONS GROUPS: Bludgeons, Bows, Brawling, Heavy Blades, and Light Blades

EQUIPMENT: Machete, Spear, Sling* Light Leather Armor

Dartsmen only

THREAT: MINOR

known for bending swamp water and swamp plants to their will. They also utilize a special poison from a particular species of toad, the recipe for which has been passed down through the tribe for centuries.

POLTERGEIST WHIRLWIND

A poltergeist whirlwind is an unusual form of unliving, as they were never actually alive and do not rise from the remains of a single departed creature. They seem to manifest in locations where great trauma or tragedy created a psychic scar. They appear as whirlwinds of small objects, which they fling at anyone near them. They cannot change locations, and cannot move to other rooms in a house or dungeon.

Truly defeating a poltergeist whirlwind relies on purifying the area of the emotions that caused it. Accomplishing this can be as simple as destroying the physical location it is tied to, or as complex as banishing all other

Fen Shaman

ABILITIES (FOCUSES)	
0	ACCURACY
-2	COMMUNICATION
0	CONSTITUTION
3	DEXTERITY (ACROBATICS, STEALTH)
3	FIGHTING
3	INTELLIGENCE
1	PERCEPTION
3	STRENGTH
3	WILLPOWER (SELF-DISCIPLINE)

SPEED	HEALTH	DEFENSE	ARMOR RATING
13 (LAND/SWIMMING)	45	13	0

WEAPON	ATTACK ROLL	DAMAGE
VINE WHIP	+5	1D6

SPECIAL QUALITIES

FAVORED STUNTS: Knock Prone, Mighty Blow, Poison

DRAINING ROOT: A shaman can conjure a draining root from the ground to touch an enemy's ankle or leg. The touch of the root drains the enemy's life force, inflicting 1d6 penetrating damage. The shaman can direct the other end of the root to burrow underground and touch an ally's ankle or leg. Any Health drained from the enemy then heals the ally. This attack uses Intelligence.

PLANT SHAPING: The shaman can use the Plant Shaping arcana using Willpower (Self-Discipline) for any requisite tests.

POISON (2 SP): A shaman can inflict an additional 1d6 penetrating damage against the target of a successful attack who fails a TN 13 Constitution (Stamina) test. This damage occurs again at the start of each of the shaman's turns until the target has made a successful test. This stunt may only be used against a target who took at least 1 damage from the shaman from the attack that generated this stunt.

SLIPPERY CUSTOMER: Any enemy of the shaman ending their turn within 3 yards of them must make a successful TN 12 Dexterity (Acrobatics) test or fall prone as swamp water pushes and pulls around their legs, trying to undermine their footing.

VINE WHIP: Once per round, when hit by an enemy, the shaman can lash out with a green tendril at any target within 3 yards using their Willpower (Self-Discipline) to attack. This attack does 1d6 damage.

THREAT: MODERATE

unliving in the area (whose negative emotions may have given rise to the poltergeist in the first place). Attacking a poltergeist can weaken it, causing it to drop all the objects in its whirlwind, but it will eventually recover. Its Health is based on the number and weight of the objects in the whirlwind.

Poltergeist Whirlwind

ABILITIES (FOCUSES)	
3	ACCURACY (WIND)
-2	COMMUNICATION
0	CONSTITUTION
6	DEXTERITY (STEALTH)
2	FIGHTING (SLAM)
2	INTELLIGENCE
3	PERCEPTION (HEARING)
2	STRENGTH
2	WILLPOWER

SPEED	HEALTH	DEFENSE	ARMOR RATING
16 (FLYING)	25	16	0

WEAPON	ATTACK ROLL	DAMAGE
SLAM	+4	1D6+5

SPECIAL QUALITIES

FAVORED STUNTS: Knock Prone, Lightning Attack, Seize the Initiative

AIR WHIP: Whenever the poltergeist hits an enemy with a Slam attack or Hoard Buffet, the enemy must succeed at a TN 12 Strength (Might) test or lose their grip on their main weapon and be disarmed. The weapon is incorporated into the whirlwind and serves to heal the poltergeist whirlwind to the amount of the weapon's normal damage. This healing can exceed the poltergeist's starting Health.

ETHEREAL: Poltergeist whirlwinds are ethereal, being comprised purely of dense air. They ignore the effects of terrain. Only arcane attacks can truly harm them, though physical attacks can be used to knock objects out of the whirlwind, lessening its Health by 1d6, regardless of the physical attack's normal damage.

HOARD BUFFET: A poltergeist can create a sudden and powerful gust of wind to hurl small objects at nearby creatures, allowing it to perform the Knock Prone combat stunt on anyone within 4 yards of the poltergeist, rather than a single opponent.

WIND SHAPING: The poltergeist whirlwind can use the Wind Shaping arcanum using Accuracy (Wind) for any necessary tests.

THREAT: MODERATE

Shrieking Specter

Shrieking specters are grotesquely obese creatures with unnaturally slender, twig-like fingers. Two empty pink sockets gape where their eyes should be. They are most commonly found after the death of someone who perceives themselves to have been gravely wronged. It seems that,

Shrieking Specter

ABILITIES (FOCUSES)	
2	ACCURACY (ARCANE SCREAM)
0	COMMUNICATION
3	CONSTITUTION (STAMINA)
0	DEXTERITY
3	FIGHTING (CLAWS)
1	INTELLIGENCE
4	PERCEPTION (SMELLING, TASTING)
0	STRENGTH
1	WILLPOWER

SPEED	HEALTH	DEFENSE	ARMOR RATING
12	45	10	3

WEAPON	ATTACK ROLL	DAMAGE
ARCANE SCREAM	+4	2D6+3
CLAW	+5	1D6+3

SPECIAL QUALITIES

FAVORED STUNTS: Knock Prone, Lightning Attack, Mighty Blow

CANNIBALISTIC REGENERATION: Each round a shrieking specter draws blood in combat, it regains lost Health equal to its Constitution (usually 3). It cannot regenerate if reduced to 0 Health.

FRENZY: When attacking someone they have drawn blood from, or who is seriously wounded (lost at least half their Health), shrieking specters may perform the Lightning Attack and Might Blow combat stunts for 1 SP less than their normal cost.

SCENT OF DEATH: A shrieking specter gains the Perception (Tracking) focus to follow the trail of any target that is wounded or bleeding. They may also use this power to track and locate nearby corpses.

TOUGH: Shrieking specters have a natural armor rating of 3. Resentment is a difficult ghost to kill…

WEAKNESS TO LIGHT: Prolonged exposure (2 or more rounds) to bright light or sunlight inflicts 2d6 damage on shrieking specters.

WEAKNESS TO FIRE: When damaging a shrieking specter with fire, roll damage as normal, then double the resulting number.

THREAT: MODERATE

if someone harbors enough resentment and malice in life, these negative emotions actually coalesce into an independent spirit when their originator dies.

Shrieking specters hate the light, and flee from it whenever possible. They would rather retreat and find their targets again later—hopefully in darkness—than try to fight them in the light. Sunlight in particular causes shrieking specters to suffer physical pain.

THE SIXTH BEAST

The Sixth Beast is a *Blue Rose* adventure suitable for a group of four to six heroes, levels 1 to 4. As the bandit Five Beast Army ravages the Pavin Weald, characters must unearth the conflicts that spawned it: a sixth "beast" of old grudges, intolerance, and lies.

The adventure concerns the Trebutane, a people who fled violence in Kern to settle in the Pavin Weald, so the Narrator should familiarize themselves with **The Pavin Weald** and its subsection, **The Trebutane**, in **Chapter 6: Kingdom of the Blue Rose** in the *Blue Rose* core rulebook. The Ashlock region and the Trebutane found therein are different in some ways, but whenever a custom isn't covered in this adventure, assume the description in *Blue Rose* takes precedence.

INTRODUCTION

INTO THE ASHLOCK

Named for the deep green leaves of its trees, which appear black in direct sunlight, the Ashlock weaves a dark streak through the Pavin Weald, from the northernmost fork of the Rose River to the threshold of the Ice-Binder Mountains. The forest folk don't like the Ashlock, and skirt its edges only when they're desperate to hunt and forage. They say it's filled with cruel wolves and stone-hearted people. They also insist the folk there put on masks and engage in petty banditry. Everyone knows there's an

Aldin fort there, too, but its masters evidently do little to reign in the lawlessness.

Trebutane live in the Ashlock, but even other Trebutane find them off-putting. They belong to two clans, or factions, related partly by blood, partly by religious affiliation. The Makvael clan traditionally works as smiths or builders and honor Goia above Aulora. The Daradmor clan gives primacy to Aulora, and performs healing, farming, and animal care in her name, though, like the Makvaels, members do belong to other professions as well. Consumed with infighting, these two clans didn't escape Kern during Iran Highblood's rebellion, instead fleeing later under the influence of a mighty Hara (a Trebutane priest-scholar) called "the Grimspeaker." She led them over the mountains and appointed a successor, creating a tradition that kept the Makvaels and Daradmors from turning on each other.

The united clans made new, rough lives for themselves in the Ashlock until thirty years ago, when the so-called "Errant Master" came down from the chill mountains. It was one of the unliving: a mad, ranting thing wearing rotten finery from the age of the Sorcerer Kings. It demanded that its "slaves" among the Trebutane serve it once more. Three Knights of the Blue Rose joined the Grimspeaker of the time and destroyed it, but this didn't bring peace.

The knights lost one of their own in the battle and the two survivors, Markion and Valan, settled in the Ashlock and built a fort, promising to protect the region. The

Grimspeaker quarreled with them, then left her people to become a hermit. No one has seen or heard from her since. Even though the Aldin knights were made Protectors by the kingdom and given the power to administer justice, the Trebutane clans hide disputes from them. Even the ones (primarily Makvaels) who garrison the Protectors' fort at the trading town of Kaerith Ashlock keep their mouths shut.

The Protectors have a daughter, Mayran. Valan, who gave birth to her, is a *laevvel* man, but the Trebutane understanding of gender, with its strict divisions, does not encompass this Aldin tradition. The Trebutane are kind to children, but do not understand Mayran's parents. Throughout her childhood, they treated Mayran as if she had no true mother, and she became alienated from her birth parents as she became a teenager.

Mayran has now vanished. Rumors of bandits, members of a so-called "Five Beast Army," had recently reached the Protectors' ears. These tales were brutally confirmed when they attacked Kaerith Ashlock in a lightning raid, stealing supplies and captives; her parents fear Mayran is one of them. It is up to the heroes to uncover the truth.

OVERVIEW OF THE ASHLOCK

Despite the name, the Ashlock doesn't have many ash trees. It actually gets its name because its woods resemble a dark lock of hair spilling down from the mountains. The leaves and needles of its trees are so dark as to seem black. Old foresters recognize architecture from the Empire of Thorns in certain tumbled, pitted stones among the Ashlock's trees, and suspect the darkness might be residue from some ancient curse. Before the Daradmor and Makvael clans came, the place had been devoid of people for generations, save for an aggressive pack of rhy-wolves called the Valtyre.

The land is all rocky soil and hard granite, making it hard to till a straight line or find a good path for horses. As a result, the region is far better for herds than crops, so settlers keep goats, hunt, trap, and tend small gardens to get by.

The Ashlock region contains three main settlements, but most Trebutane (several hundred, but the exact number is up to the Narrator) live in scattered single family homesteads, visiting the larger communities only to trade. In the settlements, the Trebutane build their traditional homes: multi-family dwellings wrapped around a courtyard. In the woods, families live in small cabins, with a single wall or sheet to acknowledge the traditional separation of genders. Old-style Trebutane homes are found in Kaerith Ashlock, the largest, fortified settlement, and in Shadowell, three days north of it. Keening Stray contains a single large compound, and was once the home of the Grimspeaker, now gone these thirty years.

THE ASHLOCK — HERMITAGE — KEENING STRAY — SHADOWELL — CABIN — ROSE RIVER — KAERITH ASHLOCK

PART I

JOURNEY TO THE ASHLOCK

The scenario begins in Kaerith Ashlock. The characters may visit either as part of some greater journey, due to rumors of unrest, or because they were summoned by Valan and Markion, the Protectors. Once Mayran goes missing, they send messengers down the Rose River, asking for aid. The heroes could hear such a message straight from the boat, or after it reaches a noble with the power to assign them to the task. The easiest way to get there is by boat, but heroes—being heroes— undoubtedly find their own paths to adventure. By river or land, the route takes them through the northwestern Pavin Weald. As they travel, gentle hills give way to the Ashlock's rocky terrain.

Read or paraphrase the following to begin:

Crisp air blowing from the Ice-Binder Mountains banishes any drowsiness as you enter Kaerith Ashlock, a fortress town on the Pavin Weald's frontier. The fort consists of a squat stone tower surrounded by twenty-foot-high wooden walls and a few outbuildings. The town lies beyond, and is in turn girt by scattered three-foot-high fieldstone walls designed to pen goats, not repel invaders.

ADAPTING THE ADVENTURE

The Sixth Beast puts an Aldean spin on a classic adventure type: defending a plucky community against bandits. You can adjust its pace and difficulty level in many ways. As presented herein, the Ashlock is no more dangerous than the rest of the Pavin Weald, but this can easily be changed. For instance, the Errant Master may have brought shadowspawn with him, some of whom still roam the forests. Feel free to set the Trebutane communities farther apart, and fill the wilds between them with harsh weather, confusing paths, and rough terrain. (Don't overdo it, though; some people love to play through every moment spent traveling through the woods, but others would rather just get straight to the next scene.)

The easiest way to make the adventure tougher is to make the leading Five Beasts and the other bandits stronger as per the **Beefing Up Adversaries** section in *Blue Rose*, **Chapter 12: Adversaries**. You could also make the Merciless Hand more potent, so that anyone wielding it becomes an even greater threat. See the Hand's description at the end of the adventure for further details.

The adventure assumes the heroes are friends of Aldis: either members of the Sovereign's Finest, or a group with less prestige but just as much willingness to help. If the characters are more likely to be motivated by profit, let it be known the Five Beast Army attacked boats plying the Rose River, and anyone defeating them is entitled to a portion of those ill-gotten gains in reward. Non-Aldins might be called to act as neutral third parties, as relations between the Ashlock's Trebutane and the Protectors are so poor. The most sinister option would be to run the adventure with agents from Kern. They've come to probe the frontier's defenses and learn more of the Errant Master. That's not in the usual spirit of *Blue Rose*...unless the story leads infiltrators to question their loyalties and start out on the road to redemption

TREBUTANE: GENDER, SEXUALITY, AND CONFLICT

One of this adventure's minor sources of conflict comes from the Trebutane's attitudes toward gender and sexuality. To the Trebutane, same-sex romance is immature and selfish for adults to indulge in, though permitted for the young. The culture also adheres to a strict binary conception of gender. This is an unspoken assumption in rituals that govern how men and women must behave toward one another.

The Protectors are two men, one of whom gave birth to a daughter with his own body. This lies far enough outside Trebutane cultural norms that when the Grimspeaker left, many Trebutane believed the Protectors' relationship and Valan's nature were to blame. Trebutane will not display open hostility toward laevvel or *caria* heroes, however—they tend to avoid talking to all outsiders on general principle.

It's hard to tell how many people live here. There's room for a hundred, maybe more, in houses built in the Trebutane style: a large, single floor wrapped around a central courtyard, with few doors or windows facing the exterior. Five of these hug the riverbank in the fort's shadow. Seven more sit away from the water, near the edge of the uncut forest. A large field filled with old, burnt tree stumps stands between them. A road crawls from the dock through the empty field to the fort's gate, and a large log cabin stands by the road near the fort.

Once the characters enter the town, proceed to the first scene.

SCENE 1

AT KAERITH ASHLOCK

ROLEPLAYING ENCOUNTER

If the heroes were summoned by the Ashlock's Protectors, they need to go to the fortress. If they're following rumors or are traveling with no particular goal, they are directed toward the trade-house. Two old human women patrol the docks and perimeter acting as lookouts. Unless they sneak into town, the heroes meet them upon entry. If they dawdle and wander suspiciously, these human Trebutane pointedly tell them to go to the trade-house. Despite their staves, the pair are not capable combatants, but they can certainly holler for assistance, if required. These local toughs have the same traits as **minor bandits**, listed in the **Supporting Characters** section at the end of this adventure.

Observant characters notice a few oddities as soon as they arrive. First, neither woman appears able to look the other in the eye and they pointedly don't talk over one another; in fact, they barely acknowledge each other's presence. One of them has a bruised cheek. This is Moirag Makvael, and she got it in the bandit raid that occurred six days ago. If the heroes interrogate her about it, the other watcher (named Genra Daradmor) shoots her a withering glare and Moirag hurriedly changes the subject. She might be willing to talk if she's away from Daradmor eavesdroppers, but, following Trebutane tradition, is reluctant to speak directly to an outsider.

The Makvaels live near the river, and the Daradmors live near the woods. The bandits stole simple supplies from both clans, but mostly from the Makvaels. Moirag (or another Makvael witness, if the characters wander about) saw them kidnap two Makvaels as they left, and a third person wrapped in a cloak. She also knows that three more were taken, but didn't see them herself.

Barring an exceptional event, characters entering Trebutane compounds without an invitation are considered trespassers, and residents raise a hue and cry, drawing the notice of garrison staff (basic **Warriors** as described in *Blue Rose* **Chapter 12**). Heroes who brazenly ask questions

BLUE ROSE

SIX OF SWORDS

about the bandits, or interrogate Daradmors, might suffer an ambush from one minor bandit per character. The bandits lay on a beating and, if successful, tie the characters up, loot their possessions, blindfold them and dump them downriver a day or two away.

If the heroes wander about town, players may roll a TN 7 Perception (Seeing) test and consult the table at right to see what they notice.

If the heroes go to the trade-house they can expect a simple meal and a place to sleep on the floor, at no charge. Characters can also restock some of their supplies. Food and herbs are cheap, but the only metal weapons available are those that double as hunting and woodcraft tools. No armor is available. The trade-house is a large structure with two rooms: one for meeting and sleeping, and one for storage, with a cot for the proprietor, Vatric Daradmor.

Vatric serves the heroes with quiet, unfriendly efficiency. His brother, Vikor, is **Greenasp**, one of the Five Beasts, and a notorious suspected poisoner who was banished years ago. Vatric has seen Greenasp in the woods with the other bandits, but the Beast always wears his mask. Vatric suspects, but doesn't know for sure, that Greenasp is Vikor, and he doesn't really want to know, one way or the other. Vatric is a bit of a drinker, however, and might open up to a friendly hero who joins him cup for cup through the night. A successful TN 13 Constitution (Drinking) test earns the hero what Vatric knows.

At some point during the heroes' visit, a Makvael man comes in to pick up supplies. Observant characters note the peculiar nature of the transaction: the Makvael leaves

OBSERVATIONS AT KAERITH ASHLOCK	
TEST RESULT	OBSERVATIONS
7	Heroes feel the weight of less than friendly gazes from any adults milling about.
9	Some of the houses and fieldstone walls near the river look like they've been recently repaired.
11	People circulate among each of the clusters of houses, but nobody moves across the road between them.
13	A few of the Trebutane walk with a certain stiffness, as if they're getting over injuries; or they sport visible bruises.
15	While most people content themselves with a sidelong look as they go about their business, the heroes' arrival prompts one woman to head into the woods. The woman, Sheena Daradmor, is on her way to Shadowell to tell **Redhawk** that suspicious-looking characters have come to town. If the heroes appear to be ordinary traders she goes anyway, but this time the news is merely ordinary gossip.
17	The heroes find a stick with one end whittled into the shape of a wolf's head half buried in the road, along with a few links of chainmail.

THE FORTRESS TOWER AND SECRET ENTRANCE

Stairs lead up and down from the meeting hall to the tower's other floors. Upstairs, the second floor contains quarters for the fort's staff. The third floor contains rooms for Mayran and the Protectors, and an iron ladder leading to the crenelated roof.

The stairs down lead to the basement, which contains, off a hallway, the following chambers, in order: a (currently empty) holding cell, a locked storage room, and an unlocked room filled with preserved food and other supplies. The locked room contains the fort's modest treasury, spare furniture, and mementoes the Protectors acquired during their adventures. Under a drop cloth, a plain, locked box holds the genuine Merciless Hand.

The storage room features a large shelf that swings on hidden hinges: a secret door. This leads to a three-foot wide, six-foot tall tunnel that extends about fifty yards down to the riverbank, around the bend from the docks. The riverside entrance is hidden by a sod-covered wooden door. The tunnel was built as an emergency escape route and a shortcut to the water in case of fire. The laborers who built it moved away from the Ashlock and it's never been needed, so only the Protectors and Mayran known of it.

Mayran tells the bandit leader **Blackdire** about the tunnel. In **Part 4: Return and Reconciliation**, Blackdire uses it to reach the Merciless Hand. Thus, while the tower probably won't be of interest to begin with, it is included here in case the characters decide to snoop around—not that the Protectors or their staff appreciate such nosiness.

money or barter goods on one table. Vatric then brings the supplies to another table without looking at or speaking to the customer. If questioned, Vatric says it's a Trebutane custom, but characters familiar with the culture know that's only true if the two belong to rival factions.

At the Narrator's discretion, other traders might be present, bringing with them stories and opportunities that connect this adventure to the greater series.

SCENE 2

THE PROTECTORS

ROLEPLAYING ENCOUNTER

If the heroes stayed at the trade-house or dawdled in town, a messenger from the fort summons them to attend the Protectors forthwith. Otherwise, they are greeted at the fort's gate upon arrival. Either way, read or paraphrase the following:

The small fort is made of rough local stone and wood. Its walls contain the town smithy and enough room for the local population to take shelter. The gate has a single guard, and the rest of the fort's staff attends to their duties at an unhurried pace. They are dressed in rumpled blue surcoats embroidered with crossed golden antlers: the device of the local Protectors. The gate guard nods to one of the other staff: a young, male, vata'an who scowls, straightens his surcoat, then leads you into the stone tower.

He seats you at a round table on the ground floor. Stacked benches at the walls indicate this is a meeting hall, though the benches are covered with dust. A three-by-one-foot metal cage hangs from the ceiling. Inside rests a two-foot-long scepter made of black iron—specifically, six rods twisted together as one until they sprout into a six-clawed hand with two thumbs, one at each side. The palm of the hand bears a peculiar glyph.

The man who led the heroes in is Oshrak Makvael, of the fort's staff. (Use the **Warrior** from *Blue Rose* **Chapter 12: Adversaries** for the fort's **guards**, if stats are required.) Oshrak explains the Protectors will join them shortly, and offers them food and drink. If the characters accept, he runs to fetch it, and leaves them unattended for about ten minutes. If asked about the scepter he says, "It's the Merciless Hand. The Protectors got it before I was born." If asked for more details, he tells the story of the Errant Master, and how the Protectors, "along with one of our people," destroyed it. He omits further mention of **the Grimspeaker** and subsequent events, and won't talk about conflict between the factions. He considers it improper to discuss such matters with foreigners.

The cage containing the Merciless Hand hangs eight feet up, suspended from a four-foot chain. It's a fake; the real thing is locked up on the floor below. A successful TN 15 Intelligence (Evaluation) test gives the fake away as a product of local metalwork. It was commissioned in secret thirty years ago, from the current town smith's now-deceased mother. Characters fluent in written Kernish note the symbol in its palm resembles an initial of some kind. A successful TN 13 Intelligence (Sorcery Lore) test reveals it as the language of the Sorcerer Kings, spoken as "Mev" or "Mar."

MEET THE PROTECTORS

The Protectors arrive after the heroes have waited for about twenty minutes; they are friendly but obviously worried. They explain that bandits raided Kaerith Ashlock six days ago and appear to have kidnapped their daughter, **Mayran**. They suspect several townspeople were also kidnapped, but they're not sure who or how many, as the raiders stayed away from the fort and nobody raised the alarm. Even the fort staff has been uncooperative. It's not the first time the locals have refused to tell them anything about a violent incident, but it's the worst example to date. Unless a matter involves outsiders, the Trebutane keep to themselves, which has caused some friction with the neighboring forest folk, who've also suffered assaults and robberies near the edge of the Ashlock. But, again, nothing has come of the Protectors' inquiries. The forest folk have recently given these bandits a name: "the Five Beast Army."

The Protectors did manage to find out that after the attack on Kaerith Ashlock, the bandits fled toward Shadowell. The two men provide a map, a week's provisions, and, if necessary, mundane weapons and shields, though they don't have armor to spare. They want the characters to find Mayran, discover the bandits' origins, and pacify them. That won't be easy; the bandits are most likely Trebutane who've befriended or intimidated those around them into silence. They share the following additional information:

- Along with describing their daughter, Mayran, they admit to an estranged relationship with her. Valan acidly notes the Trebutane "gave her some poisonous local attitudes about laevvel," but Mayran herself has been accepted by them. They're worried, but can't think of anyone who would harm her, even among the least friendly of the Trebutane.

- The Trebutane "seem to always be arguing about something, but they don't want anyone interfering." The Protectors know the local Trebutane belong to two factions, but as far as they can tell they only argue about small things, and deal with them quietly. (The Protectors are wrong about this.)

- Thirty years ago, the Protectors joined with the Trebutane chief Hara, called the Grimspeaker, to destroy the Errant Master, but she abandoned the community when the Aldins refused to give her the Master's weapon. *"If only she'd confided in us why she wanted it,"* Markion says, *"but she wouldn't even tell us that. We can't just throw some cursed thing into the woods and hope for the best."* They don't know if the Grimspeaker still lives.

- As far as they can tell, the Five Beast Army has been operating for at least three months, perhaps even longer. Some of them are well equipped. They're named for their leaders, who wear wooden masks carved to look like animals, each painted in distinctive colors. They were originally just called the "beast-masked bandits" but apparently prefer their newer, grander name for themselves. The Protectors are afraid that if they lead an expedition to deal with them, they'll earn open enmity from the bandits' allies and relatives. The heroes should avoid killing whenever possible—better peace than justice, if it comes to it.

- Wolves are holy to the local Trebutane, because rhy-wolves aided their escape from Kern. Killing or hindering a wolf is forbidden. The wolf is the symbol of the Grimspeaker.

Having relayed the above, the Protectors ask them to leave for Shadowell at once.

PART 2

To Shadowell

Directed by the Protectors, the heroes depart for Shadowell, three days away. In the Ashlock's treacherous terrain, horses won't get them there any faster, but they do make it easier to carry supplies. The Narrator may introduce challenges along the way, but they shouldn't be so arduous that the characters are significantly injured. At night, the heroes hear distant wolf howls. These are **the Valtyre**, the Ashlock's rhy-wolf pack. They've taken an interest in the outsiders but, for now, keep far enough away that it's unlikely the characters spot them.

SCENE 1

Cabin Ambush

COMBAT/EXPLORATION ENCOUNTER

Half a day from Shadowell, the heroes come across a one-room cabin just off the trail. This is a typical structure for a semi-permanent hunting camp or supply cache, not a homestead. Introduce it by reading aloud or paraphrasing the following:

A cabin appears to the left of the trail, up a rocky slope sheltered by two of the Ashlock's great, dark trees. It looks like it was once a way station for hunters, but is now in poor repair, as if abandoned. It doesn't have a door, and is filled with leaves and branches a foot deep. Other fallen leaves cover the surrounding area. The path to Shadowell continues past it, bending around the rise.

Players who attempt an Intelligence (Natural Lore) or Perception (Tracking) test, provided they score 11 or higher, note the following, based on how well they succeed. They don't have to leave the path to spot these details.

A result of 17 or higher on the Intelligence test provides a +2 bonus to subsequent Perception (Seeing) tests to spot anything hidden on the other side of the trail. Scoring 13 or higher on the Perception (Seeing) test reveals a leaf-covered blind 15 feet up a tree. Tonn Daradmor hides behind it, as he was told to do whenever anyone approaches. Tonn is a sixteen-year-old human Shadowellian. If a hero falls into the pit or rummages through the cabin's debris, he yells "Assassins!" in Kernish, slips down the tree, and runs away. Locals know the Five Beast Army uses the cabin, so only unwanted visitors would take a closer look.

There aren't any boot prints in front of the cabin because the bandits dug a pit trap there and covered it with dry sticks and leaves. The pit is seven feet wide and only five feet deep, but it's filled with sharp, fire-hardened stakes

TABLE HEADER		
TN	**INTELLIGENCE OBSERVATION**	**PERCEPTION OBSERVATION**
11	The cabin is filled with more debris than natural events would deposit there.	A charred stick pokes out from under the leaves outside the cabin.
13	Some of the leaves on the ground outside the cabin didn't come from the trees above.	Some of the leaves look wet and crushed, as if recently stepped on.
15	Filling the cabin with that much debris would require bringing it from elsewhere, since nearby plants haven't been stripped of foliage.	The debris in the cabin looks like it was stacked in two piles, which have since collapsed, leaving two subtle bumps.
17	Anyone who approaches the cabin must go uphill, where they can be easily observed from beyond the tree line on the other side of the trail.	The remnants of tracks and furrows in the dirt indicate that at least four people dragged two objects toward the cabin before the leaves came down, and despite the boot prints on the odd leaves, an area immediately in front of the cabin has no tracks on it at all.

that inflict 1d6 damage. Roll a TN 13 Perception (Seeing) test for a hero to detect the pit trap if they are immediately adjacent to it.

If the characters rummage through the pile of leaves, they find two bodies underneath: a human man and a vata'an woman. They are two of the Makvaels who disappeared in the raid on Kaerith Ashlock. They've been clubbed to death. Between them lies a bundle of blood-stained Aldin clothes. They're Mayran's, though only their size and style indicates this.

If a hero cries out after falling into the pit, or Tonn Daradmor yells "Assassins!" a gang of Five Beast Army bandits hidden around the bend move in to strike (use the minor bandits from **Supporting Characters** at the end of the adventure, but note that two of them have a bow and a dozen arrows each). There's one bandit for each hero, plus two more, and all wear hoods and masks. Ten yards of movement brings the bandits around the bend and able to use ranged weapons, but it takes another 10 yards to get to the cabin.

Two of the gang hang back to use their bows while the rest wade into close combat. They try to push characters into the pit whenever possible. If the heroes draw blades, the bandits do likewise. Otherwise, they bludgeon characters with clubs until they've knocked them out or driven them back toward Kaerith Ashlock. If the heroes kill one of them, one flees to warn the rest of the Five Beast Army's forces in Keening Stray (see **Part 3: Secrets of the Trebutane**). As a result, they get the heroes' descriptions and try to kill or capture them whenever they come across them. Any captured heroes are taken to Redhawk in Shadowell.

INTERROGATING THE BANDITS

Captured bandits refuse to talk unless a sufficiently persuasive or intimidating character cracks them. Test the appropriate attribute for the hero's strategy vs. that bandit's Willpower (Morale). If made to talk, the bandit reveals the following:

- They didn't personally carry out the raid in Kaerith Ashlock. One of the Five Beasts, Redhawk, led a raiding party that gathered in Shadowell, and passed through on the way back while traveling to Keening Stray. Redhawk stayed in Shadowell to keep an eye on the people there, while the others went on ahead.

- The raiders brought five young Trebutane (three women, one of whom was a vata'an, and two men) with them, and one young Aldin woman. (The bandits come from outer settlements and don't know Mayran by sight.)

- Redhawk showed them the bodies of two of the captives two days later. He ordered them to dispose of them and watch the trail for visitors. The rest presumably went to Keening Stray.

- The bandits operate in cells that recognize the overall authority of the Five Beasts. The cells' members are mostly Daradmors, though a few Makvaels "know their place." (Every member of this cell is Daradmor.) They don't know the Fives Beasts' true identities, but can describe the way they look with their masks on. They don't know how many members the Five Beast Army has, but that a "host" gathers in Keening Stray.

- The bandits raid non-Trebutane beyond the fringes of the Ashlock, but their main targets are Makvaels, because they "deserve it." As the bandits tell it, every goat, weapon, coin, or anything else seized is penance for the faction's ancestral crimes. In Kern, the Makvaels were informants; they laid traps for Trebutane rebels.

Captive bandits present a dilemma. Unless they can be convinced to do otherwise, they warn their compatriots as soon as they're set free. Imprisoning them requires a journey back to Kaerith Ashlock, during which they try to escape. However, the Narrator should allow persuasive characters and compelling roleplaying to change the bandits' attitudes, or convince them to lay down their arms until the heroes resolve the situation.

If nothing attracts the bandits, they stay hidden in nearby foliage and behind an up-thrust chunk of rock around the bend; a successful TN 13 Perception (Seeing or Hearing) test detects them. After the characters pass, if the bandits remained unseen and unchallenged, they follow the heroes to Shadowell, and strike by surprise during any conflict with Redhawk in the next scene.

SCENE 2
IN SHADOWELL

COMBAT/ROLEPLAYING ENCOUNTER

A few twists in the path beyond the cabin take the heroes to Shadowell. Read or paraphrase the following:

Shadowell must be named for the rocky rift in which it lies. It's fifteen yards deep, one hundred long, and fifty wide. A natural stone ramp leads to the interior and the five Trebutane compounds which lean up against the cliffs within. Goats wander freely about the settlement, and a few sure-footed ones look down on you from cliff ledges above.

The bandits on the road are the only strong, adult Daradmors left near Shadowell. The rest joined the Five Beast Army at Keening Stray, and took nine teenage Makvaels with them as captives. Eight Daradmor elders and sixteen children currently dwell in the village. Eighteen adult Makvaels also remain, with half as many elders and children. Redhawk rules them all. The remaining Makvaels won't raise a hand against him, because they're afraid their captive kin will suffer if they do.

Redhawk reacts to the heroes based on the resources and situation at hand. If Shadowell's bandit cell returned ahead of them, he sets up an ambush where they loose arrows from inside Makvael houses, leading characters away from the Daradmors and, possibly, getting Makvaels caught up in the fight.

Without the bandits, Redhawk cajoles staff-wielding, fighting-age Makvaels to stand by him in a show of force. A successful TN 10 Perception (Empathy) test reveals the Makvaels' fearful reluctance. Spurred by concern for their press-ganged relatives, they fight when Redhawk orders and, if the heroes kill any of them, they defend themselves with all the energy they can muster. Redhawk uses Fire Shaping and other arcana against obvious adepts or the most heavily armed hero.

The heroes are almost certainly outnumbered, and unless they understand the Makvaels' involuntary participation and convince them to stand aside or turn against Redhawk, this is a dangerous situation for them. If the Makvaels oppose Redhawk, he takes a hostage from among their children or elders, offering to release them at the edge of the forest in exchange for safe passage. He also warns everyone that if he isn't in Keening Stray in three

days, his allies will kill the captives. Redhawk believes this to be true, but it isn't. Greenasp has no intention of losing his "experiments" unless he must.

If captured, Redhawk resists interrogation, but if the heroes prevail in a test of their Communication (Deception) or Strength (Intimidation) vs. his Willpower (Morale) they learn the following:

- The bandits attacked Kaerith Ashlock to test its resolve (it was weak), resupply, and capture Makvaels who could be "made loyal." Redhawk doesn't know how this is done, but the Beast called Greenasp has found a way. They were ordered to capture young people past puberty, but short of full maturity.

- The two dead Makvaels seized axes and tried to escape. They were killed in self-defense.

- He knows the real names and rough capabilities of the other Beasts, though he lies about them if he can get away with it.

- The host at Keening Stray gathers to invade Kaerith Ashlock, drive out the Protectors, and install the Beast Blackdire as leader.

If Shadowell's Makvaels trust the heroes to free their kin from Keening Stray, they agree to keep Redhawk as their prisoner.

PART 3

SECRETS OF THE TREBUTANE

In order to stop the Five Beast Army and rescue the kidnapped Makvaels, the heroes journey to Keening Stray, a hamlet two days from Shadowell or four days from Kaerith Ashlock. Unless the Narrator wishes to add another challenge—like an encounter with some shadow-spawn—the journey presents no difficulties beyond the rocky terrain.

SCENE 1

SHADOWED BY WOLVES

ROLEPLAYING/COMBAT ENCOUNTER

If the heroes attempt any hunting along the way, they can't find any game besides small birds. A successful TN 15 Perception (Tracking) test reveals large wolf tracks close to the trail. At night, the heroes hear the wolves howl again, only closer this time. By day, a successful TN 15 Perception (Hearing) test reveals the soft sound of animal footfalls ahead or behind. When the characters stop moving, the sound stops as well.

The Valtyre, a pack of rhy-wolves allied with the exiled Grimspeaker, are close by. When the characters entered the forest, the Valtyre psychically alerted her, and at her request have monitored the heroes closely ever since, starting with the bandit ambush near Shadowell. Six follow the characters, close enough to eavesdrop on conversations. If the heroes treat the Trebutane with respect and mercy, the Valtyre report it. If they kill Trebutane or express contempt for them, the rhy-wolves report that, too.

They Valtyre have been told to avoid direct contact if at all possible. If tracked, they'll flee, though not before the tracker sees them. If attacked, a rhy-wolf bites the assailant once on the wrist or ankle. Among the Ashlock's Trebutane, such a wound is a sign the recipient disrespected the wolves, and deserves nothing but contempt in return.

Despite the Valtyre's agenda, a successful Communications (Etiquette) test vs. their Willpower (Self-Discipline) (+1 bonus for predatory rhydan or Trebutane, +2 for fellow rhy-wolves) prompts them to stop and speak. If a player generates stunt points on a roleplaying test with the rhy-wolves, they learn the following for 1 stunt point each:

- The Grimspeaker lives. She sent them to watch the heroes because she's afraid they'll harm the Trebutane and wants to know if they are worthy; though for what task, the rhy-wolves don't know.

- At any mention of the Protectors, one growls derisively and says something to the effect of, "She sees them not. This land is for Trebutane and wolves." They don't know why she feels this way or why she went into exile, but know the clans "forgot to be one people."

Characters who have been kind to the Trebutane and treated the Valtyre with respect (and, perhaps, succeed at further Communications vs. Willpower tests, with the target number adjusted to take into account their behavior) might be invited to follow them to the Grimspeaker, bypassing Keening Stray entirely. In that case, the full Five Beast Army marches to Kaerith Ashlock unhindered, and the Narrator should skip to **Scene 3: The Grimspeaker's Hermitage**. It's undoubtedly an honor, but probably a tactical mistake.

SCENE 2

KEENING STRAY

COMBAT/EXPLORATION ENCOUNTER

Read or paraphrase the following for the players, but note it assumes the heroes go straight to Keening Stray from Shadowell. If they take more than two days to arrive, the bandits and captives have already started marching to Kaerith Ashlock as a second wave of attack, and only a few children and elderly residents remain.

Read or paraphrase the following to the players:

Keening Stray stands upon a great, rocky hill. The settlement contains one large Trebutane compound, surrounded by neglected gardens and a few sheds. A circular fieldstone wall as tall as an average human's chest surrounds it, except at one gate, marked by posts carved into wolf's heads on either side. Seven guards watch the solitary entrance to the "town." The whole area must be about seventy-five yards in diameter. You see at least a dozen people at any given time, and as they circulate you know there must be more out of sight, or in the compound building. They're mostly human with a few vata, all dressed as Trebutane and, as is customary, men and women gather by different fires to eat and talk. Some load narrow handcarts built to move through these woods, or tend to weapons: thick clubs, improvised pole arms, bows, and swords.

The wall makes invaders easy to spot. Even in starlight, anyone inside the wall easily sees silhouettes passing over it. This imposes a -4 penalty to Dexterity (Stealth) tests whenever anyone is looking at any part of the wall a hero is trying to slip over unseen. However, there is another gate besides the obvious one: a gray wooden door, used by hunters and herders, on the opposite side to the main gate. It's only a foot and a half wide, but crouching char-

acters could sneak through it. During the day, heroes see it with a successful TN 11 Perception (Seeing) test if they look while hidden behind the line of foliage. At night, the TN increases to 15, though characters can find this gate automatically if they're standing within a few feet of it, day or night.

THE FIVE BEAST ARMY

If the Five Beast Army knows the heroes have been searching for them, leader **Whitebear** sends out a perimeter patrol: two **minor bandits** led by a **veteran bandit**, all of whom are vata'sha, capable of seeing in the dark. She also sets a checkpoint at the gate staffed by four minor bandits, two veterans, and Fionar Daradmor, an **Adept** (see **Chapter 12** of *Blue Rose*). The patrol attacks with bows once or twice, then flees to warn their comrades. If necessary, its veteran leader stays and fights to help the others get away.

The gate guards have orders to stand and fight, using lethal force unless the heroes surrender. Besides the gate guards, patrol, and leaders (see following), twenty Daradmor bandits occupy Keening Stray: sixteen minor bandits and four veterans, under the command of Whitebear (see **Allies and Adversaries** at the end of this adventure). A dozen of them are outside at any given time, attending to various tasks. During the day, Whitebear is visible leading them through military drills, and they're

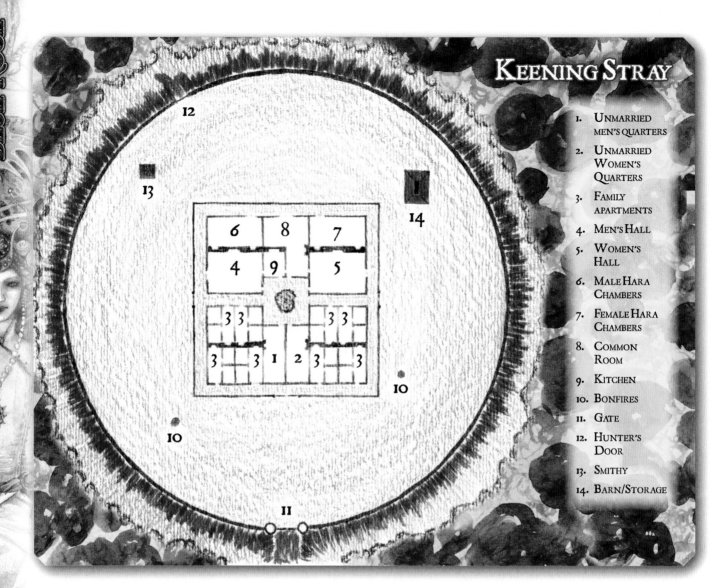

12

13

14

6   8   7

4   9   5

3 3   3 3

3   3   1   2   3   3

10

10

11

1. **UNMARRIED MEN'S QUARTERS**
2. **UNMARRIED WOMEN'S QUARTERS**
3. **FAMILY APARTMENTS**
4. **MEN'S HALL**
5. **WOMEN'S HALL**
6. **MALE HARA CHAMBERS**
7. **FEMALE HARA CHAMBERS**
8. **COMMON ROOM**
9. **KITCHEN**
10. **BONFIRES**
11. **GATE**
12. **HUNTER'S DOOR**
13. **SMITHY**
14. **BARN/STORAGE**

fully armed and armored. At night, half the bandits are equipped, though none of them are ever far from a sword or axe. As Greenasp doesn't wish to be disturbed, the bandits set up fires outside the building. This is notable to anyone familiar with Trebutane society. Bandits gather around, some dozing lightly, though few can sleep, given the march and battle ahead.

In direct combat, bandits fight in groups of five: a veteran and four minor subordinates. They encircle and employ lethal force, but do accept surrender, tying prisoners up in the compound courtyard. In addition, Whitebear has a certain fondness for "honorable combat." She won't volunteer such an arrangement, but if one of the heroes offers to duel her, she accepts terms to let them go if she's beaten, or demands unconditional surrender if she wins. (In the latter situation, she keeps the heroes bound until the conquest of Kaerith Ashlock, after which she pays a boat to take them out of the Pavin Weald. If the heroes escape, they're clearly "dishonorable," and she'll try to kill them.) Clever characters might be able to negotiate other terms as well, such as the release of Makvael captives.

Two elderly men (Kavel and Starly Daradmor) and three women (Afina Makvael, Kaya and Virna Daradmor)

walk the compound freely. They are the only residents of Keening Stray who didn't join up or run away when the Five Beast Army gathered. They might help heroes who don't look eager to kill anyone and, out of bandit earshot, they happily voice concern for the "poor Makvael boys and girls" in the heart of the compound.

The camp is filled with empty sacks, scars from other fires, trash piles, and well-used latrine trenches, indicating a larger number of transient inhabitants who left a short time ago. This was the Five Beast Army's first wave of thirty-five, led by Blackdire and Bluecat, with Mayran in tow. It set off a day before the characters arrived, or sooner, if the heroes visit the Grimspeaker first. Heroes encounter the first wave in **Part 4** of this adventure.

MAKVAEL PRISONERS

If the heroes get into the compound's central courtyard they find a blazing fire and the twelve disoriented, bruised Makvaels sweating around it. These are the captives the bandits took from Shadowell and Kaerith Ashlock. Some of them sit, rocking back and forth; others shuffle about listlessly, but a few spar with using thin, green branches, attacking each other with a mindless fervor. They all share a blank, open-mouthed expression. Discarded cups filled with the dregs of some sort of tea lie scattered all around.

The young Makvaels are Exhausted (level 3 fatigue). They acquired 1 level of fatigue from being kept awake by the fire; the rest comes from being drugged with a Kernish poison called "warweed." Kern's commanders used to feed it to Trebutane spear-fodder, making them slow, fearless, and suggestible. An hour or two after being administered, the drug causes 2 levels of fatigue, but adds +2 to Strength and a +3 bonus to Willpower (Courage and Morale) tests, while also inflicting a –3 penalty to Willpower (Purity) tests. Combined with threats and other stresses, warweed makes its victims willing to carry out orders they would normally refuse. It doesn't inflict Strength and Willpower changes or this state of suggestibility on mature adults, hence the strict guidelines on who could and couldn't be kidnapped.

This whole state of affairs is Greenasp's doing. The poisoner lectures and beats the captives, sometimes forcing them to fight each other to test their suggestibility. If the captives continue to obey him, he considers the experiment a success. Once the Five Beast Army takes the Ashlock, he'll grow enough warweed to keep dozens of young Makvaels in his thrall.

Read or paraphrase the following speech for an example of the sort of thing Greenasp screams at the captives.

"Your sins will be forgiven! Your kin will be spared when you join us against the Aldins and their collaborators! Did we not battle the living, the dead, and the chill mountains to free ourselves, and live according to our true ways? Aldins speak of tolerance, but they drove away our Grimspeaker. She forgave your clan's crimes, but that's done. Now you must earn forgiveness! Who will prove to me that they're ready to serve? To save us? You two! Get up! Fight!"

If confronted, **Greenasp** flees inside after ordering the Makvaels to attack. They use improved clubs (–1 to attack rolls) or attempt to grapple the heroes. Otherwise, use the stats for the villagers in the **Supporting Characters** section, but with +2 Strength due to the warweed. They can be talked out of attacking with a Communication (Deception or Persuasion) or Strength (Intimidation) test vs. their Willpower. Due to the warweed, threats work poorly (they're resisted by the Courage focus), but they can be manipulated by the same sort of strong speech Greenasp uses, which targets Purity-based Willpower tests. Greenasp warns the bandits to guard the compound's exits, if he can. When the heroes emerge from the building, he throws poison needles while Whitebear attacks with her sword; other nearby bandits assist their leaders.

Mayran isn't with the captives. If questioned, the bandits tell the heroes the girl is one of them now: Blackdire's adopted daughter, given the name Graylark.

WOLVES AND HEROES

Sheer numbers make Keening Stray a formidable challenge, but under the right circumstances, the heroes don't have to go it alone. If the Valtyre rhy-wolves judge them worthy, they render aid, as follows:

If the heroes avoided killing Trebutane and treated them respectfully, the six Valtyre who've been tracking them run to their side at the point where they might be overwhelmed. They put themselves between the heroes and their assailants. The bandits won't harm a wolf, or try to push by one. Only Whitebear and Greenasp would dare do such a thing, but the warweed-addled Makvaels might obey an order to attack, if they fail a TN 11 Willpower (Purity) test.

If the heroes successfully sneak in and out, the Valtyre meet them when they leave.

If the heroes communicated with the Valtyre before and left a favorable impression, the six intercept them just before they reach Keening Stray. They agree to help the heroes rescue the Makvaels, but refuse to fight other Trebutane. They operate by stealth unless they need to protect characters when they're about to be defeated (as per the previous bullet point).

SCENE 3
THE GRIMSPEAKER'S HERMITAGE

ROLEPLAYING ENCOUNTER

Assuming the characters earn the Valtyre's support and get out of Keening Stray alive, the rhy-wolves lead them through the woods and along a small stream in the rocky hills for six hours before finally reaching their lair and the Grimspeaker's home. If the heroes want to go back to Kaerith Ashlock first, the rhy-wolves tell them it would be a fool's errand. They are too few and need the Grimspeaker's aid if they are to prevail.

If the heroes wantonly killed or insult Trebutane and the Valtyre witness it, the Grimspeaker knows. They have failed to earn her trust. This scene doesn't happen, and the heroes most likely fail.

Once the characters arrive, read or paraphrase the following:

The stream disappears into the rocks and the spring that spawned it. A worn bucket sits close-at-hand. Beyond, a fire sputters in front of a cave—one of many in the broken rock face. Wolves loll nearby, gazing at you with the unmistakable intelligence of rhydan. A solidly-built woman with long, gray hair sits by the fire. She pushes herself to stand with a cane and slaps the dust off her sweeping, black Trebutane robe. "They call me the Grim-

speaker," she says in thickly-accented Aldin. "I have questions for you. Answer them truly or I have no use for you, and my friends will see you on your way." She points to a wolf, who nods in confirmation.

To injured heroes, the Grimspeaker's first question is, "What's wrong with you, then?" She treats injuries with sufficient mundane skill and arcana to heal them of all Health and Fatigue losses, as well as any lingering poison effects. If the characters brought drugged Makvaels with them, she takes them to her cave to rest, and brews a warweed antidote while she interrogates the heroes.

After gathering intelligence through her Valtyre allies, the Grimspeaker needs to confirm the strangers' good intentions. If the characters prove worthy, she shares things she's kept secret for a very long time. She starts by asking questions she already knows the answers to—for example, about the heroes' actions up to that point, especially if they're not especially proud of them—to establish they are being truthful with her. She has a fairly complete picture of their actions from the ambush near Shadowell onwards. She then follows up with questions about the heroes' motives and desires; keep each character's Calling, Destiny, and Fate in mind as they answer. The Grimspeaker has powerful psychic gifts and a keen intuition, so she sees through most attempts at deception; however, the Narrator should let particularly eloquent, well-portrayed falsehoods pass.

If the heroes lie, display blatantly selfish intentions, or have a low opinion of the Trebutane as a people (although she does not censure them regarding a dislike for a specific individual or custom), the Grimspeaker curtly dismisses the characters, saying, "Begone." The Valtyre escort the heroes away with as much insistence as required.

Ultimately, the Narrator should decide the Grimspeaker's response based on the following questions: Do the heroes seem decent and kind? Have they acted that way? If the answers are "yes," she shares the deep lore of her people, from the distant past to recent history.

THE GRIMSPEAKER'S SECRETS

"From the ice we came as two people. Through the ice we come as one." That was the first Grimspeaker's chant, when she brought the Daradmor and Makvael Trebutane out of captivity. During the fall of the Sorcerer Kings, Jarek freed them from a rival lord in the Ice-Binders, but enslaved them anew and settled them among others of their kind. His agents encouraged the two factions to hate each other, but forced them to share the same village. Worst of all, he used them to subvert the other Trebutane. Makvael smiths made swords for rebels, and then told the Knights of the Skull where to capture them. He employed Daradmors as well-poisoners, and

they produced drugs to stupefy and addict communities. They hated each other and themselves too much to join the Trebutane Highblood rebellion.

The first Grimspeaker got her name because she devised a ritual and ethos to bring the clans together and renew their pride. The Hara commanded the elders of each clan to admit their sins to her and, through her, to Anwaren. Then, with Anwaren's authority, she forgave them and commanded them to forget the past and escape. They followed her over the Ice-Binder Mountains, where they would have perished if a pack of rhy-wolves, the Valtyre's ancestors, hadn't led them down to the Ashlock, finding them food and shelter along the way. The first Grimspeaker trained the next, and so on, keeping past Makvael and Daradmor sins a secret, while ordinary members of each faction eventually forgot about them, except as vague legends. If there wasn't a great need and they hadn't demonstrated their worth, she never would have told the heroes any of this.

When the Aldin knights came, the Grimspeaker greeted them, and though the people found them strange, they appreciated their aid in bringing trade and safety to the Ashlock. But after she helped them defeat the Errant Master, she saw that its weapon, the Merciless Hand, held a Makvael smith's mark. She was bound by oath to demand the artifact but not to reveal why. The Protectors refused to hand it over without a reason, humiliating her in front of her people. So, she exiled herself.

The Valtyre told her the factions were quarreling anew, so the Grimspeaker decided to find a successor. She taught a precocious young woman named Veldra Daradmor the people's secret history, but discovered Veldra had a cold ambition and a taste for the Shadow Art of sorcery. Veldra abandoned her studies, but not before learning enough to shame the Makvaels and dream of bringing the clans under her control. She took the name Blackdire, and founded the Five Beast Army.

PEACEMAKING

Having found trustworthy outsiders, the Grimspeaker wants to come out of isolation and put a stop to her people's strife. But sacred obligations prevent her from taking the side of any one faction, inflicting violence on any Trebutane, or taking the side of the Protectors against them. She needs the heroes' aid to stop the conflict and negotiate with the Protectors to grant most of the bandits amnesty. Without the last condition, there's no reason for the Five Beast Army to stop fighting. However, she fully understands the leading Five Beasts may have to be punished. If the heroes wish to argue the details, she insists such discussions take place after they act.

Furthermore, the Grimspeaker taught Blackdire about the Merciless Hand, and has no doubt she wants it to amplify her sorcery and accomplish what the Grimspeaker could not. It's a dangerous artifact with powers over cold, death, and psychic anguish, and one that could bring disaster to her people and those around them.

She assures the heroes that any young Makvaels they brought will recover from warweed and stay safe at her hermitage. She wishes to leave as soon as she's explained herself, with the heroes and twelve rhy-wolves by her side.

PART 4

RETURN AND RECONCILIATION

It takes four days to reach Kaerith Ashlock. The best route passes through Keening Stray, where at the sight of the returned Grimspeaker and the Valtyre, rank and file bandits throw down their arms. The Grimspeaker commands them to abandon their mission, return to their homes and await word of what will come next. White-bear also submits, but Greenasp flees at the first sign of her approach; the poisoner knows his crimes won't be forgiven. The Narrator might decide he tracks the heroes and sets an ambush with the help of bandits who owe personal loyalty to him. Otherwise (and unless the heroes stop him) he takes money and supplies from his bother Vatric (see **Part 1**, **Scene 1**) and flees the Pavin Weald. After that, the Narrator can use the poisoner however they deem appropriate. Besides such complications and anything else the Narrator wishes to introduce, the journey back to Kaerith Ashlock contains no special surprises.

This section assumes the first wave of thirty-five Five Beast Army bandits reaches Kaerith Ashlock before the heroes do. Blackdire leads them, while her last lieutenant Bluecat commands them. As "Graylark," Mayran walks with them. They've got enough of a head start to avoid pursuit, but are occasionally slowed by rough terrain and the need to forage. Thus, the final part of the adventure assumes the heroes arrive at the beginning of the attack.

SCENE 1

ATTACK ON KAERITH ASHLOCK

COMBAT/ROLEPLAYING ENCOUNTER

By day or starlit night, the heroes arrive to witness the attack has begun. Read or paraphrase the following:

The smell of smoke assails you as soon as you reach the tree line. It's coming from two burning houses by the river, where residents furtively battle a dozen torch-bearing bandits. The defenders raise clubs, woodcutter's axes, and hunting spears against the bandits' swords and scale armor.

They fight with less intensity than in a true pitched battle. When a blow strikes, the person who delivers it seems reluctant to land another. The bandits toss incapacitated defenders behind their line as captives, but the Trebutane townsfolk let their wounded enemies flee.

Twenty-one bandits assail the fortress. The gates are closed, so they exchange arrows and flung stones with the defenders on the walls. Beyond their line, you see the trade-house's roof has collapsed after a crew of six dragged a rafter beam out. If they manage to gather together around ten people, they'll be able to use the beam as an effective battering ram to break down the front gate. A broad-shouldered figure in a blue cloak and a cat mask supervises them. A slight figure in oversized Trebutane woman's garb and wearing a plain, unpainted mask sits slouched on a boulder by the trade-house.

Most of the force are minor bandits, but one in five is a veteran. The group by the waterfront has been ordered to burn Makvael homes and take the occupants hostage. The bandits at the walls have been ordered to harass the fort so the guards won't come out, giving Bluecat (the figure in the blue cloak and mask) time to organize a battering ram attack. If the heroes draw close enough, they hear the Protectors directing the fort's defenders, shouting, "Try to just scare them away!" and similar non-lethal instructions. The fort's wooden walls are vulnerable to fire but Black-dire has ordered her men not to burn it. The bandits don't know why.

The figure on the boulder is Mayran, the Protectors' daughter. After confirming details about the secret tunnel to the fort (see following), Blackdire left her with Bluecat. She now suspects she has been double-crossed but can't leave; Bluecat keeps her close with veiled threats and suggestions that her parents will never take her back now she has betrayed them. Blackdire has ordered him to keep the girl as a possible hostage, while she dares the tunnel.

ENDING THE SIEGE

The Grimspeaker and Valtyre rhy-wolves make it easier to stop the siege. The Valtyre don't attack except in self-defense, but put themselves between the bandits and their targets. These bandits are better trained than the second wave in Keening Stray, and might summon up the courage to fight the rhy-wolves with a successful TN 15 Willpower (Morale) test.

The Grimspeaker won't fight, but no Trebutane would raise a hand against her unless she seemed responsible for some horrendous act committed by the heroes who accompany her. As a direct consequence, characters must grant bandits mercy in defeat to keep her person sacrosanct. If they do, for every bandit they defeat without killing in the presence of the Grimspeaker, they can demand another to surrender in her name. Roll a Communication (Leadership) test vs. the bandit's Willpower (Morale) to make it happen.

Bluecat and his six minor bandit subordinates fight rhy-wolves and ignore all calls to surrender. If attacked, they flee with Mayran to the woods, or fight to the end from a strategic spot if they can't shake their pursuers. Bluecat cares about Blackdire's safety, and after that, his ability to escape with her. He'll threaten to kill Mayran to negotiate these objectives. Bluecat won't say where Blackdire is, but during any talk with the heroes where Mayran is present, a successful TN 11 Perception (Empathy) test indicates fear is keeping Mayran from saying something important. She knows Blackdire made for the secret tunnel, but not why. If present, the Grimspeaker reminds characters that Blackdire wants the Merciless Hand.

Once the bandits are subdued, the Protectors come out under a flag of truce to negotiate. The Grimspeaker greets them with silence, but the armistice holds. If told Blackdire is headed for the Merciless Hand, the Protectors admit the one in their hall is a fake, and tell the heroes where the real one is hidden. In any event, they are fully occupied with the surrendered bandits and the Grimspeaker, so it's up to the characters to stop Blackdire.

AGAINST THE MERCILESS HAND

Mayran told Blackdire about the fort's secret entrance (see **Part 1**) and where the Protectors keep the Merciless Hand. While the heroes deal with the siege, Blackdire takes two veteran bandits into the secret passage and the fort's basement to find the artifact. The fort is short-handed: one Makvael guard watches the basement, and he's only just been told the tunnel exists.

The Narrator should stage Blackdire's progress based on how swiftly the heroes follow her, but with an eye towards setting the confrontation at a dramatic moment, such as when she acquires the Merciless Hand. Unless interrupted, her force bursts in, kills the guard before he can call out, breaks the lock on the treasury room, and, after a few moments of searching, smashes open the box containing the artifact. If allowed to continue, she kills or subdues anyone in her way and opens the gate, expecting to find her bandits ready to rush in.

If the tide has turned, she escapes with as many bandits as possible to regroup at Keening Stray. Surrendered bandits won't attack her, and the Makvaels are too frightened of her to try anything.

Unaware of how rapidly it spreads Corruption, Blackdire uses the Merciless Hand in an uninhibited fashion to battle heroes but she won't touch the Valtyre or the Grimspeaker, who remain bound by their oath not to harm her unless she harms them. If Bluecat is still active, he fights by her side, taking Mayran hostage, if possible. While Blackdire would attack the Protectors, the Narrator should ensure they are busy with the aftermath of the siege, securing prisoners and putting out fires.

In victory, the scene likely ends in Blackdire's death or capture. Once either of these is revealed to the Five Beast Army, its remaining forces flee or surrender, depending on each bandit's situation.

SCENE 2

RECONCILIATION

ROLEPLAYING ENCOUNTER

It isn't enough to just overcome the Five Beasts and end the violence. The community needs to be healed. This scene assumes the heroes defeat Blackdire and force the Five Beast Army to back down. Read or paraphrase the following:

> *Allies and enemies gather in the field near the trade-house, between the two halves of the village. The sharp smells of smoke and blood assail you. Rhy-wolves wander the field. Villagers crouch here and there to pick up stones and fallen weapons, while bandits look at them with alarm before glancing at the weapons they surrendered, lying perhaps only a short dash away. The atmosphere is tense, and the truce could break at any minute.*

The Makvaels want revenge. Unless the characters intervene, they start throwing stones and closing in to assault the bandits, or worse. If threatened with close combat, the bandits reclaim their fallen weapons.

The Grimspeaker doesn't do anything unless someone gives her the Merciless Hand. Otherwise, she says words to the effect of, "These people are governed by the Aldins now, are they not? It is they who must lend me their trust." The Protectors stand between the Makvaels and the bandits, but don't have enough loyal staff to prevent a melee. On top of that, they still don't understand the symbolic role of the Hand, which the heroes should bring to their attention. Once the Grimspeaker takes possession of the Hand she gestures the Valtyre to step between the factions and put a stop to any further bloodshed.

Now the heroes must work with the Grimspeaker and the Protectors to resolve the following issues:

Amnesty for most of the bandits is one of the Grimspeaker's conditions for renewing relations. The Makvaels who suffered their predations won't agree to this unless they receive reparations for their injuries and lost property. At the very least, the former Five Beast Army must confess its crimes.

What is to be done with the Five Beasts? If captured, Whitebear and Redhawk submit to the Grimspeaker's judgment. Bluecat agrees to anything he believes will keep Blackdire safe. If they didn't kill any Trebutane, the community takes them back. If they did (and Redhawk might be considered responsible for the deaths of the two Makvaels who were killed near Shadowell) they are never allowed back, but can't be simply banished to become somebody else's problem. If the Grimspeaker commands it, they are sent to an Aldin court in the south to be judged, but she won't do that unless the rank and file bandits gain amnesty.

Greenasp not only drugged and abused young people, but has a history of poisoning people in the past. The Makvaels want him executed, but that's not the Aldin way. The Protectors are unlikely to agree to it, though they admit it may not be safe to transport him somewhere where he can be properly dealt with.

If Blackdire lives, the Grimspeaker wishes to take custody of her and cure her ailing spirit, but the Protectors don't want one person minding her and the Merciless Hand at the same time.

The Protectors need the Trebutane to trust them with community conflicts and problems. To make that happen, the Grimspeaker must lend them her support on an ongoing basis, perhaps through shared meetings. Furthermore, the Grimspeaker must absolutely condemn the Trebutane's confused intolerance of the Protectors' relationship, and Valan's laevvel identity. This last is simple as the Grimspeaker was wise enough for that when they first met decades ago. But, unless both conditions are met, the Protectors leave, and the Ashlock will be weakened against future aggressors.

The Narrator should make negotiations as easy or as difficult as the players would enjoy, but there are few definitively right or wrong answers. This is about finding a balance of interests amidst the various feuds, and creating a basis for members of the community to trust each other.

If the negotiations succeed, the Grimspeaker, Protectors, and Trebutane from both clans ritually sanctify their promises before Anwaren, much as the first Grimspeaker did to liberate the clans from Kern, but this time, everyone will remember their errors. There's a moment of peaceful silence, but a chill wind slithers down from the Ice-Binder Mountains, where the Errant Master's long lost fortress still lies hidden. A story for some other time, perhaps…

REWARDS

Successfully completing the story of *The Sixth Beast* should be sufficient for the heroes to gain a new level, particularly if they were successful in overcoming the bandits and their schemes. Success is also likely to bring the heroes some noteriety and the attention of their superiors in the city of Aldis.

If the heroes put an end to banditry in the Ashlock, each of them earns one of following honorifics, based on the character's most notable actions: Champion of Justice, Defender of the Weald, or Rhydan Friend (though for this last one, the character should have made an exceptional impression on the Valtyre). If they help negotiate lasting peace, the Protectors send word to Sylvan Ford and beyond. Eventually, word catches up with them: they've each earned the Peacemaker's Ring of Aldis. The Narrator may decide that events have also inspired one or more companions to stand with them; Mayran is the most likely candidate.

ALLIES & ADVERSARIES

The Sixth Beast is ultimately a character-driven adventure. Use the following information to add complexity to its scenes, inspire side stories, build new relationships, and prepare future series.

SUPPORTING CHARACTERS

The following characters can be taken from **Chapter 12** of the *Blue Rose* core rulebook with little or no adjustments.

MAYRAN, AKA "GRAYLARK:"

Mayran is the sixteen-year-old daughter of Protectors Markion and Valan. Treat her as a baseline human (0 in all ability scores, 10 Health); her talents have yet to surface. After early childhood, she grew to resent her parents for raising her in the wild, but discovered the Trebutane tradition of collective childrearing applied to her. The people treated her well, except when the subject of her parents came up. The Trebutane blamed them for the Grimspeaker's absence and instilled in her their own personal biases. Mayran left the fort, and Blackdire stepped in to act as a parental figure.

VILLAGERS

When the adventure lists a character without noting anything beyond a name, use the baseline humans (stats 0, Health 10), as listed in **Chapter 12** of the *Blue Rose* core rulebook. About one in twenty of the Ashlock's Trebutane are vata (vata'an and a handful of vata'sha), not human. They share the same baseline traits as humans, but possess a Novice arcane talent from lose listed for the vata in *Blue Rose* **Chapter 2**. Elders and youngsters have lower ability scores, especially Strength and Constitution, as well as having less Health. They typically flee violence or surrender to assailants if escape is not possible. The young, drugged Makvael captives in **Part 3, Scene 2** of this adventure use the stats of baseline humans, but with +2 Strength and the Willpower test adjustments listed previously.

THE VALTYRE

The Valtyre are a pack of eighteen rhy-wolves allied with the Grimspeaker. They possess the **rhy-wolf** stats given in **Chapter 12** of the *Blue Rose* core rulebook.

MINOR BANDIT		
ABILITIES (FOCUSES)		
2	ACCURACY (BOWS, LIGHT BLADES)	
1	COMMUNICATION	
2	CONSTITUTION	
2	DEXTERITY (STEALTH)	
2	FIGHTING (BLUDGEONS)	
0	INTELLIGENCE	
1	PERCEPTION (TRACKING)	
1	STRENGTH (INTIMIDATION)	
0	WILLPOWER (MORALE)	

SPEED	HEALTH	DEFENSE	ARMOR RATING
12	15	12	3

WEAPON	ATTACK ROLL	DAMAGE
CLUB	+4	2D6+1
DAGGER	+4	1D6+2

SPECIAL QUALITIES

FAVORED STUNTS: Knock Prone, Skirmish

TALENTS: Armor Training (Novice), Single Weapon Style (Novice)

WEAPONS GROUPS: Bludgeons, Bows, Brawling, Heavy Blades, and Light Blades

EQUIPMENT: Club, Dagger, Light Leather Armor

THREAT: MINOR

VETERAN BANDIT		
ABILITIES (FOCUSES)		
3	ACCURACY (BOWS, LIGHT BLADES)	
1	COMMUNICATION	
2	CONSTITUTION	
2	DEXTERITY (STEALTH)	
3	FIGHTING (BLUDGEONS, HEAVY BLADES, POLEARMS)	
0	INTELLIGENCE	
1	PERCEPTION (TRACKING)	
1	STRENGTH (INTIMIDATION)	
1	WILLPOWER (MORALE)	

SPEED	HEALTH	DEFENSE	ARMOR RATING
10	20	12	5

WEAPON	ATTACK ROLL	DAMAGE
DAGGER	+5	1D6+2
SPEAR	+5	1D6+4
SWORD	+5	2D6+1

SPECIAL QUALITIES

TALENTS: Armor Training (Novice), Pole Weapon Style (Novice), Single Weapon Style (Novice)

WEAPONS GROUPS: Bludgeons, Bows, Brawling, Heavy Blades, Light Blades, and Polearms

EQUIPMENT: Dagger, Medium Chain Mail Armor, Spear, Sword

THREAT: MINOR

MINOR BANDITS

These are the rank-and-file bandits of the Five Beast Army. Some are armed with better weapons, as given in specific encounters. Beyond specific locations in the adventure, the number of bandits isn't set. When necessary, the Narrator can introduce groups from distant single family settlements or ones who previously left the Ashlock to raid other communities in the Pavin Weald.

VETERAN BANDITS

These are the more seasoned and better-trained members of the Five Beast Army. Veteran bandits wear medium armor (chain mail or metal plates over leather) and carry spears that enable them to strike from behind a line of minor bandits. They resort to their swords if enemies close in.

MAJOR CHARACTERS

The following characters don't get detailed stats for a different reason: they're noncombatants by choice and circumstance. The Narrator should handle their interventions through in-game descriptions, adding capabilities (arcana, talents, and so on) only if required. If provided with a full write-up, each of them would be 5th level or higher, though age and inactivity has begun to take the edge off their powers.

THE GRIMSPEAKER

Sheena Makvael was a gifted adept and, as a Makvael, was considered the proper successor to the previous Daradmor Grimspeaker. And so, she became a Hara and settled inter-clan disputes among the Ashlock's Trebutane. When the Errant Master came down from the frozen mountains she helped three Knights of the Blue Rose defeat it, but the future Protectors refused to entrust her with

the Merciless Hand. Sworn to silence about her people's history, she couldn't tell them why she needed it, nor why she was offended. She didn't expect her people's unity to fray so quickly, and once she realized her mistake, she made the grave error of selecting Veldra Daradmor to succeed her. As her student gathers belligerent Daradmors to conquer the Ashlock, Sheena searches for a solution.

The Grimspeaker is a skilled adept and lore-keeper of her people. She uses her arcana to heal and refresh characters for the challenges that await them at the adventure's end. She is a 5'10", tough-looking woman of 61, with long, iron-colored hair and green eyes.

MARKION AND VALAN, PROTECTORS

Markion and Valan became lovers on the road. They were members of the Rose Knights, driven by wanderlust, a desire to do good, and the visions of Selena, the adept who first brought them together. In fact, it was her visions that led them to the Ashlock. The three knights lingered to help the Trebutane through various crises, such as conflicts with the forest folk, Kernish infiltrators, and strange creatures hidden in the Pavin Weald.

When the Errant Master came, the Trebutane turned to them once again, and even their religious leader aided them. They defeated the unliving creature, but at the cost of Selena's life. As she lay dying, she warned them to guard its scepter. They refused the Grimspeaker's request to take possession of it, and in doing do, lost her trust. The Noble Council titled them Protectors, charged with defending the region. As they settled in, they had little idea that Trebutane unity was unraveling around them. The two factions began to argue about petty things, even though they had lived peacefully for generations before.

Softly-spoken Markion is a graceful, bald, long-fingered man of 63 who wears dark, form-fitting clothes over his 6-foot frame. The small, concealed dagger he always carries is a habit kept over from his days as a covert emissary for the Sovereign's Finest. Valan is 54, but looks a decade younger. He wears his hair close-cropped and has kept his sword arm strong. To the Trebutane, Valan, who gave birth to his daughter Mayran, is a woman, but the aging warrior is, in reality, a laevvel man. Neither Protector will take up arms against the Trebutane, though they might keep them occupied with defensive action. They perform with as much or as little competence as the Narrator requires, though age has slowed them, particularly Markion.

THE FIVE BEASTS

The Five Beasts answered Blackdire's call to drive out the Aldins and enslave the Makvaels in penance for their ancestors' crimes. The Grimspeaker's hour is done, and it is time for retribution and pride to defeat quiet shame. Each Beast uses a mask and matching codename. Their real names aren't general knowledge.

BLUECAT (KAELIC DARADMOR)

Born among Trebutane who were part of the original Highblood rebellion, Kaelic Daradmor (nee Sharphand) was a hunter and peacemaker for hire who stalked the outer Pavin Weald. He never had much use for Aldins, but he wasn't a criminal, either. If forest folk had the coin, he guarded them and caught their fugitives. But notorious outlaws, the Wistland Sisters, got the better of him. They knocked him out, stole everything he possessed, and left him to die in the mountains. Veldra Daradmor saved him before he froze to death, having stumbled across him as she wandered the Ice-Binders in search of the tomb of the Errant Master.

BLUECAT

His gratitude quickly transformed into love and unwavering loyalty. He took up Veldra's cause, believed everything she had to say about the "treacherous" Makvaels, and became Bluecat, first of the masked beasts besides Blackdire herself.

Bluecat is a hale, broad-shouldered 6'1" human male. His blue cloak is always dusty. His cracked mask bears the knot-work image of the Saithca, a lynx-like arcane cat from Trebutane legends. He owns nothing which hasn't been marked by the road with dirt, scratches, and frayed edges. His shaggy hair is an iron-shot black. He keeps two sharp, one-handed axes by his side, along with a bow and a round, hide-covered shield. He looks every battered day of his thirty-three years.

BLACKDIRE (VELDRA DARADMOR)

On the whole, Veldra Daradmor's visions terrified her. She grew up on an isolated homestead north of Shadowell, and though the adept's gifts sometimes opened her inner eye to the bright beauty of living things, at other times she saw the shadows grow claws, and a cold, skeletal thing in rotting finery. Her parents told her it was the Errant Master who'd come before she was born and there was nothing

BLUECAT

ABILITIES (FOCUSES)	
2	ACCURACY (BOWS)
0	COMMUNICATION
4	CONSTITUTION (STAMINA)
1	DEXTERITY
3	FIGHTING (AXES)
0	INTELLIGENCE
3	PERCEPTION (TRACKING)
2	STRENGTH (INTIMIDATION)
1	WILLPOWER

SPEED	HEALTH	DEFENSE	ARMOR RATING
9	50	13	5

WEAPON	ATTACK ROLL	DAMAGE
AXE	+5	2D6+2
BOW	+4	1D6+4
UNARMED	+2	1D3+2

SPECIAL QUALITIES

FAVORED STUNTS: Knock Prone, Skirmish, The Upper Hand (when tracking opponents)

TALENTS: Armor Training (Novice), Weapon and Shield Style (Journeyman)

WEAPONS GROUPS: Axes, Bows, Brawling, Heavy Blades

EQUIPMENT: 12 Arrows, Axes, Bow, Medium Shield, Scale Mail

THREAT: MODERATE

BLACKDIRE

ABILITIES (FOCUSES)	
0	ACCURACY
4	COMMUNICATION (LEADERSHIP, PERFORMANCE, PSYCHIC)
2	CONSTITUTION
2	DEXTERITY
0	FIGHTING
4	INTELLIGENCE (NATURAL LORE, SORCERY LORE)
3	PERCEPTION
-1	STRENGTH
4	WILLPOWER

SPEED	HEALTH	DEFENSE	ARMOR RATING
11	42	12	1

WEAPON	ATTACK ROLL	DAMAGE
STAFF	+0	1D6
UNARMED	+0	1D3-1

SPECIAL QUALITIES

ARCANA: Light Shaping (Wild), Move Object, Psychic Shield, Second Sight, Sorcerer's Grip (Wild), Suggestion, Torment (Wild), Visions

FAVORED STUNTS: Mighty Arcana, Passionate Inspiration, Skillful Channeling, The Upper Hand

HEROES' ARMOR: Veldra is considered to have an armor rating of 1, or the rating of the armor she is wearing—whichever is better—even if she is not wearing armor at all.

TALENTS: Bard (Novice), Lore (Novice), Medicine (Novice), Shaping (Novice), Visionary (Novice), Wild Arcane (Novice)

WEAPONS GROUPS: Brawling, Staves

EQUIPMENT: Staff

THREAT: MODERATE

BLUE ROSE

SIX OF SWORDS

for her to fear from it now. She left the Ashlock as a teenager to escape the visions, but they never went away. Indeed, she called on them when she was alone, to focus her power. When a drunk woman accosted her, she imagined her hand was the iron claw; her harasser screamed and fled. It was her first taste of sorcery. She returned home, where rhy-wolves led her to the Grimspeaker.

BLACKDIRE

Veldra was a poor student. She remembered the Makvaels' ancient crimes, but not the Daradmors'. She abandoned the Grimspeaker and searched the mountains for the Errant Master's lair. She never found it but, instead, met Bluecat, and after that, others: Daradmors who'd left the Ashlock but hated Aldin "decadence;" people that wanted the Ashlock to have only Trebutane customs and to put the Makvaels in their place. They became the Five Beasts, and raised an army of malcontents. She plans to take up the Merciless Hand, restore honor to her people, and ignore the laughing, skull-faced man of her visions, who seems to delight in every spark of hate she feels.

Blackdire stands barely five feet tall. Beneath her black robes she seems drained of color, with hair like dry straw and a thin, ashen face that makes her look older than her twenty-six years. But that face is hardly ever visible as she rarely removes her black wooden mask, carved into a snarling wolf's visage.

GREENASP (VIKOR DARADMOR)

While the other Beasts left the Ashlock of their own accord, Vikor Daradmor was exiled. The herbalist originally sold plants and preparations through Kaerith Ashlock's trade-house alongside his brother, Vatric, but used the same knowledge to make drugs and poisons. The community couldn't prove he was behind the deaths of two Makvaels and a foreign visitor, but their suspicions were strong

GREENASP

enough for a gang to beat him unconscious, tie him up, and put him on a raft with a warning to never, ever return.

Blackdire found him in Kella's Ford, where travelers fell victim to his experiments. She offered him a chance to take revenge on the Makvaels; in return, he offered to find a use for them through his recent work with warweed. Greenasp knows that even though he stands with the Daradmors, they'd never trust him if they knew he was Vikor, suspected poisoner. He doesn't feel guilty

about it. Point of fact, he's never felt guilty about much of anything.

Greenasp wears a dark green, snake-headed mask and cloak over leather clothes covered with pouches. The herbs he carries make him smell like vanilla and fresh-dug clay. At 5'7", he has a thick, short-limbed build, and a bowlegged gait that makes him look less agile than he truly is. He is twenty-five, with short brown hair and watery blue eyes.

GREENASP

ABILITIES (FOCUSES)	
3	ACCURACY
0	COMMUNICATION
0	CONSTITUTION
3	DEXTERITY (CRAFTING, STEALTH)
2	FIGHTING
4	INTELLIGENCE (HEALING, NATURAL LORE)
2	PERCEPTION
0	STRENGTH
1	WILLPOWER

SPEED	HEALTH	DEFENSE	ARMOR RATING
13	35	13	3

WEAPON	ATTACK ROLL	DAMAGE
DAGGER	+3	1D6+1
NEEDLE (THROWN)	+3	1D3 + POISON
UNARMED	+3	1D3

SPECIAL QUALITIES

EXPERT'S ARMOR: The poisoner is at home in Light Armor and is considered trained in its use without the need of the Armor Training talent.

PINPOINT ATTACK: Once per round, if Greenasp's Dexterity is greater than his target's, he does an additional 1d6 damage on a successful attack.

POISON NEEDLES: If Greenasp strikes with one of his needles and it inflicts at least 1 point of damage, spend 2 SP (if available) to inflict an additional 1d6 damage and 1 level of fatigue. This may be resisted if the victim succeeds at a TN 13 Constitution (Stamina) test. Successive needle attacks have cumulative effects.

STUNT BONUS: Greenasp is adept at finding the weak spots in his opponents' armor, physically and otherwise. He performs the Pierce Armor or Taunt combat stunts for 1 SP instead of the usual 2.

TALENTS: Medicine (Novice), Thievery (Novice)

WEAPONS GROUPS: Bows, Brawling, Light Blades, Staves

EQUIPMENT: 2 Daggers, 10 Poison Needles, Light Leather Armor

THREAT: MODERATE

Redhawk

ABILITIES (FOCUSES)	
3	ACCURACY
0	COMMUNICATION
2	CONSTITUTION
-1	DEXTERITY
0	FIGHTING
3	INTELLIGENCE (SHAPING)
3	PERCEPTION (TRACKING)
0	STRENGTH
3	WILLPOWER

SPEED	HEALTH	DEFENSE	ARMOR RATING
9	30	9	0

WEAPON	ATTACK ROLL	DAMAGE
STAFF	+0	1D6
UNARMED	+0	1D3

SPECIAL QUALITIES

ARCANA: Body Control (Wild), Fire Shaping (Wild), Move Object, Psychic Shield, Psychic Weapon (Wild)

FAVORED STUNTS: Mighty Arcana, Skillful Channeling

TALENTS: Observation (Novice), Shaping (Novice), Wild Arcane (Novice)

WEAPONS GROUPS: Brawling, Staves

EQUIPMENT: Staff

THREAT: MODERATE

REDHAWK (AROWAN MAKVAEL)

Redhawk is Arowan Makvael, an adept who discovered his potential as a teenager. In a moment of anger, he burned down his family's forest homestead. Already bullied by Daradmors, the family left the Ashlock on a trader's boat. They brought Arowan along, but refused to speak to him because of what he'd done. He slipped away at a rest stop, fending for himself at the edge of the Pavin Weald. A year later, the other Beasts came south for supplies and recognized his rags were once Trebutane clothing. He was hungry and impressed with Blackdire's sorcery, so he posed as a Daradmor from a family that had settled in Aldis.

REDHAWK

He is ashamed of what he's become but he's angry, too: at his family who took him away but withdrew their love for him, and at the Makvaels for being weak and allowing themselves to be bullied.

Whitebear

ABILITIES (FOCUSES)	
2	ACCURACY
0	COMMUNICATION
4	CONSTITUTION (RUNNING, STAMINA, SWIMMING)
0	DEXTERITY
4	FIGHTING (HEAVY BLADES)
0	INTELLIGENCE
0	PERCEPTION
4	STRENGTH (CLIMBING)
2	WILLPOWER (COURAGE)

SPEED	HEALTH	DEFENSE	ARMOR RATING
10	54	10	3

WEAPON	ATTACK ROLL	DAMAGE
TWO-HANDED SWORD	+6	3D6+4
DAGGER	+2	1D6+5
UNARMED	+2	1D3+4

SPECIAL QUALITIES

FAVORED STUNTS: Knock Prone, Mighty Blow (1 SP)

TALENTS: Armor Training (Novice), Two-Handed Style (Journeyman)

WEAPONS GROUPS: Bludgeons, Brawling, Light Blades, Heavy Blades

EQUIPMENT: Dagger, Light Leather Armor, Two-Handed Sword

THREAT: MODERATE

Redhawk is named for the color and design of his mask, but observers may mistakenly believe it is because he is garbed in nothing but red clothing, cut in the Trebutane style. Blackdire paid an Aldin tailor to make them; they're all he wears, and they're getting somewhat grubby. Underneath the robes, he's a long-limbed man of twenty with thick brown hair, dark brown eyes, and a perpetually flushed face.

WHITEBEAR (KALIA DARADMOR)

Kalia Daradmor's family lived in an isolated homestead north of Keening Stray. A bad year of hunting and trapping forced them to move to Kaerith Ashlock and rely on clan charity. Always quick to use her fists, Kalia fought Makvael children incessantly, and as she grew taller and faster than the rest, became known as a bully, until in a moment of humiliation, she was

WHITEBEAR

censured in a community gathering. She was a teenager, barely old enough to leave, but leave she did, making her way as a trapper until she found a place for her size and aggressiveness with a Rezean mercenary band. But a terrible battle in the Golgan Badlands (she won't talk about it) prompted her to return home, where she settled in an old hunting cabin.

The Five Beast Army only had three Beasts and a handful of followers when they stumbled into her home, hoping to use it as a supply cache. She fought them off with a log and thrown rocks until Blackdire intervened. She became their military trainer. For her it's not about the cause, but a sense of purpose.

Kalia is twenty-eight years old. She's a broad, muscular 6'1", and under her dirty white cloak and white bear mask, her shaved head is covered in small scars; near misses from her military career.

ARCANE ITEMS

An item of great power is a part of the action of **The Sixth Beast**, the weapon known as the Merciless Hand.

THE MERCILESS HAND

When the Shadow Wars consumed the Sorcerer Kings, Karthod of the Ice stood aside to let the his enemies destroy each other. He wasn't interested in Aldea and its kingdoms of earth and flesh, but in a place beside the exarchs. He interrogated darkfiends, and searched for the basic sentience of the Shadow itself: the ineffable voice that called Anwaren at the dawn of all things. He kept to his fortress in the Ice-Binder Mountains, with two castes of servants. One captured mortals for him, using weapons and armor they forged themselves; the other prepared captives for his twisted experiments. Karthod believed the Shadow required a host to manifest in to speak, but the subject needed to withstand immeasurable corruption, beyond even that inflicted by sorcery. If one of his victims survived, he would use the method on himself.

After tormenting numerous experimental subjects, Karthod believed he'd found a way: to "share" the inherent corruption of his process with an artifact. Karthod's spies reported rivals falling one by one, and he believed he was ready to act, but Jarek's army attacked before he could fully summon the Shadow into himself, or his scepter, the Merciless Hand. The Lich King of Kern was short of troops able to dare the Ice-Binders, so he offered Karthod's servants their

freedom in return for betraying their master. The lie worked well enough to turn them. They impaled Karthod, sealed his fortress and went to Kern, unaware that they, the Daradmors and Makvaels, would be made into slaves once again.

Jarek knew nothing of the scepter's significance, and so didn't search for it. The Daradmors and Makvaels of the Ashlock remembered nothing about serving Karthod other than tales of a bogeyman with an iron hand; a Merciless Hand. They called Karthod's weakened corpse the "Errant Master" because it came down from the mountains bearing the scepter, babbling about its lost slaves.

The Hand is a scepter of six strands of braided wrought iron that blossom into an inhuman hand, with a mark—a Makvael maker's sign—etched into the palm. It confers the following abilities:

The Merciless Hand is a bludgeon that inflicts 2d6 damage + the wielder's Corruption score.

It provides its wielder with an armor rating of 5. This doesn't stack with other armor. Blows that would otherwise cause injury strike but do not inflict wounds or bruises. The area struck takes on a corpse-like pallor instead, and cuts do not bleed. Such marks fade within a day.

The Hand grants its wielder access to the following arcana: Cold Shaping, Imbue Unlife, Psychic Shield, and Psychic Blast. Using an arcanum through the power of the Hand risks a Corruption test regardless of its intended purpose.

If the Hand's wielder is an adept, as a major action they can simultaneously use one of the Hand's arcana as well as their own, rolling any arcana and fatigue tests separately.

Most dangerously, an adept holding the Hand feels the cold power inside it. The scepter seems to shift and twist in their grasp, as its energy yearns to be released. The adept knows the Hand will absorb any Fatigue inflicted through the use of arcana, or any other source, but not that it bestows a point of Corruption per level of Fatigue absorbed. Unlike other sources of Corruption, its effects on Willpower and Constitution do not take effect until the Hand passes out of the wielder's possession or scores in either ability drop below –5. Thus, its user may tap into its power without realizing the sickness of body and spirit that will inevitably follow. The only overt signs afflicting the user are a persistent chill and an ever-increasing pallor.

The Merciless Hand offers additional powers to stronger characters. The Narrator may design these freely, and develop it into a campaign-altering item if they wish.

The heroes, envoys of the Sovereign's Finest, have a mission: they must travel deep into the Veran Marsh and infiltrate the Silence's notorious Night Market. Once there, and without drawing undue attention, they must recover a shard of the Shadow Heptagram, a powerful arcane item, before it can be sold at auction.

The Night Market is designed for a group of four to six *Blue Rose* heroes, levels 3 to 5. The envoys are chosen for this mission because they have some experience under their belts but are not likely to have enough notoriety to be easily recognized by the agents of the Silence.

This adventure focuses primarily on roleplaying and exploration encounters, although chances are it ends in a big fight. Some suggestions are included for groups who prefer more combat in their adventures.

INTRODUCTION

A RARE FIND

A few months ago, a sea-folk looter working with the Silence uncovered a treasure trove of riches scattered among the wreckage of a merchant ship at the bottom of the Leviathan's Teeth. He turned the booty over to his masters, who discovered a shard of the fabled Shadow Heptagram among the recovered loot. How it came to be on board when the ship went down remains unknown.

Eventually it made found its way to one of the Silence's agents, Lady Lianca, the manager of the Night Market.

The collection of items salvaged from the wrecked ship has just the right air of mystery to draw wealthy and obsessive bidders to the next Night Market, held in the depths of the Veran Marsh for its isolation and the influence smugglers already wield there. Invitations go out to those with a known interest in such black market goods. Fortunately, the invitation to the Arcanist Einur was intercepted by the Sovereign's Finest.

Having this accurate intelligence, and knowing that most of those interested in such items would only bid through a proxy, the Queen called upon Knight-Captain Grayson. Her task is to assemble a team of envoys to infiltrate the Night Market and recover the remnant of the Shadow Heptagram. The player characters are the members of that team.

The heroes make their way into the Veran Marsh, encountering various hazards and threats along the way. When they reach the site of the Night Market, they use guile and their fake credentials to gain entry and explore, interacting with some of the worst criminals in Aldis. They have the opportunity to size-up the opposition, and potentially have a few run-ins. Finally, they must find and seize an opportunity at the auction to grab the Shadow Heptagram and escape with it, as well as any other dangerous artifacts up for sale they can get their hands on.

ADAPTING THE ADVENTURE

While this adventure is designed for characters of levels 3–5, it can be modified for higher level heroes. Most of the adventure revolves around investigation and roleplaying encounters, so the Narrator should only have to modify the target numbers for those scenes by a few points, if necessary. For combat encounters, the Narrator can modify the antagonists using the guidelines in the Beefing Up Adversaries section of *Blue Rose* **Chapter 1**2.

While the adventure is written to involve members of the Sovereign's Finest, it can also be adapted to work with a variety of other protagonists. The player characters can just as easily be agents from Jarzon or any other interested nation. The Narrator should modify the nationality of Dez Taliviour and his people accordingly, in that case.

If you are running a *Blue Rose* game featuring rogues and scoundrels, the player characters could be members of a rival organization out to deal a blow to the Silence, weakening their control over the criminal elements of Aldin society.

THE VERAN MARSH

The Night Market is set in the Veran Marsh, with most of the events taking place on the southern passage or in the ruins of Veran-Norpar.

Located on the eastern edge of Aldis, the Veran Mash serves as a natural buffer with the theocracy of Jarzon. The region was decimated during the Shadow Wars, which has made the area volatile when certain shaping arcana are used. There are four known passages through the Veran Marsh, with the ruins of Veran-Norpar being closest to the southern passage. This route is plagued by attacks from both troglodytes and bandits venturing north from Serpent's Haven. For details on the Veran Marsh area and the southern passage see **Chapter 6** of *Blue Rose*.

The city of Veran-Tath served as the region's capital during the height of the Sorcerer Kings' reign. Before the destruction of the Shadow Wars, several outposts fortified Veran-Tath. One such—Veran-Norpar—functioned as a watch station for the lands to the south of the capital, and was all but destroyed in the battle leading to the final annihilation of Veran-Tath.

OVERVIEW OF THE NIGHT MARKET

Several years ago, the Silence acquired a small collection of rare relics dating back to the Empire of Thorns. An auction seemed the perfect opportunity to maximize profits by subtly encouraging competition, ego, and greed among the invitees. The event was a far greater success than expected. Over the years, the auction transformed into a significant

underworld event, starting with an early evening market where vendors sold various items of questionable legality, and culminating in a formal midnight auction of the rarest and most valuable items collected by the Silence. Invitations remain very limited and are highly coveted.

The Night Market, as it is now known, is a semi-regular bazaar and auction put on by the Silence which has seen steady growth under the guidance of Lady Lianca. Known to be strictly enforced neutral ground, where theft or violence against attendees provokes severe punishment, the market serves an additional purpose: it is quite useful as a meeting ground for negotiating, making deals, and establishing alliances between various criminals and outlaw groups. The Silence benefits greatly from this by gathering information, making new contacts, and recruiting potential candidates.

When the Night Market occurs fluctuates based on the items the Silence has acquired and feels would bring the best price via auction. A not-accidental side effect of this means the authorities have trouble predicting when the next event will occur. The market is never held in the same location twice in a row. While the first auction took place at a private estate in the heart of Aldis, these days the Silence prefers to host it in a remote location that won't draw any undue attention.

The marketplace officially runs from shortly before sunset until midnight, at which time the main auction begins. The crew and vendors spend most of the day setting up the market, starting with its tavern pavilion. Traveling guests that arrive early are welcome to drink and relax in the pavilion until the rest of the market is ready for visitors.

Loyal agents of the Silence deliver a nondescript envelope to those invited. The only writing on the envelopes is the name of the recipient, and the sole indication of who sent the invitation is the black wax used as a seal. The invi-

ALTERNATE OPENINGS

For Narrators wanting to expand the opening—which could be useful if the envoys are lower level—there are a couple of options.

Instead of using the read aloud text above, the Narrator could run the meeting with Knight-Captain Grayson as a roleplaying scene, and add a few minor encounters as the envoys travel to the Veran Marsh. This would allow them a chance to gain some experience before reaching the main adventure.

Another option would be to have the envoys intercept the invitation before it reaches Arcanist Einur's remote tower as part of their mission from Knight-Captain Grayson, before proceeding with the main adventure.

OPTIONAL SCENES

As noted in the **Introduction**, this adventure is lighter on combat than some groups may prefer. If your group enjoys combat scenes, add one or more of the following encounters between any of the scenes in **Part 1: Journey to the Night Market**.

TROGLODYTE CAMP

This is a scene to run after **Scene 2: Road Kill**. If the envoys want to track the troglodytes, have them roll a TN 15 Perception (Tracking) test to follow them back to their camp; if they fail the roll, the characters lose the trail. When the envoys arrive at the camp there should be one troglodyte per character, plus two others with only half their Health remaining due to injuries. See *Blue Rose* **Chapter 12** for the troglodytes' stats.

If your game's circumstances require stats for the two prisoners, you can use the Rogue write up (also in *Blue Rose* **Chapter 12**), but they should only have 5 Health each.

SERPENT'S HAVEN BANDITS

A gang of bandits from Serpent's Haven thinks the envoys are easy marks. For the bandits, use the **Night Market Guard** stats in the **Adversaries** section.

TROGLODYTE PATROL

There should be two troglodytes for every three characters in the group (round up). One of the troglodytes has two crocodiles on chains, which they unleash if combat breaks out. See *Blue Rose* **Chapter 12** for stats for this scene.

MOCK HOUNDS

A pack of five mock hounds stalks the envoys from the edges of the road. See *Blue Rose* **Chapter 12** for mock hound stats.

tation consists of a small card with the name of a location written on it and a token to give to the market guard for entrance. The current token is a small wooden disk that bears a carving of an oak tree; the pass phrase is: "Canopy of night with roots deep in the earth."

A new token is designed for each market event. Past tokens have included rare and exotic feathers, a unique piece of jewelry crafted for each recipient, and an embossed leather coin purse.

PART 1

JOURNEY TO THE NIGHT MARKET

In **Part 1**, the heroes learn the details of their mission to infiltrate the Night Market as well as their goal of recovering the shard of the Shadow Heptagram. In order to accomplish this goal, the player characters must navigate the dangers of the Veran Marsh and enter the ruins of Veran-Norpar.

To begin, read or paraphrase the following to the players:

Your band of envoys is tasked with infiltrating the elusive Night Market—the notorious moving black market and auction controlled by the Silence. Several previous attempts to root out the Night Market have failed and it is believed the Silence has members with psychic arcana as well as more mundane spies operating throughout Aldis. To avoid being compromised, your group must not reveal your true identities or mission to anyone. Besides the Queen, her most trusted advisers, and Knight-Captain Grayson, no one else is aware of this mission.

Through spies of their own, the inner council of the Sovereign's Finest has learned the next Night Market will be held in the ruins of Veran-Norpar, deep in the Veran Marsh. Along with other dangerous and contraband items, the Silence is auctioning a shard of the Shadow Heptagram, a fragment of a touchstone used by the Sorcerer Kings and a powerful arcane artifact.

Posing as agents of Einur, a reclusive adept with an unhealthy obsession for such artifacts, your group must navigate the perils of the Veran Marsh and infiltrate the Night Market. Once there, you are charged with acquiring the shard of the Shadow Heptagram, along with any other dangerous relics you can obtain. You have also been requested to gather intelligence on those who run and frequent the Night Market. To assist your mission, Knight-Captain Grayson has provided you with an ancient map of the former Veran region.

Knight-Captain Grayson is a member of the Knights of the Blue Rose and is currently assigned to Aldis as a trainer and mentor for the Aldin Guard and Knights of the Blue Rose recruits. She is a human with reddish-brown hair dusted with a few hints of steel gray, making her blue-gray eyes seem more grayish.

SCENE 1

WATCHERS ON THE ROAD

EXPLORATION/COMBAT ENCOUNTER

Making their way along the southern route through the Veran Marsh, the envoys encounter an Aldin patrol from Lysana's Crossing, consisting of a number of Warriors (*Blue Rose* **Chapter 12**) equal to the number of envoys, plus 2. The characters should make a TN 11 Perception (Seeing) test to detect the patrol's presence; not that the patrol is trying to be stealthy! If they succeed, the heroes have the option of sneaking past the patrol, subduing them, or coming up with some other creative way of dealing with them. If they all fail the test, the patrol spots them first, and sneaking past them is no longer an option.

Envoys attempting to slip quietly past the patrol must succeed on an opposed test. The patrol uses its Perception (Seeing) vs. the envoys' Dexterity (Stealth). Failure means they are spotted and the patrol begins an uncomfortable questioning session. Spotted characters can try to fast talk their way out of this predicament, which requires winning an opposed test: their Communication (Deception) vs. Communication (Investigation). Open hostility leads to combat. If this happens, the envoys may wish to avoid doing permanent damage to the patrol, as they are also loyal agents of Aldis. Let the envoys know they have the option of pulling their punches. For rules

on doing so, see the **Incapacitating** section in *Blue Rose* **Chapter 1**.

The envoys do have the option of acknowledging who they are to the patrol; this could happen at any time during the encounter but is contrary to their orders. If the characters reveal their identity to the patrol, the patrol will let them go so they can finish their mission. One member of the patrol passes the information to Vedrick, who is already at the market. Vedrick then shares the information with Lady Lianca, who puts a plan in motion (see the **Midnight Trap** sidebar in **Part 3: Midnight Auction**).

SCENE 2

ROAD KILL

EXPLORATION ENCOUNTER

Heading further into the Veran Marsh, the envoys come across a grim scene: the half-eaten and dismembered remains of what appear to be four human bandits. This scene should impart just how dangerous the marsh is. The envoys should have the option of searching the area to gather more information about the bandits' fate.

Success on a TN 11 Perception (Searching) test reveals signs of an ambush by a group of **troglodytes**. The envoys discover a roughly sketched map of the area on a test result of TN 13 or greater. This map should prove to be useful during the next scene.

Veran Marsh Hazards

D6 ROLL	RESULT
1	**Pit Trap:** A section of ground falls away when enough pressure is put upon it, dropping the unlucky envoy into a pit 15 feet deep. If the triggering character makes a successful TN 12 Perception (Touching) test, they feel the ground starting to give way and can step back before falling in. Otherwise, the character falls and takes 2d6 penetrating damage. A successful TN 11 Dexterity (Acrobatics) test halves the damage.
2	**Troglodyte Ambush:** The characters have wandered into a troglodyte ambush. There is one troglodyte for each character, with one of the troglodytes being an adept. See *Blue Rose* **Chapter 12** for stats for this scene. For the adept in the group, add the following: **Animist**—Animism talent (Novice), Communication (Animism) focus, Arcana: Animal Summoning, Plant Shaping, Psychic Contact.
3	**Ghost Weed:** The water in a ghost weed pond is tainted with the plant's digestive acids and an anesthetic toxin. Creatures coming into contact with it require a TN 13 Constitution (Stamina) test; failure means the creature becomes paralyzed. Paralyzed victims sink into the water and may drown; a harrowing hazard that inflicts 5d6 damage per round. Characters can make an additional TN 13 Constitution (Stamina) test each round to recover and escape.
4	**Strix Nest:** Traveling through the undergrowth of the marsh, the characters approach a strix nest. Heroes making a successful TN 13 Perception (Hearing) test discern the telltale buzzing of the strix and can try to avoid them. Failing, they disturb the undergrowth causing the swarm to attack. See *Blue Rose* **Chapter 12** for stats for a strix swarm.
5	**Quick Marsh:** If the envoy triggering the hazard makes a successful TN 15 Perception (Touching) test, they feel themselves starting to sink and can move back before being swallowed up by the ground. Otherwise, they must succeed on a TN 13 Constitution (Swimming) test. If they fail, they take 2d6 penetrating damage from inhaling water and muck. The envoy can make a new test each round to escape, taking further damage on a failure.
6	**Web Trap:** A pair of **ettercaps** has set up a web trap in the hope of capturing a visitor to the market. The players roll an opposed Perception (Seeing or Searching) vs. Dexterity (Traps) test to spot the web trap. Failure indicates the hero is immediately struck by a TN 15 Web attack and is surprised as the two ettercaps rush in. Succeeding on the test indicates the characters avoid the trap and are not surprised. See *Blue Rose* **Chapter 12** for ettercap stats.

With a higher test result or the use of stunt points, the envoys could uncover any of the following details, one for every two points of Outcome or one stunt point:

- Based on the tracks, seven troglodytes took part in the attack.

- At least two of the troglodytes suffered minor injuries and one was severely injured.

- The troglodytes headed south after the attack with two prisoners.

A TN 15 Perception (Tracking) test allows the envoys to follow the troglodytes back to their camp.

SCENE 3

THE RUINS OF VERAN-NORPAR

EXPLORATION/ROLEPLAYING ENCOUNTER

Having made their way as far as they can on the southern pass, the envoys must leave the trail and cross the wilderness. They need to make an advanced test to safely navigate the marsh, with a success threshold of 15 on a TN 13 Intelligence (Navigation) test; each test represents 30 minutes of travel time whether they are successful or not.

Failing a test triggers a roll on the **Veran Marsh Hazards** table. If the envoys still have the ancient map they received from Knight-Captain Grayson, it grants a +2 bonus to their rolls. If the envoys managed to find the sketch map of the Veran Marsh from the **Scene 2**, this lowers the success threshold to 10.

Once they make it to the location of the Night Market, the envoys must present the token and pass phrase to the guards. As the envoys enter, one of the guards reaches out for one of them, saying: "Wait, don't I know you?" Ask for an opposed test, the envoy's Communication (Deception) test vs. the guard's Perception (Empathy). If the envoy fails the test, the guard mistakes the envoy as a mercenary from a rival group he has a grudge with. Drawing his knife, he demands to know what business members of the Scarlet Blade Company have at the market, as well as making dire threats against them.

The characters should realize the guard has obviously mistaken them for someone else. With a successful TN 11 Perception (Empathy) test, they also pick up that he is trying to goad them into a conflict, but won't start it himself. No test is needed for the characters to recognize the Scarlet Blade Company, as the group is a well-known band of notorious mercenaries. Stats for the Night Market guards can be found in the **Adversaries** section. If circumstances require stats for any incidental brigands, or the various weapon vendors, use the Warrior stat block in *Blue Rose* **Chapter 12**.

PART 2

EXPLORING THE NIGHT MARKET

In **Part 2**, the envoys get the chance to mingle with others attending the market, and to look at the items for sale before the auction. They must navigate this nest of vipers without tipping their hands if they want to have any chance of retrieving the shard.

The envoys pass through the arched entryway to the make-shift market and onto the cracked road. Several stone spikes jut out of ground, remnants of the arcane battles that devastated the land. The only remains of the buildings that once lined this thoroughfare are piles of blackened rubble and an occasional trace of the buildings' former foundations.

Sprinkled between the piles and pillars of black stone are small wooden carts and a few makeshift stalls. The stalls are topped with brightly colored cloth canopies, which catch the fading evening light. Small glass spheres imbued with light arcana sit suspended in rope hangers on the temporary booths.

In the distance you see a large tent and can hear the unmistakable sounds of drinking and merriment, along with the smells of roasting meat and strong ale.

THE MARKET

The market is full of sellers, thieves, and hirelings, along with the guests Lady Lianca made sure to invite, as detailed in the **Adversaries** section. The market is an opportunity for Narrators to revisit antagonists previously introduced in their series, as well as foreshadowing upcoming ones, if they so desire. For the various unnamed sellers, thieves, and hirelings, feel free to use the Adept, Rogue, and Warrior entries found in *Blue Rose* **Chapter 12**, adding suitable ability focuses.

SCENE 1

CASING THE MARKET

EXPLORATION/ROLEPLAYING ENCOUNTER

Once the envoys make their way past the guard post, they have a chance to see the sights of the market, as well as getting some indication of the types of people here and observing several of the key figures. Besides the vendors selling their questionable and contraband wares, there are a few role-playing encounters which can happen as they explore.

The market is similar to what the envoys would expect of any other street market elsewhere in Aldis. The heroes approach from the southern entrance through a makeshift,

KEY CHARACTERS OF THE NIGHT MARKET

This a brief list of some of the characters the envoys may encounter at the Night Market. Full details and stats can be found in the **Adversaries** section.

MARKET STAFF

- **Lady Lianca**: A former noble from Lar'tya, she is currently the Baroness of the Night Market for the Silence.

- **Grax**: The night person head of security for the Night Market. His loyalty to Lady Lianca as her bodyguard is unquestionable.

- **Vedrick**: Corrupt junior quartermaster from the Royal College in Aldis. He is the Silence's inside man and passes along various arcane items that come into his care.

MARKET GUESTS

- **Alista Solovi**: This forest folk ranger is at the market seeking an ingredient (Widderfang Wolfsbane) for a cure for his lycanthropic curse.

- **Devlyn March**: Representative of the Onyx Court. He is looking for the shard of the Shadow Heptagram for his sister.

- **Dez Taliviour**: Captain of the Jarzoni operatives sent to discover who the leader of the Night Market is and eliminate them.

- **Kribas**: The vata'sha agent of a mysterious power from a distant land. The objective of his visit to the market is the shard of the Shadow Heptagram.

- **Lith-Kargus**: The darkfiend-bound rhy-cat desires the shard of the Shadow Heptagram, and once they see Kargus' former Talon, they will want it as well.

- **Petrovian Draven**: Charismatic former pirate and member of the Cult of the Jade Crown. He's been sent to acquire the shard of the Shadow Heptagram for the cult.

- **Vashdun**: Shadow-Taken agent of Kern out to get his hands on any of the arcane items the market has for sale, especially the shard of the Shadow Heptagram.

tarp-covered guard post. The market itself is made up of roughly two dozen vendors; their makeshift stalls have turned the remains of a ruined street into a mini-labyrinth of shopping opportunities.

At the far north end of the strip is a large, makeshift tent serving as the market's tavern, dishing up food and drink, along with gambling, dancers, and other entertainments. Among the ruins to the east of the tavern tent is a pathway circling back to the guard post. The market guard and others connected to running the market have made this their camp area. West of the tavern tent are the founda-

MARKET ITEMS	
3D6 ROLL	**MARKET ITEM**
3	Medallion dedicated to one of the exarchs
4	Ancient tome written in a personal code
5	Draught of an iridescent liquid
6	Flawless gem
7	Modified gambling items (marked cards, loaded dice)
8	Illegal drug
9	Assassin's blade
10	Slightly used common weapon
11	Forged documents / credentials
12	Hard to trace poison
13	Common weapon
14	Carved stone idol, small
15	Well-worn piece of armor
16	Charm dedicated to one of the gods
17	Foul smelling potion
18	Heirloom piece of jewelry

DRAMA DIE RESULT	
RESULT	**BENEFIT**
1	Deadly, Reinforced, Recovery, or Meditation
2	Accurate, Durable, Healing, or Memory
3	Deadly ×2, Reinforced ×2, Stamina, or Beacon
4	Specialized, Well-Balanced, Enhancing, or Sensing
5	Accurate and Deadly, Durable and Reinforced, Stimulation, or Shielding
6	Novice level of an appropriate talent

MARKET RUMORS TABLE	
3D6 ROLL	**RESULT**
3	Grax was a knight in the service of Kern. (False)
4	Lady Lianca traded her soul to a darkfiend. (False)
5	The strange vata'sha was seen talking with the market's auctioneer. (True)
6	Devlyn March is from a very wealthy family. (True)
7	There is a cursed cryston for auction. (False)
8	The last visitor who tried to steal one of the auction's pieces was torn apart by a pack of darkfiends. (False)
9	Lady Lianca is a wanted murderer in Lar'tya. (False)
10	There is a member of the Onyx Court visiting the market. (True)
11	The Silence has a bigger piece of the Heptagram they are keeping for themselves. (False)
12	There is at least one spy from Jarzon at the Night Market. (True)
13	The market guards are all part of a shadow cult. (False)
14	One of the honored guests is the consort of a darkfiend. (False)
15	The "Heptagram thing" seems to be the auction item of most interest to the market's notable guests. (True)
16	The odd one from Kern was the personal friend of a former servant to the Lich King. (False)
17	The strange vata'sha arrived at the market on a wyvern. (False)
18	A visiting merchant from Lar'tya has never heard of Lady Lianca's family. He vanished after bringing it up. (True)

EXAMPLE

The player rolls a total of 7 with a 2 on the Drama Die; the Narrator decides the envoy spots a set of jade dice, which function like an arcane stone with the Memory property.

tions of a large building where the auction house has been set up. Several guards are posted around the perimeter to keep anyone from getting too curious until it is time for the auction to begin.

While the envoys are exploring the Night Market, they might decide to check out what is for sale outside the auction. Either the players or the Narrator can roll on the **Market Item Table** to see what catches a character's eye.

MARKET ITEMS

Roll 3d6. Rolling doubles generates stunt points, granting the item a masterwork or arcane item feature. Alternate effects for Drama Die results are also listed. The Narrator should apply the result that makes the most sense for the type of item it is. For details on what these features grant, see *Blue Rose* **Chapter 11: Rewards**.

RUMORS IN THE MARKET

While wandering around the market perusing the stalls, or having a drink in the tavern tent, there are plenty of opportunities for the envoys to eavesdrop on some juicy gossip, not all of which is true. To discover what they might potentially overhear, roll 3d6 and consult the **Market Rumors** table.

SCENE 2

CLOSE ENCOUNTER

ROLEPLAYING ENCOUNTER

As the envoys explore the market, they see Vedrick walking amongst the crowd. Spotting the envoys looking at him, Vedrick begins to follow them, unsure of their identity. A successful TN 9 Perception (Seeing) test not only determines the envoys are being tailed but also that their stalker is a junior quartermaster at the Royal College.

If the characters succeed on the test, they can attempt to evade him before he realizes who they are.

To lose Vedrick in the crowd, the heroes need to win an opposed test: their Dexterity (Stealth) vs. Vedrick's Perception (Seeing). If they succeed, Vedrick feels his paranoia is simply getting the better of him and lets it go; failure indicates he catches up to the envoys and recognizes them. The envoys can attempt to bluff him with a Communication (Deception) test. If they succeed, he believes their story and mutters, "Sorry, I thought you were someone else," before wandering off. Failing means he heads directly for Lady Lianca once he is out of sight of the envoys. He tells her the market has been infiltrated; see the **Midnight Trap** sidebar in **Part 3** for how she proceeds.

If they fail to spot him in the first instance, Vedrick follows them for a while before informing Lady Lianca there are envoys in the market (see the **Midnight Trap** sidebar in **Part 3**).

SCENE 3

OPPOSING FORCES

ROLEPLAYING ENCOUNTER

While making their way around the market, the characters encounter the undercover agents of the Church of the Pure Light, led by Dez Taliviour. Underestimating his reputation outside Jarzon, Dez mistakenly thinks going by his nickname, Tal, is enough to hide his identity. While chatting with him, a successful TN 13 Perception (Empathy) test gives the characters a gut feeling something is distinctly off about Dez.

The envoys can follow up on this hunch in a number of ways:

* On a successful TN 9 Intelligence (Military Lore) test, the envoys notice Dez' military training based on his bearing.

* A successful TN 11 Intelligence (Evaluation) test tips the characters off that Dez' simple clothing is in too good condition for someone living on the road.

* With a successful TN 13 Intelligence (Religious Lore) test, the envoys note Dez' boots are standard issue gear for those in service of the Purist Church.

* On a successful TN 15 Perception (Seeing) test, the heroes spot the faint lump of Dez' holy medallion, which is hanging around his neck.

If the characters uncover more than two of Dez' tells, allow them to roll a TN 13 Intelligence (Religious Lore) test; if successful, they can put their clues together along with the name "Tal" to figure out who they are actually talking to.

During the conversation, allow the characters to make a TN 11 Communication (Investigation) test to realize Dez is scrutinizing them for clues as to their own identities. With a very good roll or a stunt point spend, give the characters the feeling Dez suspects their connection to the Sovereign's Finest. This could have severe repercussions for them during the auction (see **Final Confrontation: Cover Blown**).

SCENE 4

LIGHT FINGERS

ROLEPLAYING ENCOUNTER

While looking for an easy mark, one of the adolescent visitors to the market sets their sights on the heroes. The plan is a simple "bump and grab" to get their hands on a character's coin purse.

The targeted character gets a TN 9 Perception (Touching) test. On a success, they notice their coin purse is gone and spot the pickpocket.

Pursuing the urchin requires an opposed test: Perception (Seeing) vs. the thief's Dexterity (Stealth). If the envoys catch up to the thief, things take a turn for the worse. A dozen or so of the market guard show up and demand to know what the commotion is about. Knowing there is a zero tolerance for stealing from others in the market and the unpleasant fate awaiting any caught doing so, the envoys face the decision of whether or not to turn the thief over.

MIDNIGHT TRAP

There are a number of times during the adventure when the envoys' cover might be compromised. This section details what Lady Lianca's most likely reaction to this will be. She does have a something of a cruel streak and enjoys playing with her prey. If Lianca discovers the heroes' true identity before they enter Veran-Norpar, she ensures they gain easy access, and has them watched to ferret out any contacts they might have within the market. The same applies if she is informed of their identities after they arrive but before the auction takes place.

When entering the auction hall, the envoys are asked to hand over their weapons, "Purely as a precaution." Lady Lianca's goal is to reveal their identities at the climax of the proceedings. During the **Shell Games** scene, players succeeding on a TN 11 Perception (Seeing) test notice their characters are the only ones without weapons.

If the envoys do not hand the street thief to the market guard, they have the opportunity to gain useful information about the principle people connected to the market, as well as some market rumors. If you need stats for the thief, use the **Rogue** from *Blue Rose* **Chapter 12** and add the Dexterity (Legerdemain) ability focus.

PART 3

MIDNIGHT AUCTION

In **Part 3**, while exploring the Night Market stalls and gathering useful information about the bazaar's other visitors, the envoys meet the infamous Lady Lianca, one way or another. The heroes also have a chance to set their eyes on the shard of the Shadow Heptagram, as well as the other unique items in the auction. Unfortunately for everyone, Kribas has already cornered the auctioneer and used his monetary and psychic influence to ensure the auction goes in his favor…

A small crystal bell sounds, indicating the auction is about to begin. The market guards step out of the enclosure set up to host the auction and take up posts flanking the entranceway.

SCENE 1

ENTER THE BARONESS

ROLEPLAYING ENCOUNTER

Read or paraphrase the following to the players:

Entering the ruins of a once great hall, you see that what remains now serves as supports for the auction house's makeshift walls, with several laced-together tarps forming a canopy overhead. On the west side of the area, against the wall, are seven small carts arranged in a shallow arc, with a raised wooden platform in their midst.

As the visitors make their way into the chamber, they have a chance to examine the carts. Normally the barrows are fully enclosed, but currently the wooden top and side panels have been removed so the contents are viewable through locked metal cages. You can see small wooden number tags attached to each item by a cord, indicating the number for the various auction lots.

As the guests look around, the heroes can use any of the following abilities to gather information. With a successful TN 11 Perception (Sight) test, the envoys notice a portion of the makeshift wall behind the wooden platform is actually an entranceway. With a successful TN 11 Dexterity (Lock Picking) test, they gauge that picking the locks on the cages would be a formidable task (TN 17). A successful TN 11 Perception (Empathy) test allows the envoys to see which items seem to hold any particular guest's interest. Information regarding each item can be found in **Items of Power**; the **Key Character Reactions** sidebar and the **Adversaries** section of this adventure also contain relevant details.

When they have had a chance to look around and assess the guests' reactions to the lots, the door at the back of the platform opens up and Lady Lianca makes her entrance with Grax in her wake. Grax is casually dragging a body behind him. Making his way to the front of the platform, Grax tosses the corpse to the ground in front of the staging, clearly visible to all.

> *In a disturbingly indifferent tone, Lady Lianca says, "I see you've noticed my new accessory this evening. He attempted to remove a ring from my hand, and then had the nerve to die right in front of me. Well I had a tough choice to make, didn't I? Finally, I decided he clashed with my ensemble and I'd just have to leave him here." She coldly surveys the assembled guests. "Bad things happen to those who cross me. Terrible things." Instantly, her face seems lit with a warm, welcoming smile. "Now, let's see what's up first!"*
>
> *With that, a portly, mustachioed man makes his way to the front of the platform. He waits for Lady Lianca to exit the stage and join Grax before beginning the auction.*

SHELL GAMES

ROLEPLAYING ENCOUNTER

Once the auction begins, the envoys can keep tabs on which guests are bidding on the various items being offered. If the envoys want to bid on any of the objects themselves, this is their chance. As the scene unfolds, the heroes have the opportunity to realize something isn't right. A successful TN 11 Perception (Seeing) lets the envoys scan the room while paying attention to the bids being made. See the **Observation Table** for what they notice based on the test result.

OBSERVATION TABLE	
TN	**RESULT**
11	The envoys keep close tabs on the various bids but spot nothing particularly untoward.
13	The envoys notice the hateful expression Vashdun shoots at Kribas. If the envoys pick up on this, they will not be surprised when this escalates.
15	The envoys notice the auctioneer is missing or ignoring some of Vashdun's bids—just enough that it could be purely coincidental. But, then again…

PART 4

CROSSED AND DOUBLE-CROSSED

In **Part 4**, Kribas' manipulation of the auctioneer leads to a heated confrontation. The envoys' reactions to these events affect what happens next. Use the following as a general road map, but be prepared in case the players veer off in an unexpected direction.

SCENE 1

BITTER RIVALS

ROLEPLAYING ENCOUNTER

Vashdun is passed over once again for the winning bid and he explodes in anger. As Kribas is announced the new owner of the Ebban Codex, Vashdun leaps to his feet and launches himself bodily at the mysterious vata'sha, screaming, "I don't know how you rigged this, Kribas, but you will pay!"

Devlyn March uses his Move Object arcanum to hold Vashdun in the air, mid-assault. Shouts and jeers from the crowd escalate. The market guards go for their swords but a glance from Lady Lianca stops them, their hands on their hilts, waiting for direction.

The guests begin taking sides, accusing others of influencing the auctioneer; Devlyn March and Alista Solovi side with Vashdun, while Petrovian Draven and Lith-Kargus back Kribas' claims. As other attendees voice their opinions, Vedrick steps away from the crowd. Two of the mercenaries with Dez Taliviour appear to be whipping up both sides of the argument.

The envoys can step in and try to de-escalate the situation, if they wish. They can, alternately, stoke the fires in the hope of turning the visitors against each other, using the argument as cover to get the Shadow Heptagram shard. The least proactive option is to simply stand back and watch as the argument escalates into a physical conflict.

PERCEPTION TEST	
TN	**RESULTS**
11	Lady Lianca and Grax are clearly holding back, intensely studying everyone as they argue.
13	Dez Taliviour and a couple of his men are maneuvering themselves closer to Lady Lianca.
15	Vedrick is keeping tabs on Dez Taliviour and, based on his expression, something about Dez is puzzling him. At the same time, one of Dez' men is tracking Vedrick's movements.
17	Lith-Kargus is sneaking towards the display carts as subtly as they can.

No matter how the envoys react, the other guests have their own agendas. At some point during the proceedings, the Narrator should call for a Perception test; the accompanying table gives TNs for this test, along with their outcomes. If a player specifies their character is keeping an eye on a particular guest, a test may not be necessary.

SMOOTH DIPLOMATS

The envoys can make a TN 15 Communication (Persuasion) test to attempt to talk the various parties down. Depending on how the envoys approach the situation, adjust this target number to account for the effectiveness of their approach. Envoys may also want to find out if the auctioneer was indeed intentionally ignoring Vashdun's bids. This requires an opposed test using Communication (Investigation) or Perception (Empathy) vs. the auctioneer's 1 Willpower (Self-Discipline) with success revealing the outside influences.

Remember, each non-player character (NPC) has their own actions and agenda, regardless of the envoys' attempts to calm the situation. Just as the envoys are successful in easing tensions, Vedrick manages to put some of the pieces together, leading to the **Final Confrontation: Cover Blown** option.

FANNING THE FLAMES

The envoys may wish to encourage the argument, possibly as a cover for snatching the shard of the Shadow Heptagram. Depending on exactly what they say and do, the most likely test is a TN 11 Communication (Deception) one. If the envoys are trying to use this as a distraction, the Narrator can use quick cuts back and forth to help build tension (see **Under the Cover of Anger**). As tempers continue to rise, Vashdun snaps and strikes out with his arcana. This starts the **Final Confrontation: Hate Erupts** scene.

UNDER THE COVER OF ANGER

The envoys may not be directly involved in the argument, but they could exploit it as a distraction to get their hands on the shard of the Shadow Heptagram, or one of the other items being auctioned off. They're not the only ones, as Lith-Kargus figures this is their best chance to get it as well. Just as the envoys reach the cages, Lith-Kargus uses Move Object to overcome the lock on the one holding the shard.

BUILDING ANGER

If the envoys stand back and do nothing, after three rounds (approximately 45 seconds), Lady Lianca has enough of the situation and orders Grax to dispatch Vashdun. Just as Grax comes within a few feet of his target, Dez Taliviour makes his move to kill Lady Lianca. This leads into the **Final Confrontation: Hate Erupts** scene.

SCENE 2

THE FINAL CONFRONTATION

COMBAT ENCOUNTER

While there are a myriad of ways to get to this point, the odds are against the envoys getting out of this situation without a fight. Two of the most likely scenarios are the auction argument escalating to full-blown combat or Dez Taliviour revealing the envoys as agents of Aldis. Regardless of what else happens, the market guards move in as soon as melee ensues. See the accompanying sidebar for a quick recap of how the key characters react:

Any of the following **Final Confrontation** options could easily involve various NPCs interacting solely with each other. In order to keep the focus on the heroes, there is no need to roll dice for NPC actions unless the characters interact with them. Simply portray the outcome you, as Narrator, feel is most appropriate for your game.

COVER BLOWN

For the envoys who've been keeping a watchful eye on what Dez Taliviour is doing, odds are they've noticed Vedrick watching him since the start of the auction. Vedrick's scrutiny intensifies as the argument continues. Players succeeding on a TN 13 Perception (Empathy) test ensure their characters spot Vedrick's body language indicating he has discerned something significant about Dez. As Vedrick raises his hand and is about to yell a warning, Dez' lieutenant Tull screams "Agents of Queen Jaellin! Aldin spies!" and charges the envoys (provided, of course, Dez rumbled the heroes during their earlier conversation). At this point, combat commences.

HATE ERUPTS

When Vashdun's anger reaches boiling point, he uses Summon Spirit to call forth an elemental. Since this arcanum requires an associated shaping arcana (in this case, Earth Shaping), its use within the Veran Marsh triggers feedback, meaning Vashdun sets off an earthquake in addition to summoning the creature! See **Summon Spirit** in *Blue Rose* **Chapter 4: Arcana** for further details, and the **Arcana in the Veran Marsh** section in *Blue Rose* **Chapter 6** for the potential fallout.

AFTERMATH

Once combat begins, those outside the hall scatter into the surrounding marsh and attempt to make their way to Serpent's Haven. No matter the fate of Lady Lianca, it is

KEY CHARACTER REACTIONS

Here is a brief synopsis of how the key characters behave once combat begins. Stats for these NPCs can be found in the **Adversaries** section.

MARKET STAFF

- **Lady Lianca:** Confident in her abilities and those of Grax, she does not rush in, instead casually leaving the matter for others to attend to.
- **Grax:** He is out to protect Lady Lianca. Once Dez Taliviour—or anyone else—makes any visibly threatening move against his mistress, he forsakes everything else to protect her.
- **Vedrick:** If he is around, Vedrick quickly attempts to leave the scene, to see if he can find a way out of the market.

MARKET GUESTS

- **Alista Solovi:** Alista's first goal is to get the Widderfang Wolfsbane. This changes, however, if it appears the envoys are losing the battle. Entering the fight or being attacked triggers his beastly nature, transforming him into his man-wolf form. See **Adversaries** for further details.
- **Devlyn March:** While Devlyn might take a few parting shots at anyone attacking him, his goal is self-preservation and escape.
- **Dez Taliviour:** Dez is on a mission from the Church of the Pure Faith. He will not stop until Lady Lianca is dead or beyond his reach.
- **Kribas:** Kribas uses his Wake the Dead ability to cast Imbue Unlife on any dead combatants, transforming them into walking dead. See *Blue Rose* **Chapter 12** for the relevant stats.
- **Lith-Kargus:** Lith-Kargus goes straight for the shard of the Shadow Heptagram, fighting tooth and claw to get it.
- **Petrovian Draven:** Petrovian's primary goal is to get the shard of the Shadow Heptagram. To do so he uses his acrobatics to evade his opponents and his lock picking ability to break into the cage.
- **Vashdun:** His orders are clear: bring back the shard of the Shadow Heptagram and any other artifacts of power he can get.

quite some time before the Silence can host another such event. The damage to the Night Market's reputation may, in fact, never recover. Additionally, the heroes have (hopefully) secured one or more dangerous arcane items to return to Aldis for study and safekeeping.

Alista Solovi

ABILITIES (FOCUSES)	
2/0	ACCURACY (LIGHT BLADES / BITE)
1/0	COMMUNICATION (DECEPTION)
3/5	CONSTITUTION (STAMINA)
1/3	DEXTERITY (STEALTH)
3/5	FIGHTING (BRAWLING / CLAWS)
0/0	INTELLIGENCE (NATURAL LORE)
3/4	PERCEPTION (TRACKING / SMELLING)
2/4	STRENGTH
0/0	WILLPOWER (SELF-DISCIPLINE)

SPEED	HEALTH	DEFENSE	ARMOR RATING
11/14	21/43	11/13	3/3

WEAPON	ATTACK ROLL	DAMAGE
BITE	+2	1D6+7
CLAW	+7	1D6+6
SHORT SWORD	+4	1D6+3

SPECIAL QUALITIES

FAVORED STUNTS: Dual Strike, Lightning Attack / Mighty Blow, Pierce Armor, Threaten

EMBRACE OF THE BEAST: At times of great stress, such as during combat, Alista Solovi may transform into his cursed man-wolf form. To resist the transformation, he must succeed on a TN 15 Willpower (Self-Discipline) test.

HYBRID FORM: When Alista Solovi takes his man-wolf form, he undergoes a significant physical transformation, gaining over a foot in height, growing claws and fur, and his face takes on wolf-like features. He can only use the following abilities in his man-wolf form: Bite, Claw, and Smelling, as well the Tooth and Claw talent. Shifting between forms is a major action.

PART MAN, PART WOLF: Due to the curse placed on him, Alista is never fully human or animal. As such, he is susceptible to both animism and psychic arcana no matter which form he is in. To represent these changes, Alista's abilities are listed with two numbers, the first being his human form with the one after the "/" his man-wolf form. As an example: 3/5 Fighting indicates as a human, he has 3 Fighting and as the man-wolf, his Fighting increases to 5. The same format applies to Alista's ability focuses.

TALENTS: Armor Training (Novice), Single Weapon Style (Novice), Tooth and Claw (Novice)

WEAPONS GROUPS: Brawling, Bows, Heavy Blades, Light Blades

EQUIPMENT: Light Leather Armor (designed to stay on when he transforms), Shortsword

THREAT: MINOR/MODERATE

ADVERSARIES

The following section covers the backgrounds and stats for those running the market, along with the elite guests the Silence invited. For any incidental characters not detailed in this section, the Narrator should use a character from *Blue Rose* **Chapter 12**, adding appropriate ability focuses as required.

ALISTA SOLOVI

ALISTA SOLOVI

A small village called upon the ranger, Alista, to rid them of a malevolent force causing their crops to wither on the vine. Alista discovered the culprit—the essence of a corrupt witch—inhabiting the body of a recently deceased girl from a nearby farm. This presence slowly infected the land, killing the crops. The witch had bodyguards in the form of corrupted wolves, which the ranger dispatched. Unfortunately, he suffered several deep bites before they went down. Without her bodyguards, the witch was no match for Alista's skills, but before departing the girl's corpse, the witch cursed Alista, tying him to the spirit of her beloved wolves. Now, whenever he is overcome with rage, fear, or the heat of battle, he transforms into a man-beast.

Traveling and working as a sell-sword, Alista has consulted with healers and adepts but none have been able to find a way to break the curse; undaunted, he continues looking. Contacts made over drinks in unsavory bars have led to him uncovering rumors and folk tales of possible cures. One such contact in Rezea spoke of an elixir requiring a rare ingredient, Widderfang Wolfsbane. After months of obsessive searching, he learned of the Night Market. His single-minded goal for this event is to get his hands on the Widderfang Wolfsbane in any way possible.

Standing just over six feet tall, Alista is a broadly-built man who tends to dress in simple breeches and an over-sized linen shirt with the sleeves rolled up. Over that, he wears a loose-fitting dark brown, sleeveless leather tunic. He keeps his coppery hair and beard cropped short. When his bestial side is unleashed, he stands well over seven feet tall and his fur takes on the same coppery color of his hair, but almost as dark as blood.

DEVLYN MARCH

Devlyn is older than his fraternal twin sister by a matter of minutes. Growing up on the southwest tip of Aldis, it was clear the twins had distinctly different personalities. Laytisha, his sister, is quiet and reserved, whereas Devlin's actions are ruled by his ever-changing emotions.

The Night Market

While Devlyn March is the only member of the Onyx Court featured in this adventure, a brief overview of the Court is included for Narrators who wish to expand on its presence in this adventure, or to use it as a plot hook for later scenarios.

The Onyx Court formed a little over ten years ago, and although started by a few bored members of well-to-do families on the fringes of Aldin society, it quickly transformed into something quite different when Harthor Gotis joined.

Harthor Gotis is the son of a successful merchant family which considered themselves close allies of Lord Sayvin during the years leading up to Sayvin joining forces with Kern. Whenever their support of him is questioned, the family now plays the victim in public. Privately, Harthor fans the flames of resentment towards Queen Jaellin and has stirred up doubts about the Golden Hart's judgment. As primary examples, he uses King Valin and Queen Larai to convince others of what he sees as fundamental flaws in the process and, likewise, claims any forward-thinking visionaries are deliberately weeded out by the Test of the Blue Rose Scepter.

Harthor, Devlin, and Laytisha slowly (and quietly) continue to fill the Onyx Court with disenfranchised members of affluent families, as well as bitter, ambitious, and resentful nobles who would fail if they had to take the Test of Blue Rose Scepter today. The Onyx Court's current objective is to find a way to circumvent or destroy the Blue Rose Scepter.

Even from an early age, Devlyn would do anything to protect his sister and he made sure she wanted for nothing.

Ambition is the sole driver of the twins' motivations. Though their father was a regional noble, and as such they lacked neither means nor opportunity, both are caught up in the pursuit of more. During their teen years, Laytisha confessed to Devlyn both her desire to rule and her fear of being unable to pass the Test of the Blue Rose Scepter.

Devlyn made it his mission to help his sister secure that power, and in the process he met Harthor Gotis. Between the three of them were the shared goals that became the foundations of the Onyx Court.

Currently, the shard of the Shadow Heptagram is what Laytisha wants, as she believes it will give the Onyx Court the power to accomplish their goals. Naturally, Devlyn has traveled to the Night Market to acquire it for her.

At the Market, two things have an effect on Devlyn. Before meeting the envoys, he had a run in with Vashdun which left him annoyed so, just for spite, he'll bid on anything Vashdun is after. Also, when he notices the Sun Fire Pendant at the auction, he tries to acquire it for Laytisha.

Devlyn carries himself with a commanding mien, showing he is used to having people pay close attention to his words. While at the Night Market he dresses in clothes akin to those worn by the other travelers, but the fabrics and their condition may reveal his outfit is carefully *designed* to blend in, (such as with a successful TN 13 Perception (Seeing) test).

DEVLYN MARCH

DEVLYN MARCH

ABILITIES (FOCUSES)	
3	ACCURACY (LIGHT BLADES)
2	COMMUNICATION (DECEPTION, PSYCHIC)
1	CONSTITUTION
2	DEXTERITY
1	FIGHTING
4	INTELLIGENCE (ARCANE LORE)
3	PERCEPTION (EMPATHY, SEARCHING)
1	STRENGTH
2	WILLPOWER (PSYCHIC)

SPEED	HEALTH	DEFENSE	ARMOR RATING
12	37	12	1

WEAPON	ATTACK ROLL	DAMAGE
MAIN GAUCHE	+5	1D6+2
RAPIER	+5	1D6+2

SPECIAL QUALITIES

ARCANA: Mind Reading, Psychic Shield

FAVORED STUNTS: Disarm, Dual Strike, Pierce Armor

PINPOINT ATTACK: Once per round, if Devlyn's Dexterity is greater than his target's, he does an additional 1d6 damage on a successful attack.

TALENTS: Arcane Potential (Journeyman), Armor Training (Novice), Dual Weapon Style (Journeyman), Intrigue (Novice)

WEAPONS GROUPS: Bows, Brawling, Light Blades, Staves

EQUIPMENT: Main Gauche, Rapier, Reinforced Garb

THREAT: MODERATE

DEZ TALIVIOUR

Taliviour has served as a knight-captain in the service of Jarzon for a number of years. Orphaned at the age of eight, he was taken in and raised by the Church of the Pure Light. In return, he is devout in his service to the order. While he was still quite young, the church realized Dez was better suited to wielding a sword and shield than an ascetic life in the temple. Taking up the blade, Taliviour joined, and has even led, several assaults against the forces of Shadow. Although his campaigns have largely focused on threats from the Shadow Barrens, he has also hunted troglodytes

BLUE ROSE

SIX OF SWORDS

DEZ TALIVIOUR

ABILITIES (FOCUSES)	
3	ACCURACY (BRAWLING)
1	COMMUNICATION (INVESTIGATION, LEADERSHIP)
3	CONSTITUTION
2	DEXTERITY (RIDING)
4	FIGHTING (BLUDGEONS, HEAVY BLADES)
0	INTELLIGENCE (RELIGIOUS LORE)
2	PERCEPTION (SEEING)
3	STRENGTH (INTIMIDATION)
2	WILLPOWER (FAITH)

SPEED	HEALTH	DEFENSE	ARMOR RATING
12	38	13	5

WEAPON	ATTACK ROLL	DAMAGE
LONGSWORD	+6	2d6+3
MACE	+6	2d6+3
UNARMED	+5	1d6+3

SPECIAL QUALITIES

TALENTS: Armor Training (Novice), Purifying Light (Novice), Single Weapon Style (Novice), Unarmed Style (Novice)

WEAPONS GROUPS: Brawling, Bludgeons, Heavy Blades, Light Blades

EQUIPMENT: Dagger, Medium Leather Armor, Light Shield, Longsword, Mace (well worn), Medallion of Leonoth (under his tunic)

THREAT: MODERATE

DEZ'S SQUAD

ABILITIES (FOCUSES)	
2	ACCURACY (BRAWLING)
0	COMMUNICATION
2	CONSTITUTION
2	DEXTERITY
3	FIGHTING (HEAVY BLADES)
0	INTELLIGENCE (RELIGIOUS LORE)
2	PERCEPTION (SEEING)
2	STRENGTH
0	WILLPOWER (FAITH)

SPEED	HEALTH	DEFENSE	ARMOR RATING
12	18	13	3

WEAPON	ATTACK ROLL	DAMAGE
BRAWLING	+4	1d3+2
DAGGER	+2	1d6+2
LONGSWORD	+5	2d6+2

SPECIAL QUALITIES

FAVORED STUNTS: Mighty Blow, Pierce Armor

TALENTS: Armor Training (Novice), Single Weapon Style (Novice)

WEAPONS GROUPS: Brawling, Bludgeons, Heavy Blades, Light Blades

EQUIPMENT: Daggers, Light Leather Armor, Light Shield, Longsword

THREAT: MINOR

- **Leah** is a stern, powerfully built woman. Her scalp is shorn and tattooed, and her eyes and skin suggest possible night person heritage.

- **May** is a tall, athletic woman. Her nose has been broken at least twice. May is always toying with her knives, and somehow always seems to have another somewhere on her person.

- **Tull** is a giant of a man, standing over 6'7", and rather lanky. He has hawkish features and heavy brows. Tull is extremely religious and when not on a mission requiring subtlety, he proudly displays a talisman of Leonoth.

GRAX

Grax serves as head of the Night Market's security as well as Lady Lianca's personal bodyguard. In the past, he held numerous similar positions: a simple blade for hire for merchant caravans, a dock worker at various ports along Aldis' coast, and a short stint as a brigand that he's not terribly proud of. While he is quite capable at his job, he is self-conscious about moving in a much higher social circle than he's used to and so prefers to

and bandits in the Veran Marsh, making him an ideal choice to lead this mission.

DEZ TALIVIOURA

Dez' current objective is to discover who is in charge of the Night Market and eliminate them. Despite being in his early 30s, Dez looks like a grizzled warrior; years of battle have left his face weathered and wrinkled. His chestnut brown hair is liberally sprinkled with gray. His powerful build and broad shoulders, combined with his 6'2" frame, make for an intimidating presence.

Dez has not come to the Market alone. The following members of his squad are with him and they all use the same stat block:

- **Semyon** stands about 5'5" tall but has muscles like knotted rope and skin like old leather. A long dagger scar on the left side of his face traps his lip in a permanent sneer. Because of this disfigurement, he rarely speaks.

GRAX

	ABILITIES (FOCUSES)
2	ACCURACY (BRAWLING, LIGHT BLADES)
0	COMMUNICATION
5	CONSTITUTION (DRINKING, STAMINA)
1	DEXTERITY (RIDING, SAILING)
4	FIGHTING (AXES)
1	INTELLIGENCE
2	PERCEPTION
6	STRENGTH (MIGHT)
0	WILLPOWER

SPEED	HEALTH	DEFENSE	ARMOR RATING
11	43	12	5

WEAPON	ATTACK ROLL	DAMAGE
AXE	+6	2D6+6
BRAWLING	+4	1D3+6

SPECIAL QUALITIES

FAVORED STUNTS: Mighty Blow, Threaten

BRIGHT LIGHT SUSCEPTIBLY: When first exposed to bright light (full daylight or brighter), Grax is blind for one full round.

NIGHTVISION: Grax can see up to 30 yards in darkness.

TALENTS: Armor Training (Novice), Single Weapon Style (Novice)

WEAPONS GROUPS: Axes, Brawling, Heavy Blades, Light Blades

EQUIPMENT: Axe, Daggers, Light Shield, Medium Leather Armor

THREAT: MODERATE

NIGHT MARKET GUARD

	ABILITIES (FOCUSES)
2	ACCURACY (BRAWLING, LIGHT BLADES)
0	COMMUNICATION
1	CONSTITUTION (DRINKING)
2	DEXTERITY
1	FIGHTING (HEAVY BLADES)
1	INTELLIGENCE
2	PERCEPTION (SEEING, TRACKING)
2	STRENGTH
1	WILLPOWER

SPEED	HEALTH	DEFENSE	ARMOR RATING
11	18	13	3

WEAPON	ATTACK ROLL	DAMAGE
BRAWLING	+4	1D3+2
DAGGER	+4	1D6+2
LONGSWORD	+3	2D6+2

SPECIAL QUALITIES

FAVORED STUNTS: Mighty Blow, Piercing Armor

TALENTS: Armor Training (Novice), Single Weapon Style (Novice)

WEAPONS GROUPS: Brawling, Bludgeons, Heavy Blades, Light Blades

EQUIPMENT: Daggers, Light Leather Armor, Longsword

THREAT: MINOR

project the image of an eagle-eyed and quite silent guard.

Grax is devoted to Lady Lianca, and protecting her is his primary drive; he will not hesitate to do whatever is required to accomplish his task. In his role as head of security for the Market, he oversees a small group of people who try to keep the peace without upsetting the sensibilities of the customers—not always the easiest of tasks.

Grax is a mountain of a man, standing over 6'5" tall. Like most night people, he has ash gray skin and he keeps his long black hair braided. His finely crafted black leather armor was a gift from Lady Lianca and Grax works hard to keep it in pristine condition. He always strives to look his best as he feels his appearance reflects on his employer.

There are just over a dozen mercenaries under Grax's command at the Night Market. These men and woman have been hired to keep the peace at the market. There

are two to three posted at the makeshift entrance, with the others randomly patrolling the market in pairs. With the exception of the couple working the gate, most of them can easily be bribed if the envoys run into any trouble while exploring the market. During the final auction there will be one guard on hand for each envoy there. The following stat block can be used for any of the Night Market Guards the envoys encounter:

KRIBAS

Although he is clearly vata'shan, Kribas is an enigma, who only provides evasive replies to requests for personal information, such as claiming he is "from beyond the Plains of Rezea." The very few times someone has quite rudely pursued an answer as to who or what he serves, the most direct he has been is: "The Slumbering One," "The Stirring One," or something similarly cryptic.

KRIBAS

ABILITIES (FOCUSES)	
3	ACCURACY (ARCANE, LIGHT BLADES)
3	COMMUNICATION (DECEPTION, PSYCHIC)
2	CONSTITUTION
2	DEXTERITY
2	FIGHTING
4	INTELLIGENCE (ARCANE LORE, SHAPING, SORCERY LORE)
4	PERCEPTION (PSYCHIC, VISIONARY)
1	STRENGTH
4	WILLPOWER (FAITH, SELF-DISCIPLINE)

SPEED	HEALTH	DEFENSE	ARMOR RATING
12	46	12	2

WEAPON	ATTACK ROLL	DAMAGE
CRYSTON	+5	2D6+4
DAGGER	+5	1D6+2

SPECIAL QUALITIES

ARCANA: Fire Shaping, Heart Shaping, Move Object, Object Reading, Psychic Contact, Psychic Domination, Psychic Shield, Second Sight, Torment, Visions

AUSPICIOUS ARMOR: Kribas is considered to have an armor rating of 2, even though he is not wearing armor.

BRIGHT LIGHT SUSCEPTIBILITY: When first exposed to bright light (full daylight or brighter), Kribas is blind for one full round.

NIGHTVISION: Kribas can see up to 30 yards in darkness.

WAKE THE DEAD: With just a few drops of his own blood, Kribas is able to animate a recently deceased body. This requires a major action and a successful TN 13 Intelligence (Shaping) test.

FAVORED STUNTS: Arcane Shield, Lightning Attack, Mighty Arcana

TALENTS: Arcane Training (Novice), Psychic (Novice), Shaping (Novice), Visionary (Novice)

WEAPONS GROUPS: Brawling, Light Blades, Staves

EQUIPMENT: Shas Crystal Dagger (functions as a cryston).

THREAT: MODERATE

Anyone attempting to use arcana to get answers from his mind runs into a powerful Psychic Shield, which manifests in their mind's eye as an image of a giant stone door, sealed, and bearing a faintly glowing unknown glyph.

His goal at the market is to procure as many of the arcane items as he can, with the Ebban Codex and the Darkfiend Mask highest on his list.

Kribas has long, straight, silvery-white hair, which sharply contrasts with his night-black skin. He wears long, flowing garments, reminiscent of the Roamers and the Rezeans, as well as incorporating elements from other cultures of Aldea. While he does speak Aldin, he has an unusual accent, which the worldliest of bards are unable to place.

LADY LIANCA

ABILITIES (FOCUSES)	
2	ACCURACY (LIGHT BLADES)
4	COMMUNICATION (DECEPTION, ETIQUETTE, LEADERSHIP)
1	CONSTITUTION
2	DEXTERITY
2	FIGHTING
4	INTELLIGENCE (ARCANE LORE, EVALUATION)
4	PERCEPTION (EMPATHY, SEEING)
2	STRENGTH
4	WILLPOWER (SELF-DISCIPLINE)

SPEED	HEALTH	DEFENSE	ARMOR RATING
12	52	12	2

WEAPON	ATTACK ROLL	DAMAGE
DAGGER	+4	1D6+3
UNARMED	+2	1D3+2

SPECIAL QUALITIES

FAVORED STUNTS: Defensive Stance, Dual Strike, Stay Aware

AUSPICIOUS ARMOR: Lady Lianca is considered to have an armor rating of 2, even though she is not wearing armor.

TALENTS: Contacts (Journeyman), Observation (Novice), Oratory (Journeyman)

WEAPONS GROUPS: Bows, Brawling, Light Blades, Staves

EQUIPMENT: Daggers

THREAT: MODERATE

LADY LIANCA

LADY LIANCA

Born into the Nuit caste on the island of Ryzana in the nation of Lar'tya, Lianca is the daughter of a simple farmer. At an early age, her aspirations far outstripped what is permissible for her caste. Her relationship with her family grew tenser as her ambition turned to action as she began acting out. As soon as she came of age, Lianca gathered her meager belongings, boarded a boat for Aldis, and never looked back.

During her travels, Lianca assumed the identity of a lesser noblewoman from the isle of Grala, a fantasy she constructed as a child. Living this role for many years has replaced the truth, even in her own mind. It would take an adept skilled in psychic arcana to make her face the facts about her real life on Ryzana.

She was rapidly recruited after coming to the attention of the Silence, and in a few short years rose to a position of power overseeing the Night Market. Under her management, the market has grown from a one-time event into the highly respected (by a certain segment of the population) enterprise it is today. In addition to running and managing the Night Market, she coordinates distribution of more common illegal goods for the Silence.

Lady Lianca isn't one to have close ties, but over the years she has come to rely on a select few. Chief among them is Grax, the head of security for the market and her personal bodyguard.

Just under six feet tall, Lianca has a slightly stout build. Her shoulder-length, raven black hair has a subtle wave to it, and her light green eyes seem to pick up hints of gold from her deeply tanned skin. While her clothing is made from the heavier fabrics found in Aldis, the cut and design take obvious cues from her homeland of Lar'tya.

LITH-KARGUS

LITH-KARGUS

Lith's curiosity combined with her skills made her an excellent scout and explorer. When she came across the ruins of an ancient keep, the combination of inquisitiveness and a chance for some lesser trinkets she could sell meant she naturally couldn't resist investigating it.

Finding the intact remains of a well-concealed alchemical laboratory in the lower level of the keep delighted her. Tucked away in an almost invisible nook, she found a vial of swirling purple gas, which shimmered in the torchlight. She reached out with her mind to secure the vial, drawing it towards her. But, just before it reached her, a face formed within the swirling mist and something pulled against her arcana. She lost control of the vial, which fell to the stone floor, shattering on contact.

An unearthly voice filled the chamber, crying: "Kargus is free." The mist grew and began to enclose Lith, despite her best attempts to dodge and twist away from its enveloping shroud.

Lith exited the ruins three days later, her cream-colored fur now ashen-tinted. Since then, she's been driven to locate any scraps of knowledge concerning the forbidden arts of sorcery. Her current obsession is the shard of the Shadow Heptagram, which she is more than willing to fight tooth and claw to get her paws on. If an opportunity to get hold of the Talon of the Darkfiend Kargus arises, she will grab it as well, but everything remains secondary to getting the Shadow Heptagram.

Lith's fur is mostly a light, creamy off-white but it remains frosted with gray. Her/their eyes have turned a disturbing shade of grayish-purple after the visit to the ruins. Whenever referring to herself, she uses the terms "us" and "we."

LITH-KARGUS

ABILITIES (FOCUSES)	
2	ACCURACY (BITE)
2	COMMUNICATION
1	CONSTITUTION
4	DEXTERITY (LOCK PICKING, STEALTH, TRAPS)
2	FIGHTING (CLAWS)
3	INTELLIGENCE (REMOTE WEAPONS, SHAPING, SORCERY LORE)
3	PERCEPTION (PSYCHIC)
1	STRENGTH
1	WILLPOWER

SPEED	HEALTH	DEFENSE	ARMOR RATING
16	32	14	0

WEAPON	ATTACK ROLL	DAMAGE
BITE	+4	1D6+3
CLAWS	+4	1D6+1

SPECIAL QUALITIES

ARCANA: Manipulate Object, Move Object, Psychic Contact, Psychic Blast, Psychic Shield, Second Sight, Sorcerer's Grip

FAVORED STUNTS: Fast Casting, Lightning Attack, Skillful Channeling

NIGHTVISION: Lith-Kargus can see up to 30 feet in the dark.

WE ARE LEGION: Due to presence of Kargus in Lith's mind, they are at +3 to resists any attempts to control them via arcane or any other supernatural ability.

TALENTS: Arcane Training (Novice), Psychic (Novice), Shaping (Novice), Thievery (Novice), Tooth and Claw (Novice)

WEAPONS GROUPS: Natural Weapons

EQUIPMENT: Saddle Pack, Lock Picks

THREAT: MODERATE

PETROVIAN DRAVEN

PETROVIAN DRAVEN

Wily Petrovian has been relying on his good looks and charisma to get what he wants his whole life. Growing up in a hearth family on Amber Bay Island in the Scatterstar Archipelago, he spent his youth feeling restless. His family was sure he would outgrow it, but it intensified and he eventually left the small fishing village looking for "something new." Oddly, his family didn't seem too concerned. After a few years on the high seas as a pirate, fate returned him to them. Once ensconced back at home

PETROVIAN DRAVEN

ABILITIES (FOCUSES)	
3	ACCURACY (LIGHT BLADES)
4	COMMUNICATION (DECEPTION, PERSUASION, ROMANCE)
1	CONSTITUTION (DRINKING, SWIMMING)
3	DEXTERITY (ACROBATICS, LEGERDEMAIN, LOCK PICKING, SAILING)
2	FIGHTING
2	INTELLIGENCE (NAUTICAL LORE)
2	PERCEPTION
1	STRENGTH
1	WILLPOWER

SPEED	HEALTH	DEFENSE	ARMOR RATING
13	32	13	3

WEAPON	ATTACK ROLL	DAMAGE
SABER	+5	1D6+1
UNARMED	+3	1D3+1

SPECIAL QUALITIES

FAVORED STUNTS: Lightning Attack, Pierce Armor, Skirmish

PIERCING STRIKE: The Pierce Armor combat stunt costs Draven only 1 SP, instead of the usual 2.

PINPOINT ATTACK: Once per round, if Petrovian's Dexterity is greater than his target's, he does an additional 1d6 damage with a successful attack.

TALENTS: Armor Training (Novice), Carousing (Novice), Intrigue (Novice), Single Weapon Style (Novice)

WEAPONS GROUPS: Bows, Brawling, Light Blades, Staves

EQUIPMENT: Daggers, Light Leather Armor, Saber

THREAT: MODERATE

his family told him that Larn Andris had foretold of his journey and homecoming. Since Petrovian's reappearance and the revelation of his family's secret, he is now a full member of the Cult of the Jade Crown.

As Petrovian is one of the few members of his hearth family to travel away from Amber Bay Island, Larn has chosen him for this mission. According to the cult's summoned darkfiend, the Shadow Heptagram is his property and he wants the ancient relic returned.

Petrovian—a blue-eyed, blond-haired charmer—stands 5'9" tall with a captivating smile and chiseled good looks. As if that's not enough, he is also gifted with a voice as sweet as honey. This ruggedly handsome ex-pirate has a lithe, wiry build, which should be a clue as to just how quick and nimble he is.

VASHDUN

Born in a small mining town, Vashdun would have done anything to escape his miserable existence. His dream finally

VASHDUN

ABILITIES (FOCUSES)	
2	ACCURACY (ARCANE, STAVES)
1	COMMUNICATION
1	CONSTITUTION
2	DEXTERITY (STEALTH)
1	FIGHTING
4	INTELLIGENCE (ARCANE LORE, CRYPTOGRAPHY, NATURE LORE, SHAPING)
4	PERCEPTION (SEEING)
0	STRENGTH
2	WILLPOWER (FAITH)

SPEED	HEALTH	DEFENSE	ARMOR RATING
12	29	13	3

WEAPON	ATTACK ROLL	DAMAGE
CRYSTON	+4	2D6+2
STAFF	+4	1D6+1

SPECIAL QUALITIES

ARCANA: Arcane Weapon, Earth Shaping, Move Object, Psychic Blast, Psychic Shield, Second Sight,

FAVORED STUNTS: Fast Casting, Mighty Arcana

TALENTS: Arcane Training (Journeyman), Psychic (Novice), Shaping (Journeyman)

WEAPONS GROUPS: Brawling, Light Blades, Staves

EQUIPMENT: Cryston topped oak staff, Deep Earth Stone (allows the wearer to use the Summon Spirit arcanum as wells as reducing the time required from 1 minute to a major action), Light Leather Armor

THREAT: MODERATE

VASHDUN

seemed possible on the day he displayed a talent for arcana. He practiced in secret whenever he could and slowly began to develop his abilities. Eventually, he packed up his meager belongings and headed off to Sarn, fully confident he knew what he was headed toward.

Unfortunately for Vashdun, over the next year he was twisted and molded into a perfect candidate for the Shadow-Taken. In his newfound fervor, he was devoutly loyal to Jarek until the Lich King's destruction; since then, Vashdun has been firmly established in Lady Talis' camp.

Like so many others, Vashdun has come to the market to obtain the shard of the Shadow Heptagram, but the Blood Amber, Ebban Codex, and Darkfiend Mask are also of interest to him.

Vashdun's beady eyes, pointed nose, buck teeth, and big ears give him a rat-like appearance. This image isn't helped by his tendency to wear drab garb over his thin build.

VEDRICK

Raised in the heart of Aldis, Vedrick dreamed of joining the Knights of the Blue Rose. By his early teens, his small frame and poor health made it clear this dream was not to be. He spent long hours in the temples praying to the gods for any gifts which would allow him to serve his beloved Aldis, but those prayers went unanswered.

When Vedrick was approached by the Sovereign's Finest, he felt his opportunity had finally arrived. When he discovered they wanted him to serve as a clerk and junior quartermaster, he was devastated. Still, he accepted the offer, as he saw no other way to serve his kingdom. Over the years, his disappointment with his lot in life transformed into resentment and anger as his work turned into a series of daily reminders of his inadequacies.

Since being recruited by the Silence, he provides them with information as well as the occasional item that "goes missing" from the Royal College.

Vedrick is quite uncomfortable attending the Night Market but has done so before to meet with Lady Lianca or, like this time, to deliver a last-minute item. Vedrick has created a cover story about a chronically ill cousin to help explain these random disappearances. His own sickly appearance helps make this believable.

Actually standing at 5'3", his frail frame makes him appear even smaller. His muddy brown hair pairs badly with his pale skin, heightening his already unhealthy demeanor.

ITEMS OF POWER

There are seven major arcane items up for auction at the Night Market. The following covers each of these in detail, along with who is interested in it.

BLOOD AMBER

This piece of amber is about the size of a human thumb and has a drop of unknown blood trapped within it. It grants a +1 bonus to Healing or Heart Shaping arcane tests, and reduces the target number for sorcery fatigue tests by -2.

TALON OF THE DARKFIEND KARGUS

The preserved talon formerly belonging to the darkfiend Kargus (the same being currently skulking in the rhy-cat Lith's mind), sealed in a glass jar. With the use of Flesh

VEDRICK

	ABILITIES (FOCUSES)
2	ACCURACY (LIGHT BLADES)
2	COMMUNICATION (DECEPTION)
-1	CONSTITUTION
0	DEXTERITY
1	FIGHTING
3	INTELLIGENCE (EVALUATION)
3	PERCEPTION (EMPATHY)
-1	STRENGTH
1	WILLPOWER (SELF-DISCIPLINE)

SPEED	HEALTH	DEFENSE	ARMOR RATING
10	22	10	3

WEAPON	ATTACK ROLL	DAMAGE
DAGGER	+4	1D6
UNARMED	+2	1D3-1

SPECIAL QUALITIES

FAVORED STUNTS: Lightning Attack, Pierce Armor (1 SP), Skirmish

TALENTS: Armor Training (Novice), Single Weapon Style (Novice)

WEAPONS GROUPS: Bows, Brawling, Light Blades, Staves

EQUIPMENT: Daggers, Light Leather Armor

THREAT: MODERATE

Shaping, this talon could be used as a replacement limb. If grafted onto a character, it grants +2 Strength, a natural claw attack for 1d6 + Strength damage, and +1 to all Intelligence (Sorcery Lore) tests. It also grants the character uncontrollable access to the Visions arcanum (like the Wild Arcane talent; see *Blue Rose* **Chapter 3**). The talon is a corrupt item.

EBBAN CODEX

This well-worn tome, bound in black leather, contains the encoded arcane writings of Thadus Ebban, which has somehow made its way from the Tanglewood to the Night Market. Even without breaking any of the codes, the Codex counts as a corrupt item. The various sections in the Codex require tests to break their ciphers and unlock them. The main entry is a general discussion of the history of sorcery. A successful TN 15 Intelligence (Cryptography) test grants the user a +1 bonus on all Intelligence (Arcane Lore) and Intelligence (Sorcery Lore) tests. Unlocking this section is required before the user can attempt to decode any of the other entries.

The codex contains four additional "chapters" that can be unlocked, each permitting the user to learn a new arcanum: Harm, Heart Shaping, Sorcerer's Grip, and Torment. Each entry requires a separate successful TN 17

Intelligence (Cryptography) test to decipher. Each of these tests may be tried once a week, and the adept may make repeated attempts until they have learned all the secrets the Codex contains.

DARKFIEND MASK

This mask of carved stone is of interest to the various shadow cults in Aldea and functions as a corrupt item. While worn, the mask gives the wearer Darkvision, use of the Imbue Unlife arcana, and a +2 bonus to all Intelligence (Sorcery Lore) tests.

If the Narrator would like to connect this adventure to the **Shadows of Tanglewood** adventure in *Blue Rose,* this mask could be adjusted to be the Ebban Mask. As junior quartermaster, Vedrick could have acquired the mask from the Royal College on the behalf of the Silence.

WIDDERFANG WOLFSBANE

Consisting of seven petals with purple and crimson coloring, this variety of wolfsbane is only known to grow in the Bitter-Fang Mountains, making it difficult to get anywhere outside Kern. While it can be used in several alchemical potions and poisons, it is most notable for stories surrounding its ability to cure someone cursed with lycanthropy.

SUN FIRE PENDANT

This arcane focus is made of red and orange gemstones set in a gold-mounted pendant. Allegedly, it belonged to the adept Elthia, who used her mastery of Fire Shaping in the service of her Sorcerer King. The pendant gives the wearer access to the Fire Shaping arcanum. If the wearer already has the arcanum, they gain access to the following arcane abilities. Both require a TN 13 fatigue test after use:

- **FLAMING WEAPON:** The character can create a sheath of fire around a melee weapon they are wielding. While the flames do no damage to the weapon, they add +1d6 damage to any attacks made with it. The flaming weapon lasts for five rounds.

- **FLAME AURA:** The character can envelope their body in an aura of fire. The flames last for five rounds, and while they cause no harm to the wielder, anyone touching the character takes 1d6 penetrating fire damage.

SHARD OF THE SHADOW HEPTAGRAM

This is reported to be a piece of the mythic Shadow Heptagram used during the height of the Empire of Thorns. The Heptagram was a powerful touchstone of white marble inscribed with many sigils, including a seven-pointed star. While similar to the Touchstone in Aldis' capital, it was used in a ritual to extend and magnify the power of the participating adepts. According to legend, one lone rebel adept disrupted a ritual at a key point. The energies from the failed rite destroyed all of the participating sorcerers and transformed the white marble of the touchstone into an unidentifiable black rock, brittle and quite fragile.

The Shadow Heptagram, as it is now called, has broken into several large pieces over the centuries. Various shadow cults believe its power would rival the Aldin Touchstone's if it could be made whole again, and the rumor persists that if one shard can be found, it could lead to others.

When affecting multiple subjects with arcana, this shard reduces both the arcane and fatigue test modifiers by one half, rounded up. So affecting three subjects at once is normally +3 TN on both tests; use of this shard makes the increase +1.5 (rounded up to +2).

The villages bordering the Pavin Weald have always existed on the edge of mystery, and the people living there are used to a certain amount of wonder and uncertainty. But even these hardy folk have limits, and a series of disappearances over recent months prompted them to call for help.

A Harvest of Masks is a *Blue Rose* adventure for a group of 4–6 heroes, levels 5–8, although it can be adjusted to suit characters of a higher or lower level by adjusting the Threat posed by the adversaries and the target numbers of some of the tests. See the **Adversaries** and **Running the Game** chapters of the *Blue Rose* core rulebook for details.

INTRODUCTION

THE ROAMERS' TRAIL

A couple of years ago, a young adept stumbled upon the Mother Tree, an ancient willow whose spirit manifests as a fey that calls itself Syadays. When the adept found the grove, Syadays revealed herself as a lovely and playful maiden who invited the adept to join her in dancing and love-making, for she longed for companionship and the adept's appearance greatly pleased her.

The two fell in love and spent days wrapped in bliss and shared learning, but one day Syadays felt like manifesting as a handsome lad, and the adept became confused.

Although knowing the souls of the Eternal Dance can wear many shapes, the adept was shaken to face this truth in the flesh, and was not ready to embrace Syadays in his new form and, instead, turned away from the fey's open arms.

Tortured by guilt at the fey's hurt eyes upon his rejection, the adept found an abandoned cottage and made it into a laboratory. The solution the adept found was deceptively simple: to match Syadays' form at all times. In order to do so, the adept delved deep into dangerous sorcery. The result of his efforts was an arcane mask that would change the adept's shape as required, and the new toy delighted the faerie.

However, the adept's heart had not changed, and the mask's transformations began to create a dangerous rift between who the adept aspired to be, and whatever identity the mask enforced. Slowly, Shadow crept through that rift and corrupted the adept with the notion that nobody is truly happy with their lot in life, and everybody should have the chance to help themselves to a new one.

The adept convinced Syadays they should bring more people to celebrate joy in all its forms, and together they made other masks. The innocent fey did not detect their lover's corruption until their new "companions" began arriving, wearing the shapes of animals or people other than themselves, but by then it was far too late. The adept took the name of **Falahm**, and slowly forgot who they used to be, lost completely in the enchantment of the mask.

Falahm is the one responsible for the disappearances, and plans to spread the masks beyond the borders of the Pavin Weald. Syadays cannot leave their grove, and corruption is infecting the Mother Tree which, against her will, now produces masks instead of leaves and flowers.

Getting Started

This adventure assumes the heroes are envoys of the Sovereign's Finest, or at least aspirants who take this investigation on with a view to becoming full members. Characters from different backgrounds can definitely participate; they need only to have heard about the disappearances and want to help.

Characters who are local to one of the villages around the Weald could actually be part of a delegation sent to request help from the Crown, who then guide the Finest back to the region. Alternately, they may be independent parties who offer assistance to the distressed inhabitants.

Whatever the group's composition, they set out from the city of Verdaunen towards Dusktrail, the closest town with reported missing people. The heroes encounter a Roamer caravan and get the first hints of the trouble that lies ahead. They can then investigate the disappearances in Dusktrail, gathering clues and evidence pointing towards something sinister going on. The disappearance of a new victim leads the characters in hot pursuit and

shows them the true nature of the threat: sorcerous masks that transform their wearers. The heroes confront various victims influenced by the masks, eventually facing down the sorcerer responsible, allowing them the opportunity to free the victims and put a stop to the gruesome "harvest" of masks before the threat can spread any further.

SCENE I

Meeting the Caravan

ROLEPLAYING ENCOUNTER

Just as the sun begins to set, the Finest encounter a Roamer caravan traveling in the opposite direction.

A cloud of dust rises ahead of you on the road, and it doesn't take long for the bustling sounds of wagons and horses to reach your ears, followed by the notes of a traveling song echoing the joys of life on the road. The leading wagon is impossible to miss as it comes closer, painted in a dizzying array of yellows and reds that contrast with the greens of the surrounding hills. The driver hails you, his face lit with a big, contagious smile.

The caravan slows down and stops, asking after the heroes' destination and news of the road behind them. The caravan's headman introduces himself as Vaus Falari,

and invites the characters to make camp with them, if they wish. If they are easily identifiable as the Sovereign's Finest, his invitation carries a degree of relief and concern he makes no effort to hide; but when asked, he says the matter can wait until they have all dined and rested.

The caravan is relatively small, composed of three families, each with their own wagon, plus a communal wagon for extra supplies and assorted cargo. Vaus introduces the characters to his family first and then to the others, and the general sentiment is welcoming.

The heroes are invited to join the Roamers' famous dancing around the campfire in their role as honored guests. Vaus' own daughter, Sania, leads the dance, which is more teaching practice than actual revelry, as she demonstrates the steps to five other youths from the caravan. She welcomes any character who wishes to try, but mercilessly teases them regardless of their performance.

When the last person finishes dinner, Vaus calls the adventurers to share his fire; joining them is the caravan's Seer, Tayta Falari. It immediately becomes clear the two leaders are worried about something.

The characters can find out the following by talking to the Roamers:

- The Roamers know about the recent disappearances, and that Dusktrail is only one of many settlements where people have gone missing. Farther down the road, Madeen's Haven, Barktown, Woodside, Ralith's Crossing, and Three Homes have also lost people under mysterious circumstances.

- Vaus' caravan has suffered no disappearances, but he heard that another caravan traveling northeast did lose one of their number, but had assumed he just ran off to stay in one of the towns they'd passed through, as sometimes happens.

- Seer Tayta tells the characters the forest has more eyes than it used to, and she has felt the caravan being watched from the woods.

- Reading the Royal Road has been difficult for the past couple of weeks. The results always come up confusing and contradictory, as if Destiny and Fate change at a moment's notice. On top of this, the various Chalice cards are coming up with unnerving frequency. If one or more among the characters can read the Royal Road, they can confirm this.

- The elders are worried because some folk are laying the blame for the disappearances on the Roamers, and for the last few weeks the people have been cold—if not outright hostile—to the caravan. They left Dusktrail this morning after a single night of camping, and decided to leave the Weald border towns and head for Verdaunen until things cool down.

- Trade has been just as difficult. The only good deal the caravan has brokered recently was a chest full of beautifully crafted masks from a merchant in Dusktrail. The Roamers intend to sell the masks

THE FALARI CARAVAN

The caravan is composed of twenty-two members, comprising three families: the Falari, Venidai, and Sanvan. The head family consists of Vaus Falari, his wife Dima, their daughters Sania and Radeet, and their sons Rus, Maurus, and Dalto, plus Seer Tayta, who is Vaus' mother. Yodran and Mareesa Venidai, and Bentio and Varima Sanvan have their respective wagons and families.

The Narrator is encouraged to come up with any other caravan members who are part of the three families.

- **Male names:** *Aderio, Corto, Hesrin, Masar, Ottan, Poen.*
- **Female names:** *Binda, Emira, Jorita, Navita, Samatri, Tivi.*

in Verdaunen, hoping to get some windfall from the whole sorry trip. The Spring Equinox is approaching, and with it the Feast of Braniel, so the masks are bound to be popular. Characters can make a TN 11 Intelligence test using the Arcane Lore, Cultural Lore, or Religious Lore focuses; success reminds the characters that Braniel governs the Minor Arcana of Chalices in the Royal Road.

SCENE 2

A CHEST FULL OF MASKS

ROLEPLAYING ENCOUNTER

The masks in the Roamers' chest are the arcane masks that Falahm and Syadays have been making, but right now they are dormant. The players have no reason to suspect the masks yet, and using arcana such as Object Reading or Second Sight on them yields no particular results.

If the characters are not curious about the masks, have Vaus boast about the stroke of luck he had in buying them, and have him show some of them off. It is important to use this chance at foreshadowing, as well as providing a clue the heroes can follow up later in the adventure.

The masks are mostly doge- and volto-style masks that cover half or all of the face, respectively, with a few much larger and more elaborately decorated full-face masks thrown into the mix. They all have a velvety and pleasant texture and fragrance, and playful designs cover their outer surfaces. All the masks are different and have unique designs that never repeat.

If the heroes are interested in acquiring one, Vaus agrees to sell them it for five Aldin silver sovereigns, although he's easily talked down to two or the equivalent in trade—less than what he plans to sell them for in Verdaunen, but still to his advantage.

When dawn comes, the Roamers pack up and continue on their southward journey, wishing good fortune to the heroes as they continue north towards Dusktrail.

PART 1

THE DISAPPEARED

Read or paraphrase the following to the players.

The sun is well on its way towards noon when you reach the first field, and the smell of rich soil is almost overpowering, with the land tilled and ready to receive the first seeds of the year. A wall of trees marks the limits of the forest a short distance from a well-tended fence. A small house stands at the farthest end. You see a man at the threshold, waving at you in greeting, while at the same time ushering a boy to run off ahead along the road. Soon enough, you hear bells tolling, and spot the bell tower as you turn a bend.

People are gathering to receive you, and the look of relief you saw in the Roamers' faces is echoed in those of the townspeople. The road becomes the town's main street, leading you to a small plaza in front of the building with the bells. A short, stocky man and a tall, angry-looking woman in hunting leathers are waiting for you.

The characters receive a hero's welcome into Dusktrail, but the mood is not entirely festive. The people are visibly afraid, although the Finest's arrival brings a glimmer of hope.

DUSKTRAIL

Like many settlements within and around the Pavin Weald, Dusktrail was founded by refugees from Kern during the Great Rebellion, and initially subsisted on local hunting and gathering. The early settlers understood the rights the forest's guardians granted them and the boundaries they set. The incomers began logging modestly, planting new trees, and otherwise managing their corner of the woods with respect.

The town provides timber to smaller communities, and some precious woods are destined for the city of Aldis itself. The town has enough arable farming to provide for its needs and to trade with, and it acts as a de facto gateway between the small city of Verdaunen and the northeastern communities of the Weald. There have been no significant matters of concern in Dusktrail for some time, certainly none sufficient to require the aid of the Sovereign's Finest.

Dusktrail is home to Lord Daen Ruhl, the traveling noble who oversees the region. Ruhl is in his mid-forties and of Kernish stock, his pale skin tanned from years of traveling and working outdoors, his neat, black hair peppered with gray. It was Lord Ruhl who sent out the call for aid, and he receives the Sovereign's Finest along with the town's sheriff, his wife, Loraine Ruhl, a middle-aged woman with olive skin and piercing green eyes, who is somewhat less pleased at outside interference in Dusktrail's affairs.

SCENE 1

A NERVOUS WELCOME

Daen Ruhl welcomes the characters warmly, but with a hint of pressing concern. He calls for the inn's stable boy to take any horses they may have and invites the heroes to the town hall to talk, apologizing for not letting them rest after their journey, but wanting to get straight to the matter at hand.

If the characters mention they rested the night before with the Roamer caravan, Ruhl's face darkens for an instant, but he simply nods and asks them to follow him.

Lord Ruhl leads the party to a large room with a stage at one end. Usually reserved for public functions and artistic performances, all the hall's benches are now pushed aside and a long table takes up the space just in front of the stage. The noble and his wife sit together at the head of the table and invite the heroes to follow suit.

The atmosphere is tense as two local lads come in carrying glasses and jars of both water and wine, which the lord himself pours for the characters.

Finally, as everyone is settled, Ruhl explains the reason why he summoned the Sovereign's Finest.

"People are afraid, good envoys. Three people have gone missing in the last six months, leaving no trace. Not even the wolf-kin who live two days' travel inside the forest were able to find them, and I'm at my wits' end, for this is a story I hear, too, when I visit the other settlements under my purview. Thirty-two people are missing in total, and the worst thing is the uncertainty on the faces of their friends and families. I have no answers to give them."

"It's the Roamers," Loraine Ruhl interjects. "We had a caravan camp on the outskirts within days of the disappearances, and I've talked with people from both Woodside and Three Homes, and they all remember Roamers passing by around the time people disappeared there. I'm deputizing some folk to set a watch tonight; I hope you can help."

Lord Ruhl shakes his head as his wife speaks, and tells the characters to investigate as they see fit, and as soon as they can. He has already arranged rooms for them at the Whispering Leaves Inn across the central plaza. He suggests that once they've rested, they start by talking to the friends and families of the missing people. The villages of Woodside and Three Homes are each within a day's walk, or half a day's ride, from Dusktrail, if the characters want to investigate the disappearances that took place there as well.

Despite her belligerence against the Roamers, Loraine helps the characters get settled in and tells them where to find the friends and families of the missing people.

SCENE 2

THE SHERIFF'S BRIEFING

ROLEPLAYING ENCOUNTER

Sheriff Ruhl informs the characters about the people missing from Dusktrail and her own thoughts about them:

- TOHM DEEKIN: The first to go missing, Tohm is a middle-aged man who worked as a lumberjack for his entire life. Before he disappeared, he had begun drinking himself into a stupor every other night. His wife died in a hunting accident four years ago, leaving him childless and alone. At first, Loraine thought he had wandered into the woods to take his own life, but she never found a body.

- LEESIE BREDAINE: The second missing person is a young woman who showed great academic aptitude. Her parents—Bodric and Marine—are farmers. They were set against her leaving for the city of Aldis to advance her studies, since they needed her to help care for her younger siblings while they worked the farm. Loraine thought she had run away to pursue her dreams, but she left her precious books behind, and she hasn't been seen in Verdaunen.

- DAVEED BREDAINE: A boy in his mid-teens and cousin to Leesie, Daveed is famous among his neighbors for being a lousy farmer, but with a natural gift for pottery. He had just been apprenticed to one of the town's master potters. Loraine knows there was something romantic going on with his best friend and neighbor, Myrna Rennick, although rumor has it Daveed is *caria*; Loraine didn't think it was relevant, and Myrna clammed up when the sheriff inquired about what was going on. Daveed disappeared two weeks ago.

Loraine also describes the surrounding area: mostly cultivated fields on the south, and to the north there are a couple of hundred yards of grassy hillside before the woodlands of the Pavin Weald begin. The main roads connecting the town lead south towards Verdaunen, east towards Madeen's Haven, skirting the Pavin Weald, and north towards Three Homes and the Ice-Binder Mountains. The road to Woodside to the northeast branches off the east road a few miles outside the town limits. People avoid the woods to the northwest, as they are known to host some fey creatures, including a sacred grove half a day's walk from the northern road.

The sheriff also mentions that, aside from the Roamers and traveling merchants, the only outsiders who've visited town near the dates of the disappearances were a group of wolf-kin who often make camp near Woodside, but

live farther inside the forest. They come to town to trade hides and meat, and while aloof and stone-faced, they are honorable. Loraine already asked them during their last visit the week before whether they'd seen anything, but the hunters simply shook their heads and then seemed in a hurry to leave, which she found a bit suspicious.

SCENE 3

FACTS AND RUMORS

ROLEPLAYING/EXPLORATION ENCOUNTER

Seeking out those close to the missing persons is easy. Loraine gives the characters general directions and excuses herself, as she needs to prepare tonight's watch shifts and patrols.

RUMORS	
TN	**INFORMATION**
7	Tohm Deekin was already unhappy even before his wife died. (True)
7	Many young lads asked Leesie to run to the Mother Tree during the upcoming Feast of Braniel (see the **Braniel and the Mother Tree** sidebar). (False, but the tradition of the Mother Tree used to be true)
9	Myrna Rennick had a huge crush on Daveed and blames herself for his disappearance. (True)
9	Lord Ruhl is frantic about losing the favor of the regional noble and will do anything to get out of the mess these disappearances have caused. (False)
11	The wolf-kin visited less frequently after Leesie disappeared. (True)
11	An eerie music was heard each night people disappeared. (False)
11	Tohm's wife was a witch who grew arcane herbs in her garden. (False; they were just medicinal herbs)
11	Nobody knows who could have sold the Roamers that chest full of masks. Nobody in town makes anything like that. (True)
13	Leesie received every Roamer caravan with enthusiastic interest, and bought from or traded with them frequently. Her favorite was the Falari caravan that was in town just the day before. (True)
15	Two days before Daveed disappeared, Myrna actually confessed her feelings, but he told her he was caria and rejected her. (True)
15	Leesie developed arcane skills she kept hidden from her parents. (True)
15	A couple of days before he disappeared, Tohm got rid of the flowers in his wife's garden and replaced them with gnarly shrubbery. (True, although the new plants have not yet grown into shrubs)
17	Tohm Deekin was seen entertaining a stranger at his house before he upended his garden. (True, but the person who reveals this cannot remember *anything* about the stranger)

As the sheriff promised, the townsfolk are eager to help, and offer their own opinions and ideas while answering the heroes' questions. Characters can make Communication (Investigation) tests while walking around town to ferret out potentially useful facts (see the accompanying table). Perception (Empathy) or Intelligence tests with a relevant focus can help them discern whether a particular piece of information is just gossip or has a kernel of truth. The And Another Thing roleplaying stunt and That Makes Me Wonder exploration stunt can be used to make these additional tests as part of the first interaction.

The higher the target number for each piece of information, the less available it is to the random people the Finest interview on the streets. If the characters seek out the close friends or family of each missing person, grant them a bonus to the Communication (Investigation) test depending on how close or familiar the interviewee was to the subject. This bonus can go from +2 (casual acquaintance or distant relative) to +5 (close friend or intimate family).

SCENE 3A

THE BREDAINE FARM: LEESIE'S AMBITION

ROLEPLAYING/EXPLORATION ENCOUNTER

The large house standing behind tilled fields is noisy even before passing through the simple gate outside the property. Three children play outside and a couple of workers put away their tools as they receive their pay from a man in his early forties. When the man spots the characters he rushes to greet them. He introduces himself as Bodric Bredaine, Leesie's father, and invites them into the house.

The entire Bredaine family follows the new arrivals inside, and Bodric acts as the perfect host, introducing his wife Marine, and his three young children.

The information the heroes can gain from the family is mostly confirmation of Loraine Ruhl's briefing, plus some of the rumors about Leesie (although they don't know about Leesie's arcane skills).

While appearing calm and collected, Leesie's parents are consumed by anguish and guilt, speaking about how much Leesie loved to read. Bodric invites the characters to the young woman's study to have a look around.

Leesie's study is in the attic: a cozy space with two bookcases that could accommodate more books but instead hold a large collection of clay figurines crafted with varying levels of skill, all representing (or at least trying to) a variety of rhydan. Nonetheless, the young woman's library is impressive for a town so far from the capital.

A successful TN 9 Perception (Searching) test reveals a tome on the basics of arcane practice hidden at the back of one shelf, behind a collection of fairy tales and histories of the realm. The book is battered and well-used, but still readable. It is a treatise on the art of shaping arcana, and there is an odd bookmark in the earth-shaping chapter. The bookmark looks to be a maple leaf, but it has a velvety feel and a pair of eyes drawn on it with ink.

Characters with the Second Sight arcanum able to read arcane signatures (see *Blue Rose* **Chapter 4: Arcana**) can make the appropriate test to discover Leesie earth-shaped all the figurines on the shelves. They can also figure this out with a successful TN 13 Intelligence (Arcane Lore) test. Judging from the detail of a griffon figurine, Leesie had become quite skilled in earth-shaping, impressive for someone with no formal training.

The Bredaines are surprised if the characters mention this to them. They had no idea their daughter had arcane talents, much less had become an adept on her own behind their backs.

SCENE 3B

MYRNA RENNICK: DAVEED'S CONFUSION

ROLEPLAYING ENCOUNTER

As you leave the Bredaine farm, you see a teenage girl waiting by the gate. She looks up as she hears you approach, and it's pretty obvious she's been crying. She has fair, Kernish skin but deep black curls around her face. She shifts her weight from one foot to the other as you reach her, making her simple skirt sway from side to side.

"I…!" She blurts out before you can say a thing. "I… want to help find Daveed!"

After her small outburst, Myrna becomes timid and barely speaks above a whisper as she introduces herself. It takes some coaxing and a successful TN 11 Communication (Persuasion) test to get her talking and either confirm or mention she has feelings for Daveed. She stammers and stumbles even more if the conversation steers towards the night he disappeared, but after additional coaxing and reassurances she reveals she confessed her love to him by asking him to visit the Mother Tree with her during the upcoming Spring Equinox, and how hurt he looked when she did (see the **Braniel and the Mother Tree** sidebar).

She hates herself for not noticing he was caria and for missing the clues he was attracted to Jeril, one of his fellow apprentices at the potter's workshop.

She also tells them she followed Daveed in secret after he rejected her. He went back to the workshop and talked to Jeril about her; about how much he cared for her and regretted not being able to return her feelings. She wanted to hate Jeril, but he was so supportive and understanding, advising Daveed to fight to keep his friendship with her, that she ended up hating herself for putting her childhood friend in such a difficult position.

SCENE 3C

THE GARDEN: TOHM'S DESECRATION

EXPLORATION ENCOUNTER

Tohm's house is deserted, but well cared for. It is located on the northern outskirts of town, but there are still houses within shouting distance. The place is locked, but the garden is easily accessible. The plant stalks look odd, as if they would be more comfortable growing in the Veran Marsh rather than the thriving Pavin Weald.

A successful TN 13 Intelligence (Natural Lore) or a TN 11 Intelligence (Arcane Lore) test reveals the stalks are not natural. The Second Sight arcanum warns characters that Shadow is strong in the garden, with the influence of animism, psychic, and shaping talents. An Outcome of 2 on the arcanum test uncovers a sorcerous version of Plant Shaping is in use, while an Outcome of 3 reveals the warped Plant Shaping is somehow imbuing the stalks with the Flesh Shaping, Heart Reading, Heart Shaping, and Psychic Domination arcana.

Digging out a single stalk triggers a TN 13 Willpower (Purity) test. A character who fails this test experiences a short vision of fulfilling their Calling through their Fate. The hero now has a choice: gain a Conviction point while risking Corruption with a TN 11 Willpower (Self-Discipline) test, or reject the vision (and the Conviction point) and remain safe. Characters who pass the Willpower (Purity) test feel the pull of Shadow, but do not receive a vision. Whether they gained Conviction or not through the vision, characters with the Visionary focus have the distinct feeling the stalk was making an offer and a promise it couldn't fulfill in its present state.

BRANIEL AND THE MOTHER TREE

Dusktrail used to have a tradition on the Feast of Braniel, which consisted of young people taking a hike into the forest—either by themselves or with their lovers—to visit the Mother Tree and ask its spirit for a boon of love.

Legend says Braniel was traveling through the world and stopped to rest at a peaceful grove, where a local dryad entertained the Primordial with such lovely songs and dance, that he lay with her and gave her a gift: to be an embodiment and patron of sweet and gentle love, and for that he granted her the power to change to suit any lover's need. The dryad transcended into a powerful tree spirit called Syadays, and became known as the Mother Tree because her boons ushered many children into the world.

The simple ritual fell out of favor and now hardly anyone visits the Mother Tree anymore. Myrna and Daveed heard this tale from his cousin Leesie, who loved to tell them stories, so it was a big deal when she asked him to join her in the old ritual.

Once a stalk is pulled free, the exposed root begins to disintegrate, but it's clear that it is oddly shaped, almost like a twisted leaf. Heroes who succeed at a TN 15 Perception (Seeing) test notice it closely resembled a domino mask before it crumbled to ash-like dirt.

Fire destroys the stalks and their roots normally, releasing a foul smoke that smells like overripe fruit and rotting grass.

SCENE 4
THE FOURTH VICTIM
ROLEPLAYING ENCOUNTER

On the night the Finest follow the last lead in Dusktrail, Falahm steps up their plan and starts outright kidnapping people instead of trusting the masks to attract them.

The town hall's bells begin ringing, rousing characters who were asleep at the inn and calling on those who joined Loraine's patrols.

Lord Ruhl is outside the town hall with two other people, armed with spears. Next to them is a teenage boy trying to catch his breath.

"They took her!" The boy says. "I saw her walking by the workshop, so I followed her, and then… these… these shadows came out of nowhere and made off with her!"

The boy is Jeril, whom the characters recognize if they followed the lead Myrna gave them. He's speaking about Myrna, whom he knows through Daveed. He had wanted to talk to her about Daveed, and seeing her walk by looked like a good opportunity to do so, although he wondered what she was doing out so late at night.

When asked for details, Jeril calms down and recalls that what he saw were not exactly shadows, but a group of at least three individuals and a very large dog—maybe a wolf, even. The people wore dark clothes with minimal decorations, and their features were uniff has nervingly obscured, except for the bright, colorful masks they were wearing… including the wolf.

SCENE 5
IN PURSUIT
EXPLORATION ENCOUNTER

The sheriff has decided that action needs to be taken. Loraine Ruhl gathers a small posse of seven townsfolk, including two of her deputies and one hunter, with the rest being commoners armed with makeshift weapons. If the Finest have not yet volunteered their services, the sheriff demands they join in pursuing the kidnappers and saving Myrna.

Tracking the kidnappers through the fields proves easy as the soil is freshly tilled, but things become complicated upon reaching the edge of the forest.

Once within the trees, following the kidnappers' moves is an advanced test with a success threshold of 15. Participating characters can make TN 9 Perception (Searching or Tracking) tests, and characters who have the Second Sight arcanum can help with Perception (Psychic or Visionary) tests, as they follow the stench of Shadow that lingers over the kidnappers' trail. Each test represents 10 minutes of pursuit. When 10 points have been achieved towards the success threshold, the rescue party reaches a point where the trail splits. Loraine takes her people and follows one of the trails, suggesting the heroes follow the other.

If the advanced test reaches 1 hour of narrative time without meeting the success threshold, the characters lose the trail and are ambushed by masked creatures (see next section). When they reach 15 points for the advanced test, the characters catch up with the kidnappers and may ambush them instead.

SCENE 6
THE MASKED ONES ATTACK
COMBAT ENCOUNTER

A darkness hangs over the kidnappers' clothes and skin, draining them of color and detail except for the bright masks on their faces; masks which bear an uncanny resemblance to the ones the Roamers you met were carrying. The group consists of a handful of humanoids and one great wolf, but there is no sign of Myrna among them. One member, who is apparently the leader, is burdened by a stuffed traveling backpack and carries a walking stick that he points at you.

The group of masked ones is led by the **Pathfinder**—a transformed Tohm Deekin—and one **masked wolf** (see the **Allies and Adversaries** section), plus a number of **masked victims** equal to the number of characters minus one.

The masked ones attack savagely and without a plan, except for their leader, who tries to aid the others.

Arcana that read thoughts and emotions yield confusing results, as the adept can "hear" two consciousnesses in each masked one; an Outcome of 3 or more is necessary to separate them and recognize that one belongs to the scared and confused mind of the original person (the wolf is originally a human too) and another to the narrow-focused and driven mind of the fake persona the mask represents, which is additionally corrupt with Shadow.

Tailor the masked ones other than the Pathfinder to pairs of Destiny and Fate that resonate with the characters and their backgrounds.

A HARVEST OF MASKS

SAVING THE VICTIMS

If the group takes care to incapacitate rather than kill the masked ones, they can remove the masks without any ability test or effort. They get the clear impression the masks are extremely corrupt, but they do not entice Corruption like the "green" masks in Tohm Deekin's garden. Once removed from their hosts, the masks rot and disintegrate completely.

The victims remember everything they did while they wore the masks as if in a dream, and the memories fade just as quickly. The other masked ones are from the other settlements that have suffered from disappearances, while Tohm is the only Dusktrail citizen among them. They all remember a general feeling of bliss, like their lives were finally complete. They also have vague recollections of dancing in circles around a tree adorned with flowers and arcane symbols, following the melody of a sad song while being directed by someone who whispered inside their heads.

When conscious, Tohm tells the Finest that, as soon as they entered the forest, they forced a mask on Myrna's face, and she transformed into a shining knight who went on ahead while the rest of the masked ones slowed down to let any pursuers catch up with them. He remembers the stranger who delivered the masks to his home: it was an old merchant he used to know. He also recalls the merchant mentioned using a Roamer caravan to spread the masks even farther.

THE CROSSROADS

The heroes now have information pointing them towards the next step of the adventure: Tohm can identify the Mother Tree from the blissful images he remembers while dominated by the mask, and the characters have (hopefully) already heard of the Mother Tree's legend from Myrna or someone else in town. If they've spoken to Myrna, they certainly know the Mother Tree was important to her.

The characters are also aware the Falari caravan is carrying a chest full of sorcerous masks and is in grave danger as long as they have them; never mind the threat they pose to the people of Verdaunen, who wear masks in their celebrations of the Feast of Braniel and will gladly buy the monstrosities from the unwitting Roamers.

As such, the characters face two pretty clear choices: they can follow Myrna's trail deeper into the Pavin Weald hoping to find the Mother Tree and the source of the masks, or head back to Dusktrail and farther south to catch the Roamer caravan before it reaches Verdaunen and disaster strikes.

If the heroes choose the former, continue to **Part 2: Into the Weald**. If they opt for the latter, skip to **Part 3: After the Roamers**. They still have the people they rescued to worry about, as well as Loraine Ruhl's posse.

THE MASKS AND ARCANA

The masks' nature is to obfuscate and misrepresent, and that extends to the echoes of their power; arcana such as Object Reading, Scrying, and Visions show the victims as their masked personas (see the **Allies and Adversaries** section), as well as events that did not—and may not—happen. Such visions of past, present, and future are tinted with the victim's Fate and are so preposterous that adepts can immediately figure out the visions are false.

As described, the Sense Minds arcanum accurately detects two minds instead of one when "reading" a masked creature. An Outcome of 3 or more on the test allows an adept to distinguish between the real mind and the masked persona for one minute, after which the mask's power adapts and reasserts itself.

PART 2

INTO THE WEALD

The Sovereign's Finest go deeper into the Pavin Weald, continuing their pursuit of the now masked Myrna Rennick, and catch up with the Sheriff, Loraine Ruhl, and her posse not long thereafter. With the help of Ruhl's deputies, the envoys can pick up Myrna's trail from the original tracks left by her kidnappers, but the townsfolk refuse to accompany the Finest any farther into the forest. They can truthfully say the whole problem is now way beyond their ability to handle and they will be more useful keeping an eye on the town.

The trees feel like they are pressing together, forcing you to circle around and seek an easier path, leading you into short ravines and corridors flanked by mounds that still smell of freshly dug soil, with roots lying in wait to snag a foot or a piece of clothing. As you navigate this hostile terrain, you hear a deep howl, just as you feel a cry for help inside your minds.

Characters with Intelligence (Arcane Lore or Natural Lore) recognize the use of the Earth Shaping arcanum all around them. At this point, the uneven terrain and meandering path just make travel difficult.

SCENE 1

CRY WOLF

COMBAT & ROLEPLAYING ENCOUNTER

The howl and the psychic call come from Runs-Sharp, a young rhy-wolf chased by masked monsters. Characters who establish psychic contact with the rhydan receive panicked cries for help and the sense he's running in

81

their direction, along with a warning he's being pursued. Psychic contact grants characters the knowledge they are about to face masked creatures like the ones they fought earlier. There is one masked one for each character, divided evenly between masked wolves and masked victims, favoring wolves if there is an odd number. Both humanoid and wolf creatures bear features from other animals, such as antlers, hooves, reptilian tails, beaks, etc., but these are purely cosmetic, reflecting some twisted misinterpretation of the wearers' Fates.

Runs-Sharp bursts through the underbrush and seeks refuge behind one of the characters. He's wounded and exhausted and will not be much help in a fight, with only 5 Health remaining and suffering from 2 levels of fatigue.

The masked ones reach the heroes 3 rounds after Runs-Sharp does, and do not actually engage or initially attack them; they are focused on capturing the rhy-wolf and only attack the characters if attacked first. Runs-Sharp does nothing other than try to avoid his pursuers. If the characters engage more than half the masked ones in combat, all the creatures forget Runs-Sharp and focus on attacking them instead.

Masked creatures that are incapacitated and have their masks removed turn into the opposite of their masked persona: humanoids turn into rhy-wolves, and wolves turn into humans, particularly wolf-kin.

Runs-Sharp's Tale

When all the masked ones are defeated, Runs-Sharp thanks the heroes then collapses to the ground, panting hard, but still alive and conscious. He has been running all day, beset by his former pack mates and their rhy-bonded humans.

After time enough for a breather, or less if the characters tend to his wounds and fatigue, he psychically speaks about his ordeal.

"My pack, my friends… they are gone; they are something else inside; something that twisted their bodies as you see.

"It's a curse, a darkness growing in the forest. We felt it, and thought it better to avoid it, but it grew and deepened. We sent out-runners to investigate. They reached the big town—the one you call Dusktrail. The people asked our scouts to search for missing friends and family, and we knew… we knew we had failed in our watch.

"My bond-mate and I were sent, with the rest of our pack, to find an adept who lives near the Mother Tree to seek their help, but we were too late. In the adept's cabin was a thing that walks as a human but smells like a dead plant, with no face and a mind split into a thousand shards. It had a box, full of those things, those… masks. They flew towards us, they held onto the faces of my friends and they… they changed.

"They missed me, but not Misha, my bond-mate. She… falters. She's fading. I can feel it. She's resisting, but I can hear the whispers in her mind through our bond. She's hanging onto me for strength, but I'm tired. I'm so tired… I fear that if I sleep I will lose her. I can barely maintain our bond, but you can use it, see through my mind, see her true self and find her!"

What Runs-Sharp is suggesting is they use the rhy-bond as a substitute for familiarity regarding psychic and visionary arcana, effectively bypassing the mask's veil (see **The Masks and Arcana** in the previous section). If no one in the group has the Scrying or Visions arcana, or even Psychic Contact, Runs-Sharp uses his own arcana to link the characters to his bond-mate.

Thanks to this bypass, a successful TN 11 Perception (Searching, Seeing, Psychic, or Visionary) test shows them a first-person view of Misha shambling towards the colorful wagons of the Roamer caravan. They can hear unintelligible whispers and feel a sense of being mired in a swamp. A hand pastes something onto the side of a wagon, a tree leaf that resembles a mask, like those in Tohm's garden and in Leesie's book, and they are certain that *something* woke up inside the caravan.

Failure only yields a sense of desperation and urgency, and the cries of a drowning woman being silenced by a bestial whisper, which turns into several dozen more insidious voices.

Runs-Sharp forces himself to stay awake, but he can no longer walk on his own. He suggests the characters help him hide, but he's not averse to being carried if they can figure out how.

SCENE 2

THE ARCHITECT'S LABYRINTH

EXPLORATION/COMBAT/ROLEPLAYING ENCOUNTER

Whether the heroes decide to continue their search for Myrna and the Mother Tree, or return to town in a bid to catch up with the Roamers, as soon as they walk a few feet away from their current spot, they stumble across a narrow ravine. Characters who know the Second Sight arcanum detect a power shaping the land around them.

Framed by the walls of the ravine, a ghostly figure rounds a corner to stand before you: a young man in practical attire, holding a small portable drawing board and a pen. His clothes are darkened by clinging shadows except for the bright yellow mask that covers the top half of his face. He motions you to enter the ravine.

"Come, follow if you will, wonder at my craft! I built all of this! Me! Nobody else! Nobody can deny my genius now!" he says in a loud whisper. His speech has an eerie undertone, as if someone else is repeating the words an instant later, in a voice that sounds like a scared young woman.

Characters who succeed at a TN 12 Perception (Empathy) test realize the figure is none other than Leesie; the mask fulfilled her ambitions of becoming a shaping adept.

As soon as they attempt to talk or engage the masked man, he disappears back around the corner, leaving a scorning laugh (with a terrified undertone) echoing around them.

Following means entering a shifting maze shaped and reshaped by the **Architect** (see the **Allies and Adversaries** section). The pursuit is an advanced test with a success threshold of 10. The heroes can use any relevant focus to navigate the maze, or even try to reshape it or destroy it with their own arcana, but every such test is an opposed one vs. the Architect's own Intelligence (Shaping).

In addition to contributing towards the threshold, each success means the characters catch up briefly with the Architect. Until the beginning of the turn of the character who achieved the success, the heroes and the Architect can attack or interact with each other, but then the earth rises up into a wall between them and the chase begins anew.

Failure means the character who failed the test falls into a trap devised by the Architect, and suffers 2d6+3 damage from a variety of sources (snapping roots, a concealed pit, a crumbling wall, etc.). The character's armor rating applies against this damage.

When the group meets the success threshold, the pursuit ends and the Architect remains until defeated.

LEESIE'S TALE

Incapacitating the Architect and removing the mask reveals Leesie Bredaine. She awakens moments after, hugs the heroes and sobs, speaking about how the mask twisted all her dreams and ambitions, making her indulge in arrogance and unjustified pride. She confirms everything Runs-Sharp and Tohm told them: the sorcerer behind the masks is hiding in the grove of the Mother Tree along with a small group of followers, all twisted by the masks. She also remembers that, among the whispers in her head, there was one asking for help.

If the heroes mention her cousin Daveed and his friend Myrna have been captured by the masks, she insists on coming with them and doing what she can to help.

THE NEXT STEP

After this, the Sovereign's Finest can decide to resume their journey towards the Mother Tree, with Leesie guiding the way, or head back to town to regroup and try to catch the Roamers before they reach Verdaunen. Skip to **Part 4: The Masked Tree** if they choose to press on, or continue to **Part 3: After the Roamers** if they turn back.

AFTER THE ROAMERS

The Roamer caravan is at least a full day's travel ahead of the heroes. Even counting the wagons' relatively slow movement, the caravan is bound to arrive in Verdaunen within a couple of days. After explaining the crisis, Lord Ruhl will lend a horse to any character that does not have one already. Meanwhile, Loraine will send runners to all the villages to warn them about the masks so that at least no more victims are taken by guile.

SCENE 1

CATCHING UP

EXPLORATION/COMBAT ENCOUNTER

The heroes need to ride hard to make up for the Roamers' head start. This is an advanced test with a success threshold of 15. The characters can contribute towards success by making TN 12 Dexterity (Riding) tests, TN 14 Constitution (Stamina) tests, and TN 14 Perception (Tracking) tests. Each turn where all the characters get to make a test represents half a day of riding, resting the horses, and using shortcuts.

A failed test imposes 1 level of fatigue on a character, which others can make a TN 10 Intelligence (Healing) test to remove. This test does not count towards the success threshold; it just helps keep everyone on their feet.

If the heroes take more than two days to meet the success threshold and catch up with the Roamers, they all suffer 1 level of fatigue when they finally arrive at the caravan's encampment on a hill overlooking the city. On top of that, they are expected.

THE SILENT CARAVAN

The encampment is visible in the dwindling light of the sunset. There are fires already lit, but there is no music in the air. It's as if the caravan itself was one of the unliving: active, but without a soul. The only thing breaking the eerie silence is someone crooning a lullaby, the old voice cracking with the effort. You recognize the singer as Seer Tayta.

The heroes can see the Roamers just standing around the fires, all of them with masks on their faces, but still wearing their own shapes. Tendrils of darkness writhe over their bodies, trying to take hold but beaten back by

the Seer's song. As soon as the heroes approach, shadows finish engulfing a number of **masked victims** equal to the number of characters minus one. These then turn on the heroes, some producing shadowy weapons while others grow claws and fangs.

If, on the other hand, the characters did not succeed at the advanced test in time, there is no one visible in the camp. All the masked victims are hiding in ambush behind wagons or nearby vegetation.

Regardless, instead of straight up attacking, the masked victims try to restrain a character (the Narrator should choose one at random). If successful, a **floating mask** flies out from the chest and tries to attach to the character's face (see the **Allies and Adversaries** section).

When the heroes incapacitate or dispatch all the masked victims and active floating masks, another group is engulfed and attacks using the same tactics. This happens one more time or until there are no more Roamers wearing masks.

"Against deception, truth! Against turmoil, calm! Find the true heart and bring it forth!" the old Seer shouts.

If the characters have not yet discovered how to exploit the masked ones' False Psyche special quality, have any adepts in the group make a TN 12 Intelligence (Arcane Lore) test to decipher the Seer's words. If no one in the group knows the relevant arcana (see **The Masks and Arcana** sidebar), the test reveals the effect the Communication (Persuasion) focus has on the masked ones (see the **Allies and Adversaries** section).

DESTINY AND FATE

If a character is forced to wear a mask, they are replaced by a new masked victim who fights the rest of the group. This creature is a dark reflection of the character's Calling and Fate, making a mockery of their ideals and personality while in control.

While dominated, the character can still fight the mask from within their own mind. They are seemingly transported to a ghostly landscape echoing the material world, and are confronted by their masked mirror image selves, while something whispers promises of glory and fulfillment into their mind.

As this happens inside their mind and soul, any method the character uses to attack their double is just a representation of their will, and affects the masked victim as if it was a normal attack from outside. However, the character cannot exploit the False Psyche special quality while they battle from within (see the **Allies and Adversaries** section). Allies with the Psychic Contact or Sense Minds arcana can detect the masked character's intense internal struggle.

If their masked representation is defeated during combat, the character reappears where they were possessed, with the same Health as when the character was replaced.

ALTERNATE SCENE

STEALTHY SUCCESS

COMBAT/ROLEPLAYING ENCOUNTER

If by chance or skill the heroes manage to catch up with the caravan in half a day, no one spots their approach, allowing them to observe the camp and plan ahead. They can sneak around and notice that, among the Roamers, there is a wolf-kin woman swaying to Seer Tayta's song. The chest containing the masks the caravan's leader showed them is open; there are still masks inside, shivering as if they are alive. They find Seer Tayta sitting on her wagon's step, sweating heavily while crooning away. She notices the heroes and nods towards them, then towards her people.

Characters can try to remove the masks from the Roamers' faces and the wolf-kin woman with an opposed Dexterity (Legerdemain) test vs. the masked victim's Perception (Psychic) ability. There are 22 people in total, and as soon as an opposed test fails, combat begins as above.

HEARING THE WHISPERS

After combat ends, characters who were dominated by a mask get a chance to figure out what happened to them with the help of an exhausted Seer Tayta.

She explains the whispers come from both the mask the person wears, and another mask of greater power and evil, worn by the sorcerer who set this crisis in motion. Seer Tayta regrets having relied too much on the Royal Road, as the masks have the power to confound Destiny and Fate, throwing any card reading askew.

If the characters did not figure it out during this combat or earlier, Tayta also explains how psychic arcana can sever the link between mask and wearer, but in the absence of this power, words of encouragement and conviction can sway the heart that remains true to itself into fighting off the mask's influence.

The wolf-kin woman among the Roamers is called Misha, and the mask commanded her to bring an enchanted leaf that would awaken all the masks to dominate the Roamers. She has been resisting control thanks to her rhy-bond, and she's worried about her rhy-wolf companion, who ran from the rest of their pack when they were dominated. If the characters already met the rhy-wolf Runs-Sharp in **Part 2: Into the Weald**, they can give her news about him.

BACK INTO THE FRAY

From this point, the characters can return to Dusktrail and pick up their pursuit of Myrna and the Mother Tree. The Narrator can take them through **Part 2** if they haven't done so already, or may omit it and continue straight into **Part 4:**

The Masked Tree. Misha asks to return to Dusktrail with the characters so she can reunite with Runs-Sharp.

PART 4

THE MASKED TREE

After fighting the various victims of the sorcerous masks, the characters head for the Mother Tree, in the hope of stopping the madness and confronting the one responsible.

SCENE 1

GUARDIANS OF THE GROVE

EXPLORATION/COMBAT ENCOUNTER

After almost a full day's walk, the characters approach the grove of the Mother Tree. The forest grows quieter and quieter with each passing step. Random trees have cords and charms tied around their trunks, and circles of toadstools and small stones dot the way. Even the air itself feels laden with arcane power, as well as a growing sense of dread.

Eventually, the advancing heroes hear whispers coming from all around them. There are only a few at first, their words unintelligible, but they gradually grow louder and clearer. Characters can make out calls like: "You are not who you deserve to be," "You will never be happy as you are," "You were born for ruin, but you can change." A successful TN 11 Perception (Hearing) test helps characters make out another set of whispers, ones saying things like: "Help her," "She's in danger," "She didn't want this," and "Save her before she is changed forever."

Before they can see their destination, a group of **masked shades** attack the heroes. There is one for each character and an additional one for each companion they have with them. These creatures use the information for **shades** in *Blue Rose* Chapter 12: Adversaries, but they also have the False Psyche special quality found in the **Allies and Adversaries** section of this adventure.

These shades rose when Falahm sacrificed some of his thralls, and they are still bound to the sorcerer's will. They are the source of the whispers above, but the cries for help are spoken by a sweeter, sadder voice, coming from the masks the shades are wearing. Unlike other victims, the shades are permanently destroyed if their link to the masks is shattered through the False Psyche special quality.

NEW COMPANIONS

Depending on how the heroes act, they might be joined by Misha and Runs-Sharp, Leesie Bredaine, Loraine Ruhl, or any combination thereof as they go to face the Mother Tree. The Narrator can find their information in the **Allies and Adversaries** section.

SCENE 2

GAUNTLET OF THE PETAL KNIGHT

COMBAT ENCOUNTER

The heroes continue on their way without further interruption. Any companion or guide assures them they are almost upon the grove, and so must proceed with care.

The ground slopes downward into a basin, and the trickle of many streams echoes in the silence. The trees thin out and you can see the bottom of the bowl, covered in snaking roots thick with moss that hold puddles of many sizes; their water a disturbing shade of claret.

When you finally reach the bottom, you see the Mother Tree clearly for the first time. It may have once been a willow, but the trunk is now as thick as five humans hunched together, and the lowest branch is at least fifteen feet up, draped with hanging vines of varying length. There appear to be flowers dripping from the branches, but closer inspection reveals they are not blossoms at all, but more corrupt masks.

A young woman with green skin and a mane of auburn hair appears to be chained to the tree. She is naked but for the assorted leaves and flowers that grow from her body. You blink and instead see a young man, and then the woman again—or perhaps neither—but regardless of the shape, their unearthly beauty is marred by a look of anguish and pain, and with each whimper and moan, a face bubbles up through the tree's bark in a silent scream, only to fade an instant later.

"I sense your confusion." A soft but deep voice interrupts your surveillance. A cloaked figure walks from around the tree, brandishing a bloodied dagger. You cannot tell whether the stranger is male or female, but your attention is drawn by the intense mask on their face. "Why deny my gift? Life is a cruel joke. The Eternal Dance and the Wheel of Rebirth insist in matching us to the wrong partners. I have defied this tyranny! I have transcended the shackles of body and spirit! And I would share this gift with everyone!"

"Behold the fair Syadays," the figure says, walking besides the chained spirit. "She cannot decide who she is. How can she be happy like that? I tried to love her, but she kept changing. A man…a woman.. cannot…one cannot…"

"You call yourself Falahm because you have forgotten who you are under that mask. I am who I am," the tree spirit responds.

"True, but that can be fixed," the sorcerer scoffs. "And to you, visitors, I offer you a sample of my gift! Witness these star-crossed lovers! Yearning to be together, but separated by cruel destiny! But no more! I have brought them together!"

As the sorcerer finishes speaking, from one of the blood-soaked pools, a pair of masked humanoids emerges: the **Petal Knight** and the **Two-Faced Maiden**. The knight is the very image of a Knight of the Blue Rose, but instead of the royal symbol, the breastplate is engraved with a wilting stem holding onto its last petal. It bellows a challenge in a deep, throaty voice, saying *"I will defend my paramour!"* but paired with the masculine tones, characters recognize Myrna's voice.

The maiden also looks to have been snatched from a fairy tale, feminine and graceful and dressed in the finest clothing, except for the mask she wears, which mashes together two sets of facial features in a chaotic grimace. She utters: *"I will surrender to my lord,"* but her mousy tone echoes with the voice of a young boy.

The two are joined by a golden chain clasped around their necks, which extends and shortens so as to always appear taut.

If Leesie is with the heroes, she whimpers as she recognizes her cousin's voice and warns them of this just as the pair charge and engage in battle.

The terrain is uneven and characters can only move at half Speed, but both masked creatures move about as if in a carefully choreographed ballet, even stepping on the surface of the pools as if they were solid.

Throughout combat, the sorcerer gloats about how perfect Daveed and Myrna are now the masks have granted them their heart's desires, but Syadays refutes this and begs him to stop.

"You do not understand! You did not have to change for me to love you!" the tree spirit cries. *"And these children are not us! Look into their hearts and see what true love is! They already know they are not meant to be together, but love each other still! Their love is not a chain that binds them together, it is wings that free them both!"*

The characters should know about Myrna and Daveed's feelings if they spoke with Myrna and Jeril back in Dusktrail. If they follow this line of reasoning, prompted by Syadays, exploiting the False Psyche special quality can be devastating for their masked personas.

SCENE 3
THE HEARTLESS FACE

COMBAT ENCOUNTER

Falahm trembles in rage when the heroes defeat the Petal Knight and Two-Faced Maiden; he cries out if the heroes beat them by exploiting the False Psyche special quality rather than through physical combat. Without any more preamble, **Falahm** attacks.

During combat, the chained Syadays reveals the story of her relationship with the sorcerer, and how the masks came to be. For dramatic effect, when Falahm uses his Maskfall stunt, describe how he releases a veritable swarm of **floating masks**, only for the Mother Tree's hanging branches to animate and destroy most of them, except those attacking the characters. Despite her bondage, Syadays is trying to help.

At some point during combat, Syadays speaks of Falahm's shortcomings, and the sorcerer flies into a rage, forgetting to use any of his special qualities or arcana. Hopefully, this suggests to the heroes they can provoke Falahm themselves, either by goading him with his failure to turn Daveed and Myrna into his idea of a perfect relationship, or by debating him as to the nature of true love, acceptance, and self-worth. They can take a major action and use any Communication focus relevant to what they are trying to do, opposed by Falahm's Willpower (Morale). Falahm cannot use any special quality or arcana for one round when he loses this opposed test. Any further Communication tests to goad Falahm that round have no effect, until the following round, when the heroes can try again.

When Falahm is defeated, the mask falls off and reveals a smooth, featureless patch of skin where a face should be. The body has no recognizable features, either.

AFTERMATH

With the sorcerer's defeat, the Sovereign's Finest are left with many opportunities for further adventures and stories. The Mother Tree and Syadays remain damaged by Falahm's sorcery and require healing that may well need a power greater than the heroes possess. Many masked victims roam the forest, lost and confused, and there is also the matter of what to do with Falahm's mask, which is a profoundly corrupt item.

The characters may also take an interest in the futures of some of the people they met in the course of the adventure. The masks revealed their wearers' Callings, even if twisted by their shadow-selves, and the heroes might be inclined to help them fulfill their Destinies…

FLOATING MASK

ABILITIES (FOCUSES)	
3	ACCURACY (TOUCH)
-2	COMMUNICATION
2	CONSTITUTION (PSYCHIC)
5	DEXTERITY
-2	FIGHTING
0	INTELLIGENCE
3	PERCEPTION (PSYCHIC)
0	STRENGTH
3	WILLPOWER (MORALE)

SPEED	HEALTH	DEFENSE	ARMOR RATING
8 (FLYING)	5	15	0

WEAPON	ATTACK ROLL	DAMAGE
TOUCH	+5	SPECIAL*

SPECIAL QUALITIES

ARCANA: Sense Minds

FAVORED STUNTS: Lightning Attack, Skirmish

MINDSENSE: A floating mask has no physical senses, but uses its Sense Minds arcanum just like other creatures use their normal senses.

TOUCH: As a normal attack, a floating mask attempts to attach itself to the face of a victim. If successful, the target must make an opposed Willpower test, using any focus except Courage and Morale, vs. the mask's Communication (Psychic) ability. If the mask wins, the target is stunned until the end of their next round, at which point they may repeat the test. If the mask wins with an Outcome of 2 or more, the target is replaced with a masked victim, reflecting the target's Fate. After this point, the target must fight the masked victim from within (see the **Destiny and Fate** section in **Part 3: After the Roamers**). Success means the mask cannot attach to the target and disengages.

THREAT: MINOR

ALLIES & ADVERSARIES

In this section you will find the game statistics for the various allies and adversaries the heroes encounter in this adventure.

NEW COMPANIONS

The following are non-player characters (NPCs) who may join the heroes for part of the story. They are based on the information presented in the **Adversaries** chapter of *Blue Rose,* with some modifications.

MISHA

Use the information for a **Rogue**, but replace the given abilities and focuses with the following: Accuracy (Bows), Communication (Animism), Constitution (Stamina), Dexterity (Stealth, Traps), Perception (Tracking), Willpower (Morale), and the Arcane Potential (Journeyman) talent, with knowledge of the Psychic Contact and Animal Messenger arcana. She has a bow (attack roll: +4, damage 1d6+2) and a shortsword (attack roll: +2, damage 1d6+2).

RUNS-SHARP

Runs-Sharp is a **Rhy-wolf.** Statistics can be found in **Chapter 12** of the *Blue Rose* core book.

LEESIE BREDAINE

Use the information for an **Adept**, but reduce Willpower to 1. She knows the Dexterity (Artisan) and Intelligence (Shaping) focuses. Leesie carries no weapons and has only 10 hit points. She has the Arcane Training (Novice) and Shaping (Novice) talents, and knows the Earth Shaping, Manipulate Object, Move Object, Psychic Shield, and Second Sight arcana.

LORAINE RUHL

Use the information for a **Warrior**. She has Fighting (Pole-arms) instead of the Heavy Blades focus, and Communication (Animal Handling) instead of the Dexterity (Stealth) focus. She knows the Pole Weapon Style (Novice) talent instead of Single Weapon Style (Novice), and carries a spear (attack roll: +4, damage 1d6+4) and a short bow (attack roll: +4, damage 1d6+2).

FLOATING MASK

These enchanted masks float around on their own, looking for suitable hosts to dominate.

Falahm

ABILITIES (FOCUSES)	
3	ACCURACY (ARCANE)
2	COMMUNICATION (ANIMISM, PSYCHIC)
0	CONSTITUTION
1	DEXTERITY
0	FIGHTING (CLAW)
3	INTELLIGENCE (ARCANE LORE, SHAPING, SORCERY LORE)
0	PERCEPTION (PSYCHIC)
0	STRENGTH
1	WILLPOWER (FAITH)

SPEED	HEALTH	DEFENSE	ARMOR RATING
11	25	11	0

WEAPON	ATTACK ROLL	DAMAGE
CLAWS	+2	1d6+1

SPECIAL QUALITIES

ARCANA: Calm, Flesh Shaping, Heart Reading, Heart Shaping, Mind Reading, Mind Shaping, Psychic Blast, Psychic Contact, Psychic Shield, Second Sight, Sorcerer's Grip, Torment

FAVORED STUNTS: Imposing Arcana, Maskfall, Skillful Channeling

FORCED MASKFALL: As a major action, Falahm uses their Maskfall stunt for free. They can only do this once during the encounter.

IMITATION: As a minor action, Falahm points at a person and their mask imitates that person's face perfectly. The target resists with a Willpower (Meditative or Self-Discipline) test vs. Falahm's Intelligence (Shaping) test. If Falahm wins the test, they gain one of the following traits from the target until the beginning of Falahm's next turn: Perception, Strength, Defense, or armor rating.

MASKFALL (5 SP): Falahm's arcana causes mask-shaped leaves to fall from the Mother Tree. One floating mask (see before) per member of the heroes' group appears and acts on Falahm's turn until destroyed.

TALENTS: Animism, Psychic, Shaping

EQUIPMENT: Corrupt Mask

THREAT: MODERATE

FALAHM

Falahm is a humanoid wearing nondescript robes that shift quality from rags to the finest velvet between blinks. It is impossible to tell from their voice or mannerisms whether they are male or female, and a hood covers their head, shielding their features. They wear a mask that appears crudely chiseled from porcelain, but it has the disturbing property of becoming an actual, random face for a few moments at a time.

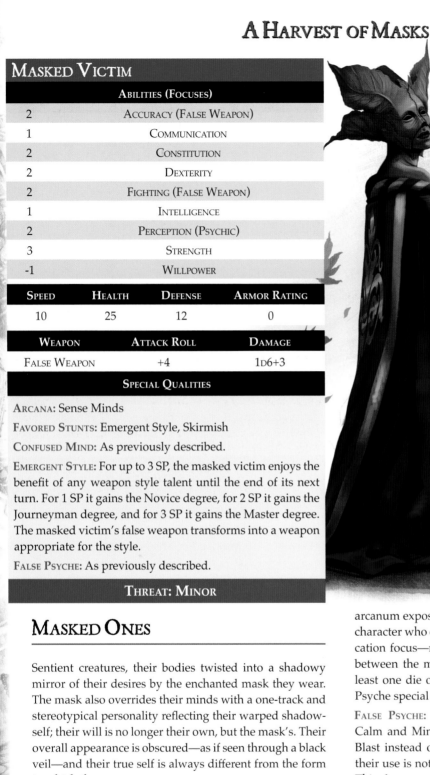

Masked Victim

ABILITIES (FOCUSES)	
2	ACCURACY (FALSE WEAPON)
1	COMMUNICATION
2	CONSTITUTION
2	DEXTERITY
2	FIGHTING (FALSE WEAPON)
1	INTELLIGENCE
2	PERCEPTION (PSYCHIC)
3	STRENGTH
-1	WILLPOWER

SPEED	HEALTH	DEFENSE	ARMOR RATING
10	25	12	0

WEAPON	ATTACK ROLL	DAMAGE
FALSE WEAPON	+4	1D6+3

SPECIAL QUALITIES

ARCANA: Sense Minds

FAVORED STUNTS: Emergent Style, Skirmish

CONFUSED MIND: As previously described.

EMERGENT STYLE: For up to 3 SP, the masked victim enjoys the benefit of any weapon style talent until the end of its next turn. For 1 SP it gains the Novice degree, for 2 SP it gains the Journeyman degree, and for 3 SP it gains the Master degree. The masked victim's false weapon transforms into a weapon appropriate for the style.

FALSE PSYCHE: As previously described.

THREAT: MINOR

MASKED ONES

Sentient creatures, their bodies twisted into a shadowy mirror of their desires by the enchanted mask they wear. The mask also overrides their minds with a one-track and stereotypical personality reflecting their warped shadow-self; their will is no longer their own, but the mask's. Their overall appearance is obscured—as if seen through a black veil—and their true self is always different from the form in which they appear.

If killed, masked ones return to their true form, and their mask disintegrates. Removing a mask from an incapacitated or unconscious creature is a major action, but requires no special tests. Removing one under any other circumstances requires a successful Dexterity (Legerdemain) test vs. the target's Perception (Psychic) ability.

All masked ones, regardless of type, share the following special qualities:

CONFUSED MIND: The masked one has a +2 bonus to resist initial psychic contact as the mask's and wearer's minds vie for attention. A successful use of the Psychic Contact arcanum exposes the mask's false mind, and allows the character who established contact to use any Communication focus—not just Persuasion—to damage the link between the mask and its wearer, and always deal at least one die of damage, as described under the False Psyche special quality.

FALSE PSYCHE: When used against masked ones, the Calm and Mind Shaping arcana function like Psychic Blast instead of having their normal effects; however, their use is not considered to be sorcery in this context. This damage cannot kill the masks' wearers, but incapacitates them instead when they are reduced to 0 Health. When the victims wake up, they recover all the damage caused by these arcana. In addition, any character can make a Communication (Persuasion) test as if it was the Psychic Blast arcanum against a masked one, provided the attacker mentions something related to the masked one's original self. The Narrator can grant additional damage dice if the attacker mentions something extremely personal to the masked one, or declare the attempt does not work if the attacker says something generic or only tangentially related to the possessed being.

The Pathfinder

ABILITIES (FOCUSES)	
3	ACCURACY (BOWS, LIGHT BLADES, STAVES)
0	COMMUNICATION (ANIMAL HANDLING)
0	CONSTITUTION (RUNNING, STAMINA)
3	DEXTERITY (INITIATIVE, STEALTH, TRAPS)
0	FIGHTING
2	INTELLIGENCE (NAVIGATION)
3	PERCEPTION (SEARCHING, SEEING, TRACKING)
2	STRENGTH (CLIMBING)
0	WILLPOWER

SPEED	HEALTH	DEFENSE	ARMOR RATING
12	15	13	3

WEAPON	ATTACK ROLL	DAMAGE
LONGBOW	+5	1D6+6
SHORTSWORD	+5	1D6+3

SPECIAL QUALITIES

ARCANA: Second Sight

FAVORED STUNTS: Rapid Reload, Set Up

CONFUSED MIND: As previously described.

FALSE PSYCHE: As previously described.

FIND THE PATH: The Pathfinder suffers no penalty to his Speed caused by natural or arcane conditions on the ground.

POINT THE WAY: As a minor action, the Pathfinder can allow an ally to move half their Speed on the Pathfinder's turn.

TALENTS: Armor Training (Novice), Scouting (Novice)

WEAPONS GROUPS: Bows, Brawling, Light Blades, Staves

EQUIPMENT: Light Leather Armor, Longbow, Shortsword

THREAT: MINOR

MASKED VICTIM

The victims of the masks adopt a shadowy visage that echoes their Fate and is a twisted reflection of their Calling. No two are alike, as varied as the nightmares of their wearers.

MASKED WOLF

Masked wolves are usually wolf-kin humans whose masks exploit their closeness to their lupine companions. A masked wolf has the same stats as a **wolf** (see the **Adversaries** chapter of *Blue Rose*) with the following alterations: Intelligence 1, Health 20. Add the Perception (Psychic, Searching) focuses, the Second Sight and Sense Minds arcana, and the Confused Mind and False Psyche special qualities as previously described. Remove the Tough special quality, which reduces its armor rating to 0. A masked wolf represents a minor threat.

The Architect

ABILITIES (FOCUSES)	
2	ACCURACY (ARCANE, BRAWLING, STAVES)
1	COMMUNICATION
1	CONSTITUTION
1	DEXTERITY
0	FIGHTING
2	INTELLIGENCE (ARCANE LORE, SHAPING)
1	PERCEPTION (SEEING)
0	STRENGTH
2	WILLPOWER (SELF-DISCIPLINE)

SPEED	HEALTH	DEFENSE	ARMOR RATING
11	15	11	0

WEAPON	ATTACK ROLL	DAMAGE
STAFF	+2	1D6+1

SPECIAL QUALITIES

ARCANA: Arcane Strike, Earth Shaping, Manipulate Object, Move Object, Plant Shaping, Psychic Shield, Second Sight, Water Shaping

FAVORED STUNTS: Powerful Channeling, Skillful Channeling

CONFUSED MIND: As previously described.

FALSE PSYCHE: As previously described.

TALENTS: Shaping (Master)

WEAPONS GROUPS: Brawling, Staves

EQUIPMENT: Staff

THREAT: MINOR

MASKED PERSONAS

The power of the masks has turned the missing people of Dusktrail into the following creatures:

THE ARCHITECT

Leesie Bredaine yearns to study in the city of Aldis and become an adept. The mask has transformed her into a version of her dream of a master shaper.

THE PATHFINDER

Tohm Deekin, a man with no sense of purpose, regrets never leaving Dusktrail to see the world. The Pathfinder is a brave explorer who will let nothing stop him from reaching his destination, even if it means leaving others behind or forcing them out of his way.

The Petal Knight

ABILITIES (FOCUSES)	
0	ACCURACY (LIGHT BLADES)
1	COMMUNICATION
3	CONSTITUTION
2	DEXTERITY
2	FIGHTING (HEAVY BLADES)
0	INTELLIGENCE
1	PERCEPTION (PSYCHIC)
3	STRENGTH (INTIMIDATION, MIGHT)
1	WILLPOWER (MORALE)

SPEED	HEALTH	DEFENSE	ARMOR RATING
10	20	14	5

WEAPON	ATTACK ROLL	DAMAGE
LONGSWORD	+4	2D6+3

SPECIAL QUALITIES

FAVORED STUNTS: Defend the Maiden, Knock Prone

CHAINED HEARTS: The Petal Knight and the Two-Faced Maiden are chained to each other by the neck, meaning they cannot move more than 15 yards away from each other. The Petal Knight can use his minor action to make the Two-Faced Maiden move up to her Speed per round.

CONFUSED MIND: As previously described.

DEFEND THE MAIDEN (1 SP): The Petal Knight uses his shield to protect the Two-Faced Maiden, giving her a +2 bonus to Defense and Armor Rating until the start of his next turn.

FALSE PSYCHE: As previously described.

HOW DARE YOU: The first time the Two-Faced Maiden is hit in a round, the Petal Knight's next successful attack deals an extra 1d6 damage.

TALENTS: Armor Training (Novice), Weapon and Shield Style (Journeyman)

WEAPONS GROUPS: Heavy Blades, Light Blades

EQUIPMENT: Medium Breastplate, Longsword

THREAT: MODERATE

The Two-Faced Maiden

ABILITIES (FOCUSES)	
3	ACCURACY (ARCANE)
2	COMMUNICATION (DECEPTION, ROMANCE)
1	CONSTITUTION
2	DEXTERITY (INITIATIVE)
0	FIGHTING
2	INTELLIGENCE (HEALING, SHAPING)
3	PERCEPTION (EMPATHY, PSYCHIC)
0	STRENGTH (INTIMIDATION, MIGHT)
2	WILLPOWER (MORALE)

SPEED	HEALTH	DEFENSE	ARMOR RATING
12	15	12	0

WEAPON	ATTACK ROLL	DAMAGE
MOVED OBJECT	+4	1D6 (+1D6/2 OUTCOME)

SPECIAL QUALITIES

ARCANA: Cure, Move Object, Second Sight, Sorcerer's Grip

FAVORED STUNTS: Arcane Shield, Support the Knight

LINKED FATES: The Two-Faced Maiden and the Petal Knight are chained to each other by the neck, meaning they cannot move more than 15 yards away from each other. While the Two-Faced Maiden is active, the Petal Knight cannot be reduced to less than 1 Health, except if the damage comes from False Psyche.

CONFUSED MIND: As previously described.

DON'T HURT HIM!: The first time the Petal Knight is hit in a round, the Two-Faced Maiden's next use of arcana gains a +2 bonus to the test.

FALSE PSYCHE: As previously described.

SUPPORT THE KNIGHT (3 SP): The Two-Faced Maiden sings a stanza of love and devotion that uplifts the Petal Knight. The next attack to successfully hit the Petal Knight only deals half damage.

TALENTS: Healing (Novice), Shaping (Novice)

THREAT: MODERATE

The Petal Knight

Myrna Rennick is wracked by guilt and doubt after her childhood friend Daveed rejected her romantic declaration because he is caria. The mask grants her the strength of will to get what she wants and keep it, colored by an idle dream of joining the Knights of the Blue Rose.

The Two-Faced Maiden

Daveed Bredaine feels badly about not being able to return Myrna's romantic feelings, and is confused by the fact he does care deeply for her. The mask tempted him with the ability to lie to himself and others about his feelings and his true nature, perverting his wish to see Myrna happy.

The heroes accept a job from an exiled Rezean witch to help free the old wintering grounds of her clan from dark and sinister influences. Unknown to them, the witch already has plans in motion and is willing to pay any price to restore the ancient lands of her people.

Storms Over Kamala is an adventure suited for a group of 4 to 6 mid-level heroes (levels 9 to 12), although it can be adjusted to suit characters of a higher or lower level by adjusting the target numbers of some of the tests and the level of Threat posed by the adversaries. See the **Adversaries** and **Running the Game** chapters of the *Blue Rose* core rulebook for further details.

INTRODUCTION

THE LAST WITCH

For generations, the earthworks of Kamala have stood deserted, untended, their life and power slowly leeching away. No foals frolic there, no clan finds shelter; the herds run wild and the bloodlines wither. The grass, they say, is endless and the sound never stops; the sawing sigh of blade on blade, the keening whine of the wind. And then there are the strange creatures filtering from the Kamala grounds, shadow-twisted and hungry for blood—or so the stories go. The tales grow with the telling, and only those with an insatiable thirst for glory and no regard for their own safety are prepared to venture into the grasslands to reclaim Kamala.

Only one still holds hope: Jessari, a powerful and cunning witch of the Kamala who fought for years to elicit some sort of aid from her fellow Rezeans, only to be repeatedly rebuffed. In response, she began to hire mercenaries and adventurers—anyone who would try the battle—but none succeeded.

As her hope faded, Jessari's path led her to the Stone Forest in search of the blue trumpet flowers she prayed would bring her visions of a way to purify the land, no matter the cost. While the flowers did not bring her the dreams she hoped for, she found another: a former Jarzoni turned vampire, Majernan the Greedy.

Desperate for a solution, Jessari decided to use the creature for her own ends. Craving power above all else, Majernan agreed to work with Jessari to free her clans' wintering grounds; in return, she would deliver him the rest of Rezea. Little does Majernan realize that Jessari has no intention of making good on her promise.

The witch installed Majernan as "ruler" of the Kamala wintering grounds with one idea in mind: to slay him after he takes ownership in order to cleanse the land of all shadows. She feels the land must be cleansed by blood, but could not convince the vampire to teach her the arcane secrets. While she sought the knowledge elsewhere, he became too powerful for her to kill on her own. Now, while she knows his death will bring the land to her hand if she strikes the killing blow, she needs allies to bring about his downfall. As a result, Jessari, last witch of the Kamala, is looking for would-be heroes to aid her in her dark task.

Getting Started

The adventure begins in Garnet, where a rogue Rezean witch needs pawns in her desperate play to free the Kamala wintering grounds from their curse (and their current overlord). She seeks brave adventurers—people who will take on a challenge without too many questions—and the rewards she promises are great.

There are many dangers lurking on the Plains of Rezea, but the greatest is one who is convinced their cause is just no matter the consequences, and no one believes in Kamala's redemption more than Jessari the Restless, the last witch of Kamala. She will stop at nothing to see her heritage restored, regardless of the cost to her, or to others.

From Garnet, the characters travel across the sea to Fallen River Trading Camp, where Jessari hires guides for them before leaving them to travel the plains on their own. She arranges to meet the heroes at the Kamala wintering grounds as soon as she has followed up on her own pieces of the puzzle. Once at the haunted serpent mound, the heroes face an unexpected—and unwelcome—surprise: a master vampire and his collection of minions.

If they succeed in their quest, the heroes have the opportunity to loot Majernan's collected treasure, which is considerable. If they fail, they will be forced to flee or become sacrifices in the vampire's play to take control of the earthworks by force.

PART 1

The Witch of the Plains

In the first part of the adventure, the heroes become acquainted with Jessari and her goals for the Kamala lands in Rezea.

SCENE 1

The City of Garnet

ROLEPLAYING ENCOUNTER

Read or paraphrase the following to the players:

The wind ceases its roaring when it nears the Kamala grounds, dropping low to the ground before skulking up into the towering rock pillars looming over the plains. Sometimes an eerie whistle escapes; a burst of sound shattering the oppressive silence. Most creatures avoid these accursed lands, risking even the storms and predators of the tall grass rather than set foot in their shadows.

It is a desolate region, devoid of the laughter and thunder of hooves that once made it a place of joy and refuge. A few shadow-twisted beasts lurk within, sharp of tooth and keen with hunger. The very air is oppressive to breathe: a clinging, damp weight that smothers sound and hope.

The sun breaks over the horizon, and a low, hissing laugh can be heard for but a moment before the deadly silence drapes over the fallen heritage of Kamala once more.

There was a time when this land was rich, the prized territory of the Kamala people and their horses. But as the Kamala faded, new masters crept into the shadows. The few people and horses who tried to stay were killed or driven mad. As time passed, silence fell over the hills, and their monuments fell to ruin.

Not everyone has given up hope. A Kamala witch, one of the most daring of her generation, has fought for years to persuade Rezea to free Kamala from its shackles, but to no avail. Finally, at the end of her tether, she has turned to outsiders for aid.

There are a number of ways for the characters to become involved with the adventure. Many in Aldea owe Jessari favors, whether in thanks for services rendered, or as a result of darker tactics. These figures may seek out the heroes, or stumble across them in other encounters, either employing them directly or coercing them into service to acquit their own outstanding debts.

Four potential ways for the heroes to be recruited are described in the following sections, if their existing adventures and contacts do not suggest an alternate method of introducing them to the plot.

The Listeners

Jessari has long advocated for and protected trade between Aldis and Rezea, as well as supporting those who hunt shadowspawn. Aldis developed its own interests in Rezea and Kamala, as well, and where Jessari's pleas might have fallen on deaf ears before, there are some who now listen more closely to her story.

The largest of those ears belongs to the Listeners, a small group of agents tasked with protecting Aldea from threats not yet seen. The agents of the Listeners work in small teams, and senior agents are allowed to pursue the threats they deem to pose the greatest danger. One of the most senior agents, **Vrenna Hrithak** (see the **Allies and Adversaries** section), has turned her eyes to Rezea, and to the suspected export of Stone Forest blue trumpet flowers and poached Kamalan horses, which are believed to be powerful components of political, family, and commercial curses.

The **Blue Merchant** has been Vrenna's special goal for many years. She suspects them of orchestrating the murder of several fellow agents, and has survived more than one attempt on her own life; whether by luck or skill, she doesn't know. Vrenna has been granted the privilege of pursuing her quarry by whatever means she finds necessary, with the full weight of the Listeners' coalition behind her. It is a secret mission, because the Blue Merchant has ears everywhere.

Now Vrenna's task brings her to Rezea, where she seeks the help of the clans to put an end to this menace, even if it means braving the Stone Forest itself. She is in Garnet, looking to assemble a group to find some answers for her. She has no interest in going into Rezea herself, as she is making some headway investigating the problem in Garnet, and has an agent in the Fallen River Trading Camp.

If Vrenna is to be the heroes' way into the adventure, she encounters them not long after they enter Garnet, approaching them at a tavern. She offers intelligence on the status of the Rezean clans, and a proposition: find where the Kamalan horses and the tainted blue trumpet flowers are coming from, and she will ensure the reward is commensurate with the risk.

If the heroes choose to accept the mission, she gives them maps of Rezea—such as they are—and documents outlining what is known of the issues she is investigating. She cautions the documents should be burned as soon as possible, as there is a great deal of sensitive information in them. She also supplies Jessari's name and suggests looking for her in the Orchard District, giving the characters the witch's last known address. Vrenna has long suspected Jessari of collaboration with the Blue Merchant, and is deeply interested in gaining access to Jessari's confidences.

The maps may or may not be useful. If there is a character present with some existing knowledge of Rezea, they can combine what they already know with what they have been given to shorten the amount of wandering they do once they enter Rezea.

MASTER AND APPRENTICE

Not all Rezeans wish to see Kamala restored. For many, the betrayal is still too fresh. For **Ganniri Hassana**, the dishonor done to the Rezeans cannot be wiped away so quickly. An elder warrior who has spent many years trying to secure Rezea from outside influence and corruption, Ganniri has directly and vocally opposed Jessari's efforts for years. She and Jessari have no use for each other, and as Jessari increases her efforts to free Kamala, Ganniri schemes against her within Rezea, hampering her efforts at every turn. She distrusts Jessari's motives and means, and actively works to discredit the woman and her efforts.

However, Ganniri is aware of the problems in Kamala, and though she has no desire to see anyone return there permanently, she does at least want to see the area cleansed. She tasks her former apprentice with finding a way to bring respite to the area and return it to the quiet memory-shrine it should be. The former apprentice, **Silvin Ashoj**, is eager enough for the task.

If Silvin is to be the heroes' way into the adventure, she comes to them with the tale, and a plea for aid. She is not kind in her depiction of Jessari, nor does she claim to have

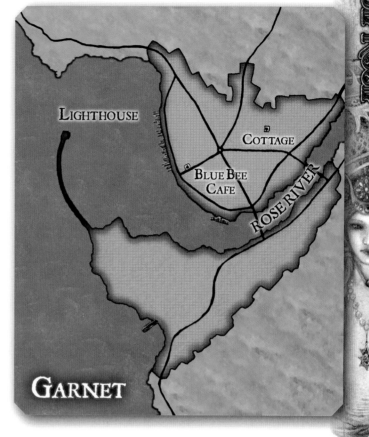

the witch's best interests in mind, but she is honest and forthright about the potential dangers.

If the characters accept the mission from Silvin, she will lead them to the witch's house.

HELSIR

Stormpoint Refuge has long sought to protect the few remaining Kamalan horses. Jessari often brings them orphaned foals and injured adults who have lost their herds. They tell stories of hunters—man and beast—preying on the herds, picking them off one by one; of finding butchered herd-mates, slaughtered friends, and the bones of missing foals. Helsir has often advocated for the protection of Kamala's heritage, but now his concern has grown immensely.

Stormpoint's ambassadors, the Rezean Jasak and the rhy-stallion Helsir, have come to Garnet to meet with local merchants to reaffirm their trading relationships. They have been staying with Jessari, bringing her up to date on the latest refugees and offering what little assistance they can.

Jasak often frequents the Blue Bee Café, as he and Jan Forthow are good friends. Helsir is more often found at City Hall or in the areas nearby, as he is friends with several officials who help coordinate Garnet's assistance of Stormpoint.

Jasak tells the party about a young stallion who recently came to the refuge, horribly burned and mourning the loss

of his mare and foal to human hunters. The stallion had been near the Kamala wintering grounds, and saw signs of regular travel into the hills there.

Further details regarding Helsir and his home can be found in the **Stormpoint Refuge** section of **Chapter 7** of the *Blue Rose* core book.

HEROES WANTED

Read or paraphrase the following to the players:

The notice boards of Garnet are always a treat to read. The latest crop of hand-scrawled missives includes: "Lost: One son to blue trumpet flower dreams." "Sailors needed! Visit foreign lands! Meet exotic folk! Make your family proud!" "Chicken stealers of the Market District: you are being watched, and you will pay for the damages we have suffered. Turn yourselves in now." Monster sightings and military recruitment posters, missing pets, folk searching for people they saw in passing, or open housing listings add to welter of threats, requests, and public service announcements on display.

The scribes sitting in their tiny shelters next to the boards take a coin, food, or items of use in exchange for writing the notices, and over time, each board develops a certain personality. One board, in particular, seems to suffer from a scribe with a penchant for flowery language and embellishments. It isn't in the richest part of the city, but even the "Firewood for Sale" posters have trees and

fires drawn on them, and comically-distorted monsters adorn a notice for someone who wants to teach you how to slay vile creatures.

But one, in particular, stands out from those surrounding it by sheer dint of its simplicity. It reads:

Skilled adventurers with shadowspawn experience to reclaim site of Rezean heritage. Must bring own weapons. Military experience preferred, knowledge of Rezean territory and dangers suggested. Compensation: based on experience.

The letters are stark and simple black on the creamy paper, and a strange sigil adorns the top of the sheet. On closer inspection, an address is visible at the bottom of the paper: the Blue Bee, a small eatery near the waterfront, known to the locals for good chicken and better beer. This is also presented as a player handout that can be found on page 133.

If the heroes decide to follow up on the notice, they discover the eatery is not far away and proves to be a popular place.

THE BLUE BEE CAFE

The Blue Bee is an old establishment, having been passed down through the Forthow family for several generations. It is near enough the docks to service the officials who oversee Garnet's rich trade, and not so far from the administrative district. The current owner, **Jan**

Forthow, has recently expanded it so that it now includes a brewery; a lucrative decision. The Forthow family has always employed orphans and children without prospects, adopting them into the family and raising them with useful skills. Jan himself is not related by blood to the Forthow family, but was adopted when very young.

The café is bustling, filled with the aroma of fresh bread, coffee, and the sweet-hot spices favored on the coast. A pitcher of excellent stout, spiced with nutmeg and cinnamon is dropped on the table within moments of walking in the door. A few minutes later, a hand-written menu on a thin sheet of wood is also left at the table.

When the characters announce they're there in response to the flyer, the server vanishes into a back room and emerges with a thin, older man, who introduces himself as Jan Forthow, proprietor and friend of Jessari the Restless. His eyes are narrow and his tone is suspicious as he questions the heroes' interests. Why do they want to help Jessari? Don't they know how dangerous this mission is? He hums gently to himself for a moment after each question is answered, as though weighing the honesty of their answers.

Finally, he shrugs and says he'll be back in a few minutes, before sending a server to take the characters' orders. After the food is brought and the beer has been refilled a few times, the proprietor returns and sits down with the party. At this point, the heroes should make a Communication (Persuasion) test and compare their result to the accompanying table to see how helpful Forthow has decided to be.

SCENE 2

THE COTTAGE

ROLEPLAYING ENCOUNTER

Read or paraphrase the following to the players:

The Orchard District is a suburb near the edge of Garnet. True to its name, it is largely composed of smaller houses, neat lanes, and small orchards of almond, plum, pear, and lemon trees. This time of year, the lemons are in full production, and the sound of workers and draft-donkeys provides a soothing backdrop. The city is growing, burying the orchards slowly as it creeps outward from the center, but here, its effects are not yet too noticeable.

Most houses have yards with chickens and the occasional pig or docile milk-cow. A few horses doze in small communal pastures, but most are in harness or under saddle, ferrying their owners into the city or working in the orchards. Neat gardens—a mix of vegetables, herbs, and a few flowers—surround the houses with color and the sound of bees. Small children play in the gardens and streets while old women sew or prepare meals in noisy circles on porches.

All in all, it seems to be a pleasant, civilized area, where people raise families and live out their lives without much fuss.

FOTHROW'S INFORMATION

TEST RESULT	INFORMATION
7	He doesn't like the look of you, and doesn't say much more than: "I don't know what else I could possibly tell you, a witch's business is her own. Hey, we have a new beer from the Scatterstars. Great with beef." Fortunately, the locals are chatty enough, and absolutely everyone knows about the quest these days.
9	Chatting him up, you learn Forthow knows the witch personally—although he won't elaborate beyond that—and where she can be found. He tells you to look for a white cottage with a blue door in the Orchard District, but nothing more.
11	Forthow likes you, so he gives you some directions—out the eatery's door, turn right, take a left at the well, find the white house with a blue door: 4, Peony Lane, in the Orchard District.
13	When you ask about the mission, Forthow shrugs. "Easy enough," he grunts. "Too easy, maybe, but it's probably something about Rezean cultural infighting and history and curses, and, long story short, they can't find anyone to go who won't piss someone else off, so they need outsiders to do it." Horses are plentiful there, after all, he explains, so why not have outsiders take all the risk, and he'd definitely do it if he didn't have the restaurant to manage. Gotta love those Rezean horses, could make a killing with a good contact in Rezea if you wanted to settle down and raise a family…
15	You know everything there is to know about the mission, the witch, and all the gossip that has wandered into the bar in the last month. Finally, you pry yourself away from Forthow and flee, following his directions toward the house with the blue door

The house that matches the address you have been given is a little smaller than those around it, and a flourishing garden nearly hides the windows. Bees hum through the many flowers, and fruit trees hang over the shoulder-height wall surrounding the yard. A white horse grazes on the shrubbery by the front door, which is every bit as blue as you might hope: a bright, cheerful blue with white flowers painted along its center panel. As you open the gate to the yard, the mare raises her head and eyes you with a certain cold intelligence. She approaches, and reaches out to speak with you.

The white horse is Misre, a Kamalan rhy-horse. She is bonded to Jessari, and guards her interests. She has patches of blue-grey over her ears, shoulders, and chest; this pattern is highly sought-after by the Rezeans, for it is considered to bring both luck and safety. The mare seems strange compared to other horses the heroes may have seen; her limbs too long and thin and set oddly together. Her eyes are ice-blue, and glimmer with an icy intellect. It is not only humans who can learn to hate.

If the characters come alone, she quizzes them on their intentions and plans, but if they arrive with Silvin, she merely asks a few questions to get to know them before stepping aside and granting them access. If the party chooses, they may ask her questions. She has traveled with Jessari for many years and knows as much as the witch. Her viewpoint may be more balanced than Jessari's, as she has not allowed anger to warp her so much.

If the party has horses, she will take them to the nearest communal pasture and negotiate care and feeding for them.

When you knock on the door, a slip of a woman—bundled in thick sweaters and scarves in every bright color imaginable—answers. Her face lights up with a smile when you introduce yourselves. Of course you're here about the adventure! With barely a pause in the stream of chatter, she ushers you into the house and—before you can draw a breath—you have tea and cakes in your hands and cats climbing your legs in hope of a treat or a new perch. Everything in the house smells of roses and baking bread. The witch isn't in right now, the woman says, but she'll be back soon, just as soon as she finishes at the market. You begin to recognize a certain resemblance to Jan Forthow, in manner if not in looks.

The endless stream of breathless, happy chatter doesn't let you get a word in edgewise until the door swings open and a tall woman in leathers stomps in. She introduces herself as Jessari the Restless, last witch of Kamala.

The witch moves too silently for such a large woman. Broad shouldered, her arms laced with sinew, she looks like a knight, not a witch. Her nose has been crushed once too often, and she is missing two fingers, which she says she lost to a fractious colt, or a sword, or a beast (it depends on how much she's had to drink when asked). The short, curved bow on her back, and the long, sweeping swords on Misre's saddle—sitting on a rack near the door, along with the bridle and her pack-saddle—are weapons made for someone with a fearless temper and powerful muscles. The fangs and talons on the bridle give further testament to the witch's bravery.

Jessari is not easy to like, but she commands immediate attention. Her attitude is brusque, and she is unlikely to win anyone over through charisma. She's seen plenty of adventurers and sell-swords promise to do what she needs but, as the characters talk, she begins to warm to them a little. She has many stories and a great deal of knowledge regarding Aldea's politics and people. If the party has other quests or questions, this is a good place to find answers.

Jessari has become something of a legend among mercenaries and those who need aid for lost causes. She's made plenty of friends, and her reputation as a fearsome ally and opponent draws grudging respect even from her enemies. She has long spoken of her desire to free the Kamala grounds, and has now begun to call in the favors she is owed. Slowly but surely, word of her mission is trickling through mercenary taverns and along merchant trails, whispered by courtesans' lips and shouted as captains' orders.

The journey is not without risk, Jessari is clear on that the moment she speaks. The plain-spoken warnings put many off, she tells them, and only the dedicated answer her call. Any stories the heroes may have heard about the disappearance of those who take up the challenge, or of them staggering into Garnet, months later, haggard and mad are fabricated, Jessari says, by her enemies, by the other clans, and by agents of the darkness in Kamala. The quest is difficult, she admits, but impossible only for those lacking the courage to persevere. Of course, with great risk comes great reward, and she has called in all her markers to secure good pay for the venture.

Jessari has a habit of constantly nibbling on things as she talks; usually nuts and dried fruit from the local orchards. She is never really still, and after a while, it rubs off on those around her as a sort of twitchy nervousness. She is willing enough to tell the story of Kamala's fall, and of its continued decline since, but is cagier about her own history until she has thoroughly warmed up to the party.

"I wish to restore the peace and safety of Kamala, and to bring the wild herds home," she says, cracking a walnut open with her bare fingers. The fire dances in her eyes, and an intense energy shimmers off her.

She lays out her dream—Kamala's lands safe, the herds returning, the remnants of her clan reviving, the respect of her people, and the safety of numbers. Conviction shines through every word, and a desperate determination to succeed no matter the cost. She explains, too, the reason Rezea will not aid its own: the vicious history of Kamala's betrayal. Grief enters her voice here, dark and personal, as she speaks of her envy toward the other clans, and the cost of watching the once-mighty herds being killed off.

Finally, she speaks of a darker threat looming over her homeland, a vampire from Jarzon, luring in shadowspawn to destroy what good remains in Kamala.

When pressed, she admits she believes this vampire is attempting to gather power in order to take the earthworks by force, to corrupt the land, and declare itself ruler over it. She says that there is only one way to stop it, if this is the case: she must be the one who deals the death-blow, and take the land for herself, to nurture and rebuild it.

The vampire has established his lair above the earthen serpent, hungering for it but still wary of its power. He seeks sacrifices to corrupt the power of the place to his mastery. He fears using Rezeans for this grim task, afraid of angering the ghosts who lurk in the ruins.

Finally, she looks up at you, tears glimmering in her eyes. The proud, fiery woman is subdued. An old grief sits on her shoulders, infectious in its strength. She needs help, she says. The vampire is too much for her alone, and with his minions, she does not stand a chance.

Jessari's grief is genuine, if calculated. She doesn't care what it takes to free her homeland.

If the heroes choose to take the mission, she provides them with a small sum of money for expenses and directions to meet her at the Blue Bee, early, two mornings from now. At this point, it is clear she is done with them; they may leave the cottage and either retire to a local inn—it is relatively late in the evening by now—or go explore the area she has named for the rendezvous and ask some questions about her. (If the characters made their way to Jessari via the Blue Bee, then they already know where they are to meet her in two days' time.)

Scene 3

Leaving Aldis' Shores

Roleplaying Encounter

It is cool and misty on the morning of the assigned meeting, and a thick fog rolls in from the sea. You meet at the agreed time at the Blue Bee Café. Jessari has already ordered breakfast for everyone: platters of eggs, bread, cheese, and tomatoes, and as she eats, she outlines the journey ahead. Highlighting, in particular, the dangers of the season, she distributes tokens of safe-travel, letters of assignment, and a briefing on the situation. It is storm season on the plains, and she is not shy about sharing stories she grew up on, such as:

> "When I was a small girl, we sheltered for a time with the Mischa clan. It was a bad year, and so they sent a party out onto the plains to try and bring back meat. Twenty hunters went, accompanied by three witches and nearly a dozen supporters to help dress and transport the kills. All were mounted on the strongest, bravest horses, and supplied as well as possible.
>
> They never returned, and no word of them came back until the clan ventured onto the plains when the storms calmed. They searched for months without luck, until one day, they found themselves in a circle of grass lying flat as a mat. The circle was as wide as six horses standing nose-to-tail, and the grass around it was twisted into knots and ropes.
>
> But in the center, they found many bones: horse and human tangled together, covered with desiccated hide, untouched by predators or scavengers. The bones were broken in strange ways, necks twisted back underneath bodies, legs and arms ripped horribly from joints.
>
> The clan said it was a curse brought upon them for harboring Kamala refugees, and as they mourned, my family and I were cast out into the plains to find our own way, never minding that my own sister lay among the dead, a young warrior cut down in her first year of adulthood.
>
> The prairie does not forgive."

Once breakfast is over, and she has handed out the necessary supplies, Jessari leads the characters, and her rhy-horse, Misre, to the docks. There, the Yellow Stag, a slim passenger ship, awaits, its captain fidgeting nervously. "The tides are turning! We must leave now!" he cries, clearly frustrated. Jessari ignores him and takes the heroes on board, showing them to their quarters. They barely have time to stow their gear before the ship casts off and sets sail for Rezea.

Part 2

Journey to Kamala

In the second part of the adventure, the heroes travel by ship to the Plains of Rezea, particularly the Fallen River Trading Camp, where they begin their journey inland to the Kamala wintering grounds.

Scene 1

The Shadow-Touched Serpent

Combat Encounter

Read or paraphrase the following to the players:

> The weather stays fairly quiet during the crossing, a strong wind from the open sea slowing the ship's pace. The captain is the nervous sort, however; a feeling that translates to everyone aboard. Sentries are constantly posted, all of them with some small adept ability, which they seem to use to scan for life. Lights are restricted at night, and noise during the day. When pressed, the captain mutters about lost ships and rumors of something preying on merchant vessels.
>
> At first, it seems only to be paranoia. The weather is calm, and nothing more ominous than a few flying fish have been seen. The sentries call out something on the afternoon of the third day, but quickly shrug it off. They notice it again later, but don't think it is anything more than a dolphin or similar sea creature. It appears to be heading for the ship, but in a winding, seemingly unfocused pattern. They even lean over the railings, trying to see if it might be good meat—perhaps a whale or an unusually large fish.
>
> Suddenly, the water erupts a few hundred feet away, and a towering, serpentine beast rises out of the sea. It is pale grey, marked with slashes of cream and black, perfectly camouflaged for the deep seas. It leans over the ship, hissing, and a bright yellow and red spiny frill erupts around its head and down its crest.

Statistics for the creature, a Shadow-touched sea serpent, can be found in the **Allies and Adversaries** section. Its first action is to attempt to coil around the boat, both to crush it and to provide itself with a stable anchor from which to unleash its other attacks. However, in doing so, it leaves its one major weakness open to assault: its spine may be heavily scaled, but it is fragile and vulnerable to crushing attacks in particular, as well as to spears. Characters can perform the Mighty Blow and Pierce Armor combat stunts against the serpent's spine for only 1 Stunt Point when making such attacks.

The beast grows more enraged and less focused as its wounds mount. At the beginning of the skirmish, it focuses on individual victims, but as its injuries worsen, it favors massive, multi-target attacks, such as Fearsome Cry and Water Jet.

After the serpent is dispatched, the crew gets busy salvaging any parts of the corpse they can find. The spines are carefully cut away from the head and placed into a metal chest; the head is cut from the body and placed in a separate chest; and the skin, blood, and flesh are secured in any container that can be found.

The damage to the ship takes longer to repair, but soon enough, the heroes are limping towards their destination once again. Before long, the steep cliffs of the Fallen River Trading Camp rise on the horizon, and Rezea looms ahead.

OPTIONAL SCENE

VRENNA HRITHAK AND THE POISON FLOWERS

ROLEPLAYING ENCOUNTER

If the characters have not been directly recruited by the Listener agent, Vrenna Hrithak, then this optional scene presents the Narrator with an opportunity to complicate their lives even further. Read or paraphrase the following to the players:

> She's been watching you since the trip started. A short woman, fat and dressed in simple but expensive clothing, no one seems to know why she's here or what she's after. Two days out from the trading camp, she approaches one of your party and asks to speak with all of you when Jessari is not present. She says her name is Vrenna, and she represents a group dedicated to ensuring the safety of Aldea from corruption and Shadow. She believes you may be able to aid her mission.

If the heroes invite the woman to their quarters, she produces a flask of a strong, apricot-scented liqueur which she shares liberally before beginning her story.

The blue trumpet flowers of Rezea are increasingly sought after throughout Aldis and its allies. Mystics, priests, lovers, and recreational users all want it. But one man controls the entire trade, choking off the supply. Recently, users are suffering from negative side-effects—nightmares, paranoia, and ill health. She believes there is either a new supplier providing bad paste, or, more troublingly, someone is tainting the existing supply coming out of Rezea with flowers from the Stone Forest.

As they drink, the woman claims she is an agent of Aldis, seeking to put an end to this poison which gives Shadow such a foothold. She herself is traveling to meet with a Rezean contact at the trading camp to try and travel with them to the Stone Forest to track the source of the

BLUE TRUMPET FLOWER TRADE

The black market export of blue trumpet flower paste is dominated by one merchant. The sale of the paste is heavily regulated by Aldin and Jarzoni officials, although demand is high from less savory places, many of which put it to uses Aldis finds distasteful and Jarzon considers heretical. All off-the-books sales of the product are licensed through this shadowy merchant, and anyone who bucks his authority gets a visit from his henchmen (see the **Allies and Adversaries** section). An older man known only as the Blue Merchant, he controls much of the drug trade in the region, and is rumored to do brisk business into Jarzon. Jessari does extensive business with him, providing the blue trumpet flowers of the Stone Forest as a particularly cruel poison, for they do not kill, insidiously destroying their consumers instead.

tainted flowers, but she sees an opportunity in the heroes to collect more information from places she cannot go. She is also somewhat suspicious of Jessari, who has become embroiled in quite a few messes over the years.

If the characters establish an alliance with Vrenna, she will provide additional intelligence about Rezea, as well as Jessari's history. She also becomes a useful ally for future use.

If, on the other hand, the heroes turn her down, she plays no further part in the proceedings.

SCENE 2

FALLEN RIVER TRADING CAMP

EXPLORATION ENCOUNTER

Read or paraphrase the following to the players:

You have heard stories of the Fallen River Trading Camp; of the danger and thrill of this rather lawless place. Bandits and honor-duels, horse-thieves dragged to their deaths through the streets, and those lost in blue trumpet flower dreams stumbling to the sea to drown while in pursuit of phantoms.

None of this prepares you for the reality; for the towering walls pressing down on you, or the thin ribbon of blue above; the bellowing of stallions and the shrill cries of young horses being weaned from their dams; or the chanting of horse-dealers as they lead their wares through the city, showing them off before the next auction. Private buyers feel over a prospective mount on one corner, while an Aldin captain studies a herd in another corral for prospective war-horses. A high-spirited young bay mare, trailing a broken rope, gallops down the street as her caretakers scramble after her, cursing and laughing.

THE HORSES OF KAMALA

Very few of Kamala's herds remain, and fewer still are tamed to the saddle. The witch and a few of her friends—most of the remaining Kamala have become mercenaries—have rounded up and domesticated a small herd of the best of what is left. Each horse has its own strengths and weaknesses, and its own personality.

SAALON

A mare the color of fresh copper, with one white foot and three long scars down her neck. She is quiet, her eyes bright with fierce intelligence. She is most likely to notice a threat the characters haven't spotted yet.

ORISTOR

A gelding the color of river-soil lit with subtle golden dappling, his thick black mane falls over a proudly arched neck and a misshapen splotch of white is emblazoned on his forehead. He is sturdy and friendly, and can carry more weight than any of the others.

HALLSET

A bay gelding with a bright, golden-brown coat and four high, white stockings, his mane and tail are thinner than the others. He is not the handsomest of them, but the witch promises he is swifter than the rest.

FRITHI

A gray mare, the color of steel all over. She is the youngest, full of fire and opinion. She has not yet been scarred and has not learned wisdom, meaning she is always the first into battle.

THANIS

A red roan stallion, his legs are marked with numerous claw marks; another scar crosses his muzzle, pulling his lips into a perpetual snarl. Thanis is not the easiest to get along with, but he has earned his scars, and will protect those in his charge.

KOLLA

A mare as black as night, Kolla has a thick swatch of white draping her shoulders and smaller patches of white on her legs. She is the handsomest of the lot, high-headed and proud. She is not the fastest, but she is fierce and strong.

NITRANI

A red-bay mare, her coat the color of blood, a single bright star blazing between her eyes. She is temperamental and powerful; anger shines in her eyes, but she softens towards humans.

RANDOM ENCOUNTERS

A number of threats lurk in the canyons, which are too rugged and labyrinthine to be completely cleared even by the most determined Rezeans. Any or all of these could be encountered by the heroes as they wend their way along the trail.

Several **brown bears** (*Blue Rose* **Chapter 12: Adversaries**) seem to have taken up residence here, levying a heavy tax on the camp's cattle and sheep. Only one has been successfully killed so far.

More deadly are the plants that some misguided soul must have thought would contribute to the safety of the camp from outsiders. The Rezeans aren't entirely sure *why* the plants are out there, but they fight an endless battle with them none the less. The most annoying of these is a corrupted **plant elemental** (*Blue Rose* **Chapter 12: Adversaries**) that wanders through the hills, attacking travelers as the will takes it.

A small nest of three **strix** (*Blue Rose* **Chapter 12: Adversaries**) also resists extermination, and moves any time its location is discovered. Currently the strix are lurking just off the main path through the canyons, waiting for some unwary prey.

There is an air of chaos here, of eel-quick change and movement so different from Aldis. Blink and you might miss it, or be run over by a small herd being moved to the docks. The season for trading is ending, according to Jessari. Most of the herds have been sold off, or are being prepared to move to the wintering grounds. This is only a fragment of what would normally swirl through the Fallen River Trading Camp, but it is mindboggling nevertheless.

THE HORSES

Jessari brings the heroes to a small tent encampment, marked by a sign painted with a black foal. After a short haggle with the owner, she shows them to a large tent in the back of the encampment. Inside, simple furnishings—designed to be packed and moved efficiently—are set up on worn, but thick, rugs. At the height of trading season, even this much would not be available.

The witch leaves the characters so she can collect the horses and supplies needed for the journey, and the noise of the camp settles over them as firmly as the tent flap. The next morning, Jessari meets the heroes outside the tent. Behind her, five Rezean mercenaries hold strings of horses. Most are packed with gear and supplies, but she brings theirs forward with a smile, seeming friendlier than last night.

The horses are of Kamalan stock, she says, a rare and dying breed, but the best of what remains. No one else will ride them through an outdated sense of respect, so if the mission is successful, they will belong to the heroes. They have suffered too, she says, but wear their scars with as much pride as any warrior. Now all that remains is for them to choose their mount.

Once the horses are chosen, it is time to leave the camp and begin the final journey. Misre, Jessari's bonded rhy-horse, has communicated the mission to the Rezean horses, and Jessari promises they will find their way to the wintering grounds if the heroes only trust them. The witch takes her leave of the characters here, promising to scout ahead and clear the path of as much danger as possible.

SCENE 3

THE EDGE OF THE GRASS FOREST

EXPLORATION/COMBAT ENCOUNTER

Read or paraphrase the following to the players:

The steep trail out of the camp seems to wind on endlessly. The Rezean horses have no trouble, their feet setting solidly with each step, their heads lowered to watch the trail. After a while, you learn to just sit there, reins loose on their necks. You lean forward until your legs tremble to ease the load on their backs, clinging to the saddle when they lunge upward over particularly steep sections of the trail. Occasionally a stone finds its way under a hoof, and the creature will pause, weight shifting to its other legs so that it can find safer footing.

Sometimes smaller canyons cut across your path, the trail dropping abruptly to cross small streams or rock-falls. The horses slither down these, sitting back on their haunches, sometimes pausing to drink from the precious rivulets.

After a while, even the horses are sweating and huffing, their huge nostrils sucking in the still, hot air of the canyons you travel through. It is slow going but, according to what the witch said before she left you, faster than the great road out of the other side of the camp, and with less chance of unfriendly characters following you.

The vegetation is sparse here, mostly rugged trees, tough grasses, and bushes. This late in the season, just before the rains begin, everything feels dry and worn.

The exception is where the streams gather in quiet pools. Cattails cluster thickly in the shade, and yellow lilies bloom around the edges of the ponds. Birds swoop over the water, diving at insects and small fish. Black squirrels pause to watch the riders, their tails jerking erratically.

Finally, the last canyon sprawls onto the plains. A huge slump of rock marks its origin, and it is here the mercenaries accompanying the heroes insist the first camp should be made. The horses are unsaddled and rubbed down before being turned loose to graze on the surrounding pastures. The camp itself is established on a small ledge above a stream which winds its way across the plains towards the sea. The night passes uneventfully.

The day is cool, and a sea breeze seems to be finding its way up the valley. In the morning light, the true extent of the canyons is revealed in all its splendor; a dizzying maze of erosion and geological shift branching off towards the sea.

To the west, the grass rolls in mighty waves under the incessant wind, heat shimmer distorting the horizon. This is where you must go, into the vast ocean of grass, at the mercy of the weather and your guides.

The horses are undisturbed. The steel-gray mare dances under her rider, pulling at the bit, eager to plunge back into the land she knows. The chestnut mare takes the lead, and the Rezeans gesture at you to follow.

The horses know where the road lies, and you can only settle into the saddle and let them choose their way through the grass.

SCENE 4
THE ELEMENTALS

COMBAT ENCOUNTER

Read or paraphrase the following to the players:

The grasslands seem endless. The gentle swell of the plains blocks sight of anything else, and the days are quickly reduced to the sound of rustling stalks and hoof beats. The scent of the dry grass baking under the sun, at first a welcoming smell reminiscent of home—at least to those from rural areas—eventually grows overbearing. The sun glimmering off the golden stalks becomes blinding after a while.

After three days of uneventful travel, Saalon takes a sharp turn from the direction she has been steadily traveling, her ears pricking up and her speed increasing. Within twenty minutes, an oasis of green grass can be seen ahead. Soon, you come upon a large spring. The ground slopes gently down to catch the water in a large pool. Fish splash noisily in the shallows, and the edges are lined with cattails, reeds, and wild iris.

This would make an excellent spot to stop for the night.

A successful TN 9 Perception (Seeing) test reveals a cache of supplies. There are also missives stored here, carved-bone messages from recent travelers the Rezean guides can interpret. The characters may replenish their packs here if desired, as well as find out information

about the way ahead, and the accompanying dangers, as detailed in the bone notes.

The next morning, Saalon easily finds her way back to the path and resumes her trek west, the others falling into their long, monotonous strides behind her. Towards evening, the horses become nervous. Swiveling ears, distended nostrils, and raised heads indicate some danger but there is nothing in sight, only a stiff breeze from the north that seems oddly hot.

If a character has Psychic Contact, or there is a rhydan in the party, they may speak to the horses and discover they smell fire, but that it seems…strange.

Soon, cinders begin falling on the heroes' shoulders, and the horizon shimmers with heat. The Rezeans curse loudly and dismount. Their leader, Weiros, dumps a pack on the ground, pulling out the materials to light a fire. Within minutes, he has a small fire going, and the Rezeans fan the flames, which race south under the wind. They lay down blankets and clothing on the burned ground. Without prompting, the horses step onto the blankets and sink down, eyes white with fear. The Rezeans show the heroes how to protect the animals' eyes and nostrils, pouring water on shirts and wrapping them over each horse, then draping the remaining blankets over their backs.

Any character with Second Sight, or who succeeds at a TN 11 Intelligence (Arcane Lore) test understand the horses' confusion: the fire has a distinct whiff of the arcane about it. But, with the preparations laid in place by the Rezeans, the characters should have safe ground to mount a defense against the oncoming trouble.

> Soon enough, the fire comes into view. A giant humanoid composed entirely of flame looms over it all, roaring with gleeful laughter as it throws burning brands far and wide. A fierce wind swirls through the flanks of the fire and drives it every which way, against any laws of how fire should move.
>
> Whether tainted by the corruption to the west, or merely rogues in their own right, the elementals appear to be working together to sow as much destruction as possible.

The elementals see easy prey in the heroes and the mercenaries and attack them immediately, cackling with glee. Statistics for both creatures can be found in *Blue Rose* **Chapter 12: Adversaries.** Their cooperation is tentative, and if the wind elemental begins to take damage, it disengages from the fire elemental and attempts to flee. The fire elemental will not stop until it is extinguished, leaving only a fast, large grass fire behind it.

The scene of devastation left by the elementals is grim. The plains are black and smoldering, deep ash and charcoal covering the ground in all directions. The Rezeans wrap the horses' hooves and legs to protect them, and drape wet rags over their noses to protect their lungs.

With these precautions in place, the long journey west begins again.

THE LAND UNDER SHADOW

The heroes arrive at the old Kamala wintering grounds, where they must face the threats lurking there, particularly the **vampire** who has claimed these lands for his own.

SCENE 1

THE KAMALA WINTERING GROUNDS

EXPLORATION/COMBAT ENCOUNTER

Read or paraphrase the following to the players:

> The grass ends abruptly where it washes up against the base of the hills. Tall stone walls mark the entrance into the hills, their eroded faces marching away into the distance on either side. A sense of desolation gathers here; there is no birdsong, not even the harsh croak of crows. It is as though every living thing has fled, leaving only decay behind.
>
> The Rezean mercenaries suddenly spur their mounts into a gallop, abandoning you where you stand. It would appear there is not enough money in Aldea to lure them into that cursed place after all.
>
> The horses pause, their ears flicking as they stare upward. They do not seem overly happy to be here, either, and hesitate to enter. Finally, Kolla takes the lead from Saalon, and the stone walls close around you, shutting off the sound and light of the plains with precipitous abruptness.

As the day wears on, even Kolla and Frithi begin to flag, their heads and high-held tails drooping. The path is rocky and overgrown, requiring frequent stops to hack a path through thorny foliage. Bones can sometimes be seen, predators and prey mixed together, an altogether disconcerting sight. Where the path is not stony, it is covered with a thick, chalky dust that coats mouths and skin and leaves a foul taste behind. The land itself is blighted and forlorn.

ENCOUNTERS: BRIGANDS AND GHOSTS

Brigands lurk in these hills, protecting the entrance to Majernan's lair as well as using it as a base from which to mount raids for horses and slaves. They pay a tax to the vampire for his protection and indulgence, and will attack any unknown parties that dare to enter. They are not overly dangerous, mostly small, dissenting bands as

likely to war with each other as a common foe—sometimes even turning on each other in battle—and are not overly-well equipped, a state of affairs Majernan has seen fit to maintain.

Even so, the party may expect to encounter them at least once or twice on their journey through the area. The bandits prefer to attack from ambush, using short swords and bows (use the Warrior from *Blue Rose* **Chapter 12: Adversaries** as required).

More problematic are the ghosts (*Blue Rose* **Chapter 12: Adversaries**). Kamala clan members who died here are tied to the region, slowly going mad from the corruption of their land. (Narrator: see the core rulebook for more on corruption, and how it may influence the characters and setting.) The ghosts regard all as interlopers, and it is not uncommon for them to attack the brigands, too. They may be appeased if a Rezean speaks to them and makes a successful TN 15 Communication (Persuasion) check. Otherwise, they attack without reason or mercy.

SCENE 2

THE VAMPIRE'S FOOTSTOOL

COMBAT ENCOUNTER

The path eventually peters out in a small valley. Here, the sense of desolation gives way to a choking emptiness. This is the Vampire's Footstool, and enchantment lies heavily on it. Fear keeps out any who have not been invited in and given the will to resist their fear. Without that blessing, the air seems to creep into lungs, choking and polluting every breath. The eyes play tricks, with swarms of spiders or snakes seeming to appear out of shadows, and the sound of hissing and a heavy, wet breathing fill the air. All characters must make a TN 7 Willpower (Courage or Self-Discipline) roll against the enchantment on entering the valley. Failure reduces Willpower by 1; this returns if the character leaves the area.

Not a single living thing grows here, not a blade of grass or even a dandelion. In the daylight, nothing moves, but by night, the place crawls with Majernan's minions searching for sustenance for their master. Not far into the Footstool, the trail levels out by a stream that does not seem overly foul, but the horses refuse to drink from it.

Any living creature that does drink from the stream falls into an arcane, unnatural slumber for 1d6+2 hours and cannot be awakened during that time. Anyone with Second Sight who looks at or touches the water of the stream feels it is unnaturally tainted. The water does not retain its properties if removed from the stream for more than an hour. It is not a wonderful place to camp, but it is the best option the characters currently have.

The attack comes just after sunset, without warning. A loud roar startles the horses and sends them scattering down the trail, except for Kolla. Three ghouls (*Blue Rose* **Chapter 12: Adversaries**) hit hard and fast, striking with

frenzied strength. The rest of the horses come back quickly, tearing into the attackers alongside their riders.

It is quickly apparent the ghouls are not trying to kill the party, but are instead attempting to capture them. If any characters drank the water and are still asleep, the ghouls automatically grab them unless they are being actively guarded.

Just as suddenly as they arrived, the surviving ghouls flee through a nearby cave mouth, taking any captives with them and triggering a spell that collapses the tunnel behind them. The only path is back to the Vampire's Footstool, and from there, upward into the cavern in which Majernan lurks. The Kamalan earthworks lie just east of the Footstool, with Majernan's lair set into a cliff face that overlooks both locations. A shadow seems to lie over the earthworks, as though the corruption of the area could bring the serpent to life at any time.

Scene 3
The Vampire

Combat/Roleplaying Encounter

At this point, the heroes can attempt to lure Majernan out to fight, leaving behind any captives in the hopes they will not be killed and he will not succeed in his sorcery. Otherwise, Majernan's tactics are to send out his minions—a mix of walking dead and beastfolk, one to two per character—to stall the party. If these are successfully defeated, he sends his surviving ghouls, all the while attempting to craft the necessary sorcery with any captives he has managed to obtain. The players have eight rounds to stop him before he succeeds, if he has captives.

If Majernan does not have captives, he will begin the sorcery and come out to fight himself. In this case, any character he kills will be sufficient to complete the curse. If he succeeds, the curse immediately comes into play. Majernan's Health does not regenerate, and his physical Strength, armor, and attack roll bonus all go down one point per round, but he is now able to summon earth elementals at will and control any corrupt creature in his territory. At this point, Jessari reappears and throws herself into the fight.

Jessari actively attempts to be the one to kill Majernan, and will ignore all other antagonists. If Jessari succeeds in landing the killing blow, it releases the land to her control, and weakens the minions. After that, the fight merely becomes a clean-up operation.

However, if a player character kills Majernan, the land falls to their control. If this happens, Jessari immediately turns against that person and seeks their death with all her might. She becomes completely antagonistic and will not stop until one or other of them is dead, which releases the land back to her, if she is successful.

Conclusion

If Jessari does not turn into an antagonist, the clean-up is simple, and the vampire's hoard is available to be looted. As the characters are doing this, they notice the witch slump as though wounded. Her dark skin turns pale and clammy. Read or paraphrase the following to the players:

"I was afraid of this," Jessari says, her lips white. "The land has been drained for too long. To fight off the sickness, blood, and death is not enough. It must have life."

Misre moves close, fear shining in her eyes, lending her strength to her owner, but the drain is too much for them. Both slowly collapse, breathing heavily. They are in obvious pain, but do not seem to be fighting it.

"It does not matter. It is free, and I am tied to it. Now the healing will begin, and the herds can return."

She knots her hand in Misre's mane, the rhy-mare's head resting heavily in her lap.

"We are together, and it is free. That is all that matters. But remember me kindly, and do me one last service: bear this news to my people. Let them know that a piece of our heritage has been reclaimed, and though it may be only a single foothold, they must now finish what I have started. Tell them!"

Your last sight of them is of two lonely creatures at the end of a hard journey, clinging together for comfort. Much later, rumor of the guardian of the hills—a ghost-woman on her white horse—begin to filter into Aldis.

If, however, Jessari becomes an antagonist and does *not* succeed in killing the heroes, the land will attempt to return to its natural form. If the affected character has high arcana, they can resist this for four rounds before succumbing to the same fate as the witch. To break the bond, they must spill their blood on the soil where the vampire was killed and renounce ownership. The land becomes free, and though the Jessari's mission was unsuccessful, the area is relieved of a little of its grief. The character who receives ownership of the land through the vampire's sorcery instinctively knows this, and may choose between renouncing the bond or allowing their life to go to the land in order to cleanse it.

Allies & Adversaries

The two main NPCs in this adventure are Jessari and Majernan the vampire. The two have very specific goals which, at the end of the day, involve betraying each other.

Jessari the Restless, Last Witch of Kamala

Jessari and her family were fostered, for a time, by the Mischa, before they were thrown out of the tribe and her father found more lucrative employment with the Tenniral clan. Most of her childhood was spent there, although she was always keenly aware of her tainted legacy, as her father was deeply, bitterly proud to be the direct descendant of Kamala. Not long after she bonded with Misre—a bond that was viewed with suspicion and intense jealousy—she had a violent disagreement with a respected elder of the tribe and left to make her name elsewhere.

JESSARI THE RESTLESS

She succeeded. Her focused rage in battle quickly became legendary, and foes much greater than she fell or fled before her arcana and her spear. She earned respect, too, from the officers and men alike, and began to teach herself languages and politics. Around this time, her dream of restoring her heritage to its former glory was born.

But in Rezea, her name bears no honor. A daughter of Kamala heart and blood, bitter from the betrayal and shunning of her heritage, she has renounced her allegiance to the nation, pursuing the freedom of Kamala at all costs. Though she has softened a little as she ages, realizing she needs allies within the clans, she is still cold and brusque to most Rezeans.

Her devotion to her lost people has made enemies, within Rezea and outside. Taking on high-risk mercenary contracts to pay for her mission, she has several bounties on her head—and has collected at least two of the ones on her herself (the arcane arts are a wonderful thing!).

But every attempt she has made to reclaim Kamala for its rightful heirs has failed, and as the bloodlines of both horse and human decline, the nearing extinction of her heritage has turned her courage to fear, and her hope to bitterness. She walks a thin line now, struggling to resist the call of Shadow, to keep a master vampire from the truth, and to fulfill her one great quest.

Jessari's strength comes from her great will and hope. She might be doing the wrong thing, but she is doing it for the right reasons, and this lends her a powerful conviction.

She carries a long oak staff set with the teeth of darkfiends, shadowspawn, and beastfolk. It serves as both a channel for her power, and as a deadly weapon.

MAJERNAN THE GREEDY

A disciple of both Ulasta and Gravicarius, Majernan marries within himself a lust for eternal life and a crushing need for dominance. He sought power through any means at his disposal, and thus became an immortal with aspirations of godhood. Unfortunately for him, he was also greedy and impatient.

The son of a minor Jarzoni lady, he first seized power after his mother's suspicious death. For a while, his hold-

JESSARI THE RESTLESS, LAST WITCH OF KAMALA			
ABILITIES (FOCUSES)			
3	ACCURACY (STAVES)		
5	COMMUNICATION (DECEPTION, LEADERSHIP, PERSUASION, PSYCHIC)		
3	CONSTITUTION		
4	DEXTERITY (INITIATIVE, RIDING)		
3	FIGHTING		
5	INTELLIGENCE (REZEAN LORE, STONE FOREST LORE)		
3	PERCEPTION (HEARING, SEEING, SMELLING)		
4	STRENGTH		
6	WILLPOWER (COURAGE, SELF-DISCIPLINE)		

SPEED	HEALTH	DEFENSE	ARMOR RATING
12	100	14	7

WEAPON	ATTACK ROLL	DAMAGE
STAFF	+5	1D6+7
UNARMED	+2	1D3+4

SPECIAL QUALITIES

ARCANA: Body Control, Calm, Psychic Contact, Psychic Shield, Second Sight

FAVORED STUNTS: Imposing Arcana, Passionate Inspiration, Stay Aware

ILLUSION: Jessari can cast minor illusions for a short period of time. This includes enhancing her Threat through appearing larger or more blood-drenched than she is, or hiding a few quiet people until the time is right for them to attack. She can cast up to two minor illusions per day. Each lasts up to four hours, but that time decreases if she is wounded.

SUGGESTION: She is able to use Suggestion once per target per day, up to three targets. The effect is mild—she is more likely to win in a rational debate than otherwise, but unable to force her will on anyone—but the effect lasts a full day.

TALENTS: Armor Training (Journeyman), Healing (Novice), Horsemanship (Master), Medicine (Novice), Meditative (Novice), Mounted Combat Style (Master), Outrider (Master), Psychic (Novice)

EQUIPMENT: Light Armor, Light Sword, Standard Lance, Throwing Knives

THREAT: MODERATE

ings grew, allegedly through trickery and the use of dark arcana, but he made too many enemies too quickly, and the few documents that mention him show only that his holding was razed in a territorial dispute. He was never seen in Jarzon again.

Not long after, a remote island in the Scatterstar Archipelago fell to Shadow. The inhabitants became twisted, raiding their neighbors and visiting atrocities on unguarded villages. Again, Majernan's reign went largely

MAJERNAN THE GREEDY

ABILITIES (FOCUSES)

3	ACCURACY (BITE, BRAWLING)
2	COMMUNICATION (DECEPTION, ETIQUETTE, LEADERSHIP, PSYCHIC)
4	CONSTITUTION
2	DEXTERITY (INITIATIVE, RIDING)
3	FIGHTING
1	INTELLIGENCE (SHAPING, SORCERY LORE)
3	PERCEPTION (HEARING, SEEING, SMELLING)
4	STRENGTH (CLIMBING, INTIMIDATION)
3	WILLPOWER (ANIMISM, COURAGE)

SPEED	HEALTH	DEFENSE	ARMOR RATING
12	120	12	3

WEAPON	ATTACK ROLL	DAMAGE
BITE*	+5	2D6+4
UNARMED	+5	1D6+6

SPECIAL QUALITIES

ARCANA: Animal Messenger, Animal Summoning, Move Object, Psychic Contact, Psychic Domination, Psychic Shield, Second Sight, Suggestion, Wind Shaping

FAVORED STUNTS: Disarm, Enrage, Knock Prone (1 SP), Imposing Arcana, Mighty Blow (1 SP), Stunned Silence, Skirmish

DEADLY BLOWS: Majernan's unarmed attacks do +2 damage (in addition to the bonus from Unarmed Style) from his raw power and claw-like nails. He also performs the Mighty Blow combat stunt for 1 SP instead of the usual 2 with unarmed attacks.

EXTREMELY HARD TO KILL: Majernan cannot be reduced below 1 Health except by sunlight, fire, or the use of the Lethal Blow combat stunt or the Lethal Arcana arcane stunt, representing decapitation or destruction of his heart or brain. Majernan also doesn't need to breath and is immune to most poisons and diseases, save those specifically targeting vampires.

MASTER'S WILL: As a minor action, Majernan may siphon the energy of his thrall, as long as they are within 20 yards. The thrall suffers 1d6 + the thrall's Constitution + Majernan's Willpower penetrating damage (in this case 1d6+7, due to his reduced Willpower), which Majernan gains in Health. A thrall may not be reduced below 1 Health in this manner, and Majernan may not gain more Health than the thrall loses.

NOCTURNAL PREDATOR: Majernan suffers no penalties for attacking or acting in darkness, natural or supernatural.

UNNATURAL ARMOR: Majernan's arcane nature provides an armor rating equal to his Willpower.

VAMPIRE BITE (4 SP): On a Bite attack, Majernan can inflict the vampire infection on his victim. A character affected by this stunt must make a TN 13 Constitution (Stamina) test or become infected. If the target character is the same race as Majernan, they suffer a -2 to this test. See **Porphyria** (*Blue Rose* **Chapter 12**) for the effects of this infection.. Majernan does not use his Bite attack unless he is certain he can kill his victim, or he specifically intends to turn them into a thrall.

WEAKNESS TO SUNLIGHT: Sunlight burns Majernan like acid, melting his flesh, causing 3d6 penetrating damage per round for partial exposure and 6d6 for being in full sunlight.

TALENTS: Animism (Novice), Psychic (Journeyman), Shaping (Novice), Unarmed Style (Master)

THREAT: DIRE

unnoticed and unchecked until his greed got the better of him, and his forces took as slaves the children of a pirate queen, who had been living with their island-folk father. The pirate queen vowed vengeance and rallied her allies, and the Shadowed Island was annihilated.

Again, the vampire escaped, and disappeared from the world, until the Rezean witch, Jessari, stumbled across him in the Stone Forest and offered him the rulership of Rezea in exchange for the freedom of Kamala. Majernan rules the empty wasteland of Kamala—for now. Many things gather to the scent of his power. Brigands and shadowspawn lurk close by, drawn by the arcane energy of the Kamala earthworks. He longs for the day when he can claim the rest of the

MAJERNAN THE GREEDY

plains as his own. Whether due to ignorance or madness, he is blind to the difficulty of his ambition, but that does not dull the threat he poses.

Unbeknownst to him, Majernan is nothing more than a dupe, but from his makeshift throne in the heart of Kamala, he does not see Jessari's treachery, nor understand the ancient hatred for Jarzon harbored in every Kamalan heart as a result of their part in Tara and Sitara's betrayal. In truth, he would not care, and for all his power, he is little more than a desperate corpse clinging to lies.

Majernan should have been much more than he is. Greed and a lust for power is what drives him, but he fears as much as he desires. A lack of conviction, and a dire failing of courage, have kept him from ever succeeding in any meaningful way, a failing he is bitterly aware of.

Nonetheless, he is a master vampire with an understanding of sorcery and no qualms about using it to gain what he wants.

BLUE MERCHANT

ABILITIES (FOCUSES)	
0	ACCURACY
6	COMMUNICATION (BARGAINING, DECEPTION, ETIQUETTE, PERSUASION)
1	CONSTITUTION
1	DEXTERITY
0	FIGHTING
6	INTELLIGENCE (CRYPTOGRAPHY, EVALUATION, HISTORICAL LORE)
3	PERCEPTION (SEEING)
1	STRENGTH (INTIMIDATION)
4	WILLPOWER (COURAGE, SELF-DISCIPLINE)

SPEED	HEALTH	DEFENSE	ARMOR RATING
11	15	11	0

WEAPON	ATTACK ROLL	DAMAGE
KNIFE	+0	1D6+2
UNARMED	+0	1D3+1

SPECIAL QUALITIES

FAVORED STUNTS: Defensive Stance, Enrage, Exciting Opportunities

TALENTS: Contacts, Inspire, Linguistics, Lore

WEAPONS GROUPS: Light Blades

EQUIPMENT: Concealed Knife

THREAT: MINOR

THE BLUE MERCHANT

THE BLUE MERCHANT

He looks so harmless if you see him on the street, a gentle old man with a slight limp and simple clothing. Someone's grandfather, perhaps, or maybe a shopkeeper or clerk. But that persona fades the moment he steps from public view.

The Blue Merchant got his start as a thief in the streets of Jarzon's capitol, Leogarth. According to some stories, he was three or four when he started, but by the time he was twelve, he'd developed a reputation for being able to acquire anything if you paid him enough. Before long, he turned that skill to blackmail and selling secrets, building a network of favors and fear that enabled him to amass a great deal of wealth.

But Jarzon became too hot for him once a large bounty was placed on his head. Taking his money, he smuggled himself into Aldis, establishing himself as a wealthy

BLUE HAMMER

ABILITIES (FOCUSES)	
3	ACCURACY (CROSSBOWS)
0	COMMUNICATION
5	CONSTITUTION (STAMINA)
2	DEXTERITY (INITIATIVE)
6	FIGHTING (BLUDGEONS)
0	INTELLIGENCE
1	PERCEPTION (HEARING)
5	STRENGTH (INTIMIDATION, MIGHT)
1	WILLPOWER

SPEED	HEALTH	DEFENSE	ARMOR RATING
12	25	12	5

WEAPON	ATTACK ROLL	DAMAGE
HAMMER	+8	2D6+8
KNIFE	+3	1D6+6

SPECIAL QUALITIES

FAVORED STUNTS: Knock Prone, Mighty Blow, Skirmish

TALENTS: Armor Training (Journeyman), Single Weapon Style (Journeyman)

WEAPONS GROUPS: Bludgeons, Brawling

EQUIPMENT: Medium Chain Armor, Hammer, Short Knife.

THREAT: MODERATE

Jarzoni heretic who'd been forced to flee for his life. Accepted into Garnet's lower-level nobles without too many questions, he quickly worked his way through the ranks to become a middling nobleman, developing the same power structure in Aldis that he'd had in Jarzon. His six children all married well, furthering his goals. Unusually, the family remains tightly-knit, and their power is now beginning to be felt outside the cities he has lived in.

No one knows his identity in Jarzon, or—if they do—they will not share the knowledge. Besides, it has been many years since he came to Garnet. Now he goes by the name "Maron Kamire," and fosters a reputation as a patron of literacy and the written word. He is an avid reader, having taught himself as a child through the use of signboards and trading favors for bits and bobs of tutelage.

Kamire hides his illegal business transactions behind a successful trade network. His legitimate wares are horses from Rezea, salt and spices, and stone. His illegitimate ones include all sorts of poisons and drugs, slaves, and refugees from Jarzon. His slave trade is particularly problematic for the Listeners, as he sells passage to skilled individuals and their families, only to take them captive once they have passed out of Aldis' waters to sell them on elsewhere.

Yet he does a great deal of good, as well, spending significant amounts of his wealth to educate and train orphans and those who lose their families to Shadow. He

VRENNA HRITHAK

ABILITIES (FOCUSES)	
4	ACCURACY (LIGHT BLADES)
5	COMMUNICATION (BARGAINING, DISGUISE, INVESTIGATION)
2	CONSTITUTION
2	DEXTERITY (LEGERDEMAIN, LOCK PICKING)
0	FIGHTING
5	INTELLIGENCE (ARCANE LORE, CRYPTOGRAPHY, RESEARCH, SORCERY LORE)
4	PERCEPTION (EMPATHY, HEARING, SEARCHING)
1	STRENGTH
3	WILLPOWER (COURAGE, MEDITATIVE)

SPEED	HEALTH	DEFENSE	ARMOR RATING
12	25	12	3

WEAPON	ATTACK ROLL	DAMAGE
THROWING KNIFE	+6	1D6+1

SPECIAL QUALITIES

FAVORED STUNTS: Efficient Search, New Friends, The Right Tools

TALENTS: Contacts (Master), Linguistics (Journeyman), Lore (Journeyman)

WEAPONS GROUPS: Light Blades

EQUIPMENT: Light Armor (Thick Robes), Throwing Knives

THREAT: MINOR

REZEAN MERCENARY

ABILITIES (FOCUSES)	
2	ACCURACY (LIGHT BLADES, BOWS)
1	COMMUNICATION
2	CONSTITUTION
3	DEXTERITY (RIDING)
2	FIGHTING (HEAVY BLADES, POLEARMS)
0	INTELLIGENCE
1	PERCEPTION (SEARCHING)
2	STRENGTH (INTIMIDATION)
1	WILLPOWER (MORALE)

SPEED	HEALTH	DEFENSE	ARMOR RATING
13	25	13	3

WEAPON	ATTACK ROLL	DAMAGE
SHORTSWORD	+4	1D6+3
SHORT BOW	+4	1D6+2
SPEAR	+4	1D6+5

SPECIAL QUALITIES

FAVORED STUNTS: Knock Prone, Skirmish

TALENTS: Armor Training (Novice), Mounted Combat Style (Master), Single Weapon Style (Novice)

WEAPONS GROUPS: Bows, Brawling, Heavy Blades, Light Blades, Polearms

EQUIPMENT: Dagger, Light Leather Armor, Shortsword, Short Bow, Spear

THREAT: MINOR

remembers all too well what it was like to be an orphan without prospects.

Berserkers and thugs, the Blue Hammers are the personal army of the Blue Merchant. They can be recognized by their blue lips and blue-painted hammers, for they ingest blue trumpet flower paste before any job or mission. They are utterly ruthless and brutal, and take a special pleasure in perverted forms of killing.

THE LISTENERS

The Listeners have a simple mission: to hear rumors of trouble before it can sprout, much less bear fruit. A clandestine operation funded and orchestrated by a small coalition of Aldeans from several nations, the Listeners collaborate to preserve peace and prevent the spread of Shadow. They are a small group, and operate outside the laws of the countries they protect, leaving them in a precarious position. Their agents operate singly, or in small teams, with a high degree of responsibility and little protection. If the agents are caught, they are on their own. If they succeed, they move immediately to a new, riskier mission. Agents of the Listeners do not have a long life expectancy, but they are efficient.

VRENNA HRITHAK

A short, round human woman, Vrenna looks like a mother or a baker, utterly guileless and inoffensive on all levels. She certainly doesn't look like one of the most accomplished and lauded Listener agents, but that's exactly what she is. Vrenna began her career relatively late in life, after her husband died. Her unassuming mien, razor-sharp mind, and prodigious memory soon brought her great success, and she rose quickly in the ranks.

VRENNA HRITHAK

Vrenna has achieved enough regard that she is now hunting her own personal targets, and calling on her Rezean contacts to help her. She specializes in finding and assimilating information, in making contacts, and in bringing miscreants to the attention of her more physically-aggressive agents.

Rezean Mercenaries

The Rezean mercenary is a typical person trained in arms and mounted combat. The weapons and armor used by these adversaries vary more than their skills, though a unique or well-trained individual could have additional focuses, talents, and higher ability scores. They prefer to fight while mounted; their Dexterity drops to 1 and they suffer a penalty of -1 Strength (Intimidation) if unhorsed.

Silvin Ashoj

SILVIN ASHOJ

It is difficult to be the daughter of the most successful Rihan warrior in living memory. Silvin's father had a habit of taking shadowspawn claws and teeth, and his huge red stallion's bridle was trimmed with these trophies. But a wound turned sour, cutting his life short, and now the clan looks to Silvin to carry on his legacy.

Unfortunately, she has no desire to be a warrior, finding her interests instead turning to the subtler arts of diplomacy. She likes making people's problems go away, and helping them work together. So, with her mother's blessing, she made her way to the Fallen River Trading Camp, hoping to find her path.

Since her arrival, she has found work as an interpreter for the Aldin envoys; not of language, per se, but of thought patterns and beliefs. She has made friends and found some success, even traveling back to Aldis with the envoys for the last two years, but she is growing homesick for the plains.

Now she finds herself in a difficult position. She does not fully support either Jessari or Ganniri, but sees wisdom in both paths. So when Ganniri sets her on this mission, she approaches Jessari and makes a devil's pact: she will aid Jessari's efforts to cleanse the area, but will do nothing to help Jessari claim the area and return it to Kamalan control.

Use the Rezean Mercenary stat block for Silvin, but swap the Knock Prone combat stunt for the New Friends roleplaying stunt.

Shadow-Touched Sea Serpent

Fifty feet of hunger and bad temper, sea serpents are dangerous enough. This one, shaped by Shadow and touched with a malevolent intelligence, is more deadly than any of its mundane kin. Whether it was intentionally set loose on Aldea's seas or escaped from a mad sorcerer's laboratory, it knows only one mission: hunt and destroy any living thing that comes within its reach.

SHADOW-TOUCHED SEA SERPENT

ABILITIES (FOCUSES)	
2	ACCURACY (BITE)
-2	COMMUNICATION
2	CONSTITUTION
1	DEXTERITY (STEALTH)
3	FIGHTING
-1	INTELLIGENCE
1	PERCEPTION
3	STRENGTH
2	WILLPOWER (COURAGE)

SPEED	HEALTH	DEFENSE	ARMOR RATING
15 (SWIMMING)	70	8	6

WEAPON	ATTACK ROLL	DAMAGE
BITE	+4	1D6+5
TAIL STRIKE	+3	1D6+4

SPECIAL QUALITIES

FAVORED STUNTS: Knock Prone, Mighty Blow, Skirmish

WATER JET: The serpent can unleash a blast of water with deadly accuracy, knocking opponents off their feet, or off their ship. The target must make a successful TN 15 Dexterity (Acrobatics) or Strength (Might) test to avoid losing 1 Health and being thrown ten feet away.

FEARSOME CRY: Serpents should not have voices, but this one does. Its scream sends shivers down the bravest spine. All players must make a Willpower (Courage) test to avoid losing their turn this round. Success against TN 16 avoids the effect entirely; succeeding at TN 12 causes a loss of 1 from their initiative for one round. The creature may use this attack every 2 rounds as a free action.

POISON SPEAR: The spines in the serpent's frill are extremely poisonous, emitting a neurotoxin that can work through skin. A light dose leads to dizziness and slowed Speed; a large dose leads to death within 5 rounds if healing is not administered. Roll a combat test for the serpent using its Dexterity ability (no focus); if the attack hits, the target must roll a TN 7 Constitution (Stamina) resistance test. If the resistance test is successful, the victim's Dexterity is reduced by 1 point for the remaining rounds of combat, as is their calculated Speed and Defense. If the test fails, the victim receives a heavy dose that reduces their Health by 20%, rounding down. A failed test also requires a new Constitution (Stamina) test against the poison's effects on each of the serpent's turns for the next five rounds. Healing may be applied to slow the effects of the poison, but eliminating the poison's effects before it has run its course requires the Journeyman rank of the Healer talent (see *Blue Rose* **Chapter 3**).

THREAT: MAJOR

The heroes are guests at a late autumn gathering hosted by a borderland noble in Aldis, which leads them to discover an unpleasant chapter in that noble's past involving an object of her affections. A vampire lord is manipulating the situation to his own advantage, and disaster may claim two sets of nobles, unless the heroes can help to resolve the matter and put an end to the corrupt forces at work.

A Wanton Curse is an adventure intended for *Blue Rose* heroes of levels 12 to 15, ideally including at least one adept, and one or more characters with Second Sight. Although the Vampire Lord Sebastian is a Dire Threat, the adventure does offer some options for dealing with him other than direct confrontation, suitable for lower-level heroes (see the **Adapting the Adventure** sidebar). Much of the adventure focuses on roleplaying and exploration encounters, and on unraveling the tangled relations between the noble ladies of Longhaven and Meridian.

INTRODUCTION

THE HUNGER

Lady Penelope Hyacanthus has been the noble of Longhaven for many years, ruling from Castle Longhaven and guiding the people of her domain in peace and prosperity. Ladies Yvayne and Talulah, married for some time, are nobles from neighboring Meridian. There has been peace between the two noble domains for generations, but that changed recently when a young woman, Vesper, came to the court of Longhaven.

Penelope was intensely attracted to Vesper at first sight. A determined woman, Lady Hyacanthus attempted to woo the young woman but, try as she might—with gifts, parties, and various luxuries—Penelope's overtures fell on deaf ears. Instead Vesper was drawn to the castle and domain across the river, where Yvayne and Talulah welcomed her with local customs and comforts not half as extravagant but far more heartfelt. The three of them fell in love and were married not long after, and Meridian prospered under their combined guidance.

Lady Hyacanthus' bitterness over Vesper's rejection grew and, sensing this growing canker in her heart, a vampire, Sebastian, whispered to her in her dreams. Penelope made a bargain with Sebastian: Vesper would no longer belong to the Ladies Meridian, if she, Penelope, would merely extend to him an invitation to feed upon a few of the folk of her domain; ones who would never be missed, he assured her. Once he gained Lady Hyacanthus' consent, Sebastian was both duplicitous and quick, using their agreement to turn Vesper into a vampire like himself, as well as hunting freely in Longhaven, leading to an extended and mysterious "plague" that has spread through the local villages.

Every year, Lady Hyacanthus hosts a party on Gravihain Eve, marking the end of the harvest festival and the beginning of the darkest time of the year. This year, the characters are invited, not yet knowing of the shadow

ADAPTING THE ADVENTURE

While **A Wanton Curse** features challenges best suited to high-level *Blue Rose* characters, it is possible to adapt the adventure for lower level heroes. In particular, the Narrator should emphasize the weaknesses of Sebastian and his vampire spawn, who differ from the standard vampires described in the **Adversaries** chapter of *Blue Rose* due to their origins. (See the **Allies and Adversaries** section of this adventure for more details.) Either have the heroes stumble upon the vampires' weaknesses early on, or make some of the supporting characters in the adventure aware of them and quick to share that information. Better still, perhaps knowledge of their weaknesses only allows the heroes to hold off the vampires, rather than finish them off outright, creating stalemate situations and rising tension as they look for a way to finally destroy Sebastian and free (or destroy) his "children" as well.

Decide as best suits your own group and series why the characters have been invited to Lady Hyacanthus' Gravihain Eve soiree. Given the level of the adventure, the heroes are likely to be quite well known and influential themselves. Perhaps some of them are fellow nobles or high-ranking members of Aldin society, meriting such an invitation, particularly if they have seen a swift rise to widespread fame in the Kingdom. The characters might have some influence or resource Lady Hyacanthus is interested in beyond just their good names, including ties with the throne or other figures within the royal court.

It is also possible the heroes are lured to Castle Longhaven under false pretenses or are on-assignment as members of the Sovereign's Finest. The Ladies Meridian might arrange for a forged invitation to bring such noteworthy heroes as the player characters to Longhaven so they can investigate the goings-on there. Alternately, the crown might wrangle the heroes an invite to attend the soiree and convey the Queen's best wishes as an excuse to visit Longhaven and quietly investigate the mysterious "illness" amongst its populace, which the local noble seems unable to manage. Whatever the reason for the invitation, the Narrator can use the **Invitation** handout from the end of the adventure as a prop for what the characters receive.

cast over Longhaven and Meridian. There are also some distinctly uninvited guests at the party, as the fallout from Penelope's bargain returns to haunt her.

PART 1

GRAVIHAIN EVE

The story opens with the characters' arrival in Longhaven. Feel free to adjust or add to the introductory text based on how the heroes came to be invited to the party, and to account for their preparations and travels beforehand. If the Narrator wishes, they can easily insert some preparatory scenes covering the journey to Longhaven, particularly if the adventure is part of an ongoing series and they want to extend things a bit.

The characters are welcomed to the Gravihain Eve party at Castle Longhaven and meet their hostess, Lady Penelope Hyacanthus. They have the opportunity to enjoy the festivities and the noble lady's hospitality before vampires attack! The heroes help drive off the creatures, and a distraught Lady Hyacanthus asks for their help.

Read or paraphrase the following to the players:

Castle Longhaven has long overlooked the Silver River in the rugged lands from which the manor takes its name. The hills are dotted with rocks and sturdy grasses, and lead to the nearby Red Cliffs. It is autumn, and the leaves surrounding the castle are just beginning to turn. The region's main road runs through Longhaven's lands before crossing the Silver River and into the domain of the neighboring Castle Meridian, about a day's travel from Longhaven.

SCENE 1

AN EXCITING INVITATION

ROLEPLAYING ENCOUNTER

Gravihain Eve celebrations are known for their elaborate costuming and masquerades, although each party has its own particular style and flair. Often the costumes are beautiful representations of nature, grim creatures, or death, or some combination of the three. Fine clothing is often accompanied by skillfully crafted masks. Ask the players to describe what their characters are wearing to Lady Hyacanthus' celebration, and what their costumes and masks represent. This is an opportunity to show off something of their characters' aesthetics or personality.

The heroes are welcomed at the bridge leading into Castle Longhaven by masked residents holding long scrolls. They check to see each character is on the guest list before allowing them across the bridge. (They are, even if their invitation was arranged under false pretenses; the group's patron has seen to it.) The small moat surrounding the castle is gorgeous; not just practical, but decorated with lotuses and a few stone statues of leaping fish. The castle itself is a fine example of elaborate gothic architecture, its arches and buttresses amply supporting the gray, stone structure.

The craftsmanship of Longhaven is evident in its subtle decorations: beautiful metal finials decorate the tops of the stair railings, wooden lotus flower patterns are carved into doors, and small stone fountains with fish heads spitting water adorn several of the walls. Castle Longhaven does not want for any luxury: large velvet drapes hang at the castle entrance; white flower petals drop onto the guests as they enter while fire pits burn all around for warmth on this chill Gravihain Eve. The party sprawls across the main courtyard at the entrance to the castle, into the large dining hall, and throughout the gardens and adjacent walkways. Much of the rest of the castle is either locked up or guarded to prevent guests from wandering into private areas.

The guests entering with the heroes seem in good spirits, most laughing and joyfully partaking in the spooky atmosphere. All the costumes are gorgeous. There are some skeletons with black capes, foxes with dresses that look like tails, a peacock with an elaborately woven, silver-threaded collar of fake feathers, and masks representing wolf skulls, cat faces, cranes, and ravens.

SCENE 2

A CONVERSATION WITH LADY HYACANTHUS

ROLEPLAYING ENCOUNTER

Lady Hyacanthus, making the rounds, comes to welcome the characters. She is a lovely, middle-aged woman; tall, with sparkling blonde hair and engaging eyes. Bedecked in blue silks, delicately embroidered with small geometric patterns, and dripping with blue jewels, Penelope is the best-dressed person at the party. She is engaging, gracious, and politic, and certainly lives up to her reputation as an excellent hostess but, every once in a while, they notice she lets her guard down and seems weary and forlorn behind her gracious manner.

Lady Penelope takes turns asking each character what it is they do and where they come from. Although she listens politely and intently to whatever they say, it is obvious her favorite topic is the majesty and history of Castle Long-haven, which has stood on this spot for generations. Her mother fought off the great shadowspawn army that once attacked these lands, in the epic and much storied "Battle of the Three Hills" which she gladly recounts to any who care to listen.

THE TALE OF THE BATTLE OF THE THREE HILLS

A momentous skirmish in Longhaven, so named because of the three hills on the Silver River at the south edge of the estate where the battle took place. Shadowspawn invaded from the north, and Castle Meridian and Castle Longhaven were compelled to join their forces together to hold off the first wave as the requested Aldin reinforcements had yet to arrive. The local militia were outnumbered three to one, and all they had were two knights to

lead them: Ilya Hyacanthus, Penelope's mother, and Sabeline Thornton, the Silver Knight. Using the terrain to their advantage, they waited to ambush the shadowspawn by the river rather than risking a full-on assault. The tactic worked, and they held the hills for five days and five nights before relief arrived from Aldis.

THE SILVER KNIGHT

Following close behind Lady Hyacanthus is a knight in decorative armor, with a great blade strapped to her back. The knight's pauldrons and chestplate are etched with gold filigree and roses. She is a much older woman with short, gray hair, who seems to be on high alert. Lady Hyacanthus introduces her as the Silver Knight. A successful TN 11 Communication (Etiquette) roll reveals it is unusual for a knight to follow a lady around her castle quite so attentively. The Silver Knight doesn't really engage much in conversation, and politely defers most questions to her mistress, answering others with a simple yes or no. She does not boast of her role in the Battle of the Three Hills, or even really mention it, unless Lady Hyacanthus puts her on the spot. Even then, she merely shrugs and explains that she did her duty, as any sworn knight would do. A TN 13 Perception (Empathy) test picks up some unspoken tension between the Silver Knight and her mistress.

SCENE 3

AT THE PARTY

ROLEPLAYING/EXPLORATION ENCOUNTER

There are a number of things the characters can do as guests at Lady Hyacanthus' party. The following provide some suggestions and guidelines, but feel free to elaborate on them to suit the interests and appetites of the main characters. Lady Hycanthus is a considerate hostess and has likely taken the interests of her guest into account.

FOOD AND DRINK

Tables groan under the weight of delicious fish dishes, local vegetables, and fresh baked breads and pies. Wine, mead, hard cider, and beer flow from various fountains. As the evening goes on, a few of the party guests may become a bit intoxicated, giving the characters some social challenges to deal with as gracefully as possible. Whatever the circumstances, a successful TN 11 Communication test adroitly handles the matter. Suitable focuses include Etiquette and Persuasion, or Deception or Romance, depending on the approach the characters take. Alternately, a similar Constitution (Drinking) test simply allows a character to harmlessly drink a troublesome guest under the table!

MUSIC AND DANCE

A troupe of actors and their animal companions dance and play music in one area of the castle. Many partygoers join in the dancing, or stand nearby to enjoy the music and performances. Characters who are musicians or singers might even join in, and any are welcome to take part in the dancing.

At some point, a graceful man wearing a fiendish-looking horned mask asks one of the characters—preferably a man—to dance with him. He is dressed in a brocaded jacket, a billowing white shirt, tight breeches, and high leather boots, and his brown, wavy hair invites caresses. He is generous with his compliments, flirtatious, and gallant. It feels as if there's something mysterious about him, and he doesn't remove his mask for the entire dance. At the end of their turn about the room, he gives his dance partner a small white flower he produces from somewhere, then disappears into the crowd. This is the **arcane vampire Sebastian**, toying with his prey prior to **Scene 4**.

LOOKING AROUND

There are several interesting things and places to see in the castle, if the characters decide to wander around:

THE TRANQUIL POOL

A branch of the Silver River runs through the castle, and is guided through masterful architectural design into a small, open air garden. The water collects in a clear pool, surrounded by beautiful lilies and decorative trees. A few guests are sitting on benches enjoying muted discourse and reflection by the water. Characters are welcome to seek respite here, or engage in quiet conversation.

THE AVIARY

Adjacent to the pool is a garden that attracts all sorts of local birds to roost and nest. There are white peacocks wandering the garden, as well as songbirds flitting about in the trees. They are incredibly friendly, and little covered dishes of seed are available for visitors to feed them.

PORTRAIT GALLERY

Some of the artwork in the castle is stunning. There are many formal portraits from the history of Castle Long-haven. Among the portraits are stately looking women, proud craftsmen, and brave warriors. Above the stair-case is Lady Hyacanthus' mother in positively regal armor, standing proud above a fallen beastman foe. In the distance behind her are the Red Cliffs.

STAINED GLASS

There are gorgeous stained glass windows at either end of the Castle's great hall, approximately 20 feet up. They're circular, and feature various blue, silver, and green pieces of glass. The images depicted are patterns of fish around the edges, followed by a circle of trees, with silver-colored water in the center. Light shines through them, and the colors of the glass dapple the castle floor.

A DANGEROUS DALLIANCE

A figure in a long, black dress and wearing a raven mask approaches a character who is alone. She speaks with them for a moment, then removes her mask, revealing a pale, but beautiful, woman's face, framed by flowing black hair. Her eyes are large and brown, and her lips red as blood. She flatters and flirts with the character, and asks if they might like to join her for a walk about the grounds.

The woman is Vivienne, an arcane vampire (see the **Allies and Adversaries** section), who tries to seduce the character into joining her somewhere more secluded. Once alone, she attacks and tries to feed on the character, making it obvious exactly what she is.

This last encounter makes a good prelude to what is about to happen, so the Narrator may want to include it right before transitioning to **Scene 4**.

THE VAMPIRE ATTACK

COMBAT ENCOUNTER

Read or paraphrase the following out loud to the players.

Two middle-aged women with dark hair enter the room, drawing the attention of the suddenly hushed crowd. They're wearing older but gorgeous red dresses that ruffle decoratively in layers and pinch in at the waist. Their hair is long and largely unbound, and they wear delicate crowns of dried flowers. The ladies' arms are entwined lovingly, and they head over to one side of the room. Lady Hyacanthus frowns at them, whispering to the Silver Knight.

A successful TN 11 Communication (Etiquette) test reveals pertinent gossip from a nearby partygoer. The Ladies Meridian, Talulah and Yvayne, have been married and leading Castle Meridian just across the river for some years now. By custom, they're entitled to attend this party, but they were definitely *not* invited. In fact, there is some unspoken bitterness between them and Lady Hyacanthus, although nobody knows exactly what it is. See the **Allies and Adversaries** section of the adventure for details on the Ladies Meridian.

RELEASE THE BATS!

The characters may approach and attempt to talk to the Ladies Meridian, but before they can, one of the windows crashes in and a swarm of **bats** flies through (see *Blue Rose* **Chapter 12: Adversaries** for statistics). In their midst is a woman with auburn hair, pale skin, and bony limbs, wearing a torn and dusty, but once fine, dress. She screams a terrifying howl of despair, revealing long fangs. She is the arcane vampire, Vesper Meridian.

Vesper attacks a person on the opposite side of the room from the heroes, and two more arcane vampires reveal themselves among the partygoers, removing their masks and attacking the people nearest them. These are Alek and Ormond, Vesper's vampire spawn. Vivienne from **A Dangerous Dalliance** rushes in to join her companions, if she has not already been dealt with. Vesper and her companions are detailed in the **Allies and Adversaries** section at the end of the adventure. Their initial attack takes place during a surprise round, allowing the vampires one round of actions before the heroes can do anything to stop them.

The scene in the room is one of chaos as the vampires and bats attack, and blood spills on the floor. Lady Hyacanthus looks at Vesper in sadness and shock for a long moment, then flees from the room on the next round, her retreat guarded by the Silver Knight.

The Ladies Meridian, on the other hand, rush towards Vesper, but hesitate when they confront her. Vesper moves for a moment as if to embrace them, then dramatically pushes them away, before fleeing. The Ladies Meridian leave as soon as Vesper does. The remaining three arcane vampires cover Vesper's escape for a round or two before fleeing themselves. Their Unnatural Swiftness ability allows the vampires to virtually disappear, running away far faster than the characters can pursue. By the time anyone can get outside of the room, the attackers are gone.

SCENE 5

AFTER THE FIGHT

ROLEPLAYING ENCOUNTER

After the attack, Lady Hyacanthus can be found in her study; a room lit with candles and a small hearth-fire and crammed with antiques and books. Dried garlic and roses hang in fragrant bunches from the ceiling beams. Penelope Hyacanthus looks pained and nervous. The Silver Knight stands guard nearby, as protective as ever. The lady does not speak until prompted by the characters, and then responds with a plea for help.

Lady Hyacanthus reveals there have been rumors and legends of a vampire haunting the Red Cliffs for generations, but there has been no evidence of it until recently. A number of local villagers have fallen mysteriously ill,

SEBASTIAN'S TREACHERY

Although Sebastian gave Lady Hyacanthus his word he wouldn't attack her under the terms of their arrangement, he didn't promise not to tell Vesper who was responsible for her current condition. He has chosen the night of the party to "let slip" to Vesper why he turned her, knowing the enraged vampire will seek revenge. He appeared at the party ahead of time to gloat to himself about what was to come. However, neither he nor Vesper expected the appearance of the Ladies Meridian, which snaps Vesper out of her bitter and deadly frenzy, causing her to flee in confusion instead.

and a few have even died, and healers in Longhaven cannot explain the cause. She suspects the Ladies Meridian of being involved with the monster as they have recently cut off all communication with her, and she doesn't know why; regardless, she doesn't trust them, part of the reason the Silver Knight remained so close at hand during the evening. (This is a half-truth: Lady Penelope feared the vampires might attack tonight because there were so many people in one place, and because it's Gravihain Eve, a fitting time for the such creatures to show their faces.) Any character who succeeds on a TN 13 Perception (Empathy) test senses Lady Hyacanthus is not telling them the entire story, but she denies this, if challenged.

At the end of the conversation, Lady Hyacanthus asks the characters if they will help investigate and deal with the vampire threat. She insists the heroes stay overnight so they can rest and recover and gather some supplies to take with them. In addition, she suggests they might want to look into what is actually going on over at Castle Meridian as a first step in their quest to root out the vampires. She then gives them dried garlic and roses—supposed to ward off the creatures according to lore—and instructs the Silver Knight to assist them with whatever else they might need, excusing herself due to fatigue from the evening and a need to deal with other matters.

After leaving Lady Hyacanthus, the Silver Knight helps the characters with any requests for supplies from the castle's armory or stores, particularly if they did not bring a great deal with them. A successful TN 11 Perception (Empathy) test reveals the knight seems frustrated, although she denies it and refuses to discuss the matter further. The Silver Knight offers to accompany the group to Castle Meridian so she can aide them against the vampires. If they agree, she excuses herself to go ask the permission of her mistress.

The heroes' sleeping quarters are finely appointed guest rooms, with canopy beds draped in gauzy cerulean silks. Each has its own copper bath fed and warmed by an arcane crystal. A leaded glass window embedded in the stone wall of each room opens outward to invite in a chill autumn breeze. The characters are free to rest or do as they please with the remainder of the night.

PART 2

MERIDIAN'S SECRETS

In **Part 2**, Lady Hyacanthus sends the characters on their journey to Meridian with food for thought. On the way, the Silver Knight relays some history about the region and herself, and ghouls attack the party on the road. Meridian proves more welcoming than expected, and its noble ladies talk about their wife, Vesper, and what has become of her. Exploration of the crypts beneath the castle reveals secrets even the Meridians didn't know were there. A potential cure to the arcane vampirism is found, along with a new weapon that could help the heroes battle the accursed creatures.

SCENE 1

AN UNEASY MEAL

ROLEPLAYING ENCOUNTER

The castle's keepers wake the heroes near dawn, having prepared a lavish meal for them. Everything in the hall is fixed from the night before, except the gaping hole where the stained glass window used to be. Only jagged bits of the colored glass remain, fish heads and bits of tree visible around its edges. In the dining hall, the characters are treated to fancy baked goods, salted meats, eggs, fruits, grains, and honey. It's quite probably the most lavish breakfast they've had since leaving home, and that they'll have for a while to come.

As they eat, Lady Hyacanthus announces—somewhat over-dramatically—that the Silver Knight will join them on their quest. It seems as if Penelope and her loyal knight have had a disagreement, as they avoid each other's gaze, and their conversation is curt and coldly polite.

Other than that, Lady Hyacanthus attempts to keep the conversation light, asking the characters about their experiences while traveling and their past exploits. She takes opportunities to praise the people and communities of Longhaven and how fortunate she is to serve as their noble. She hopes their community can continue to prosper, and the heroes can rid them of this vampire menace.

SCENE 2

TRAVEL TO MERIDIAN

ROLEPLAYING/COMBAT ENCOUNTER

Meridian is only a day's travel beyond the Silver River. Unlike its companion, Castle Longhaven, it is in something of a state of disrepair. Its crumbling walls often cause it to be mistaken for a ruin up in the hills, and its lands are overgrown and unkempt.

The river, the Silver Knight explains, is the natural demarcation between the two domains, which stretch in either direction east and west of the water. To the east are the Red Cliffs of Longhaven, named for the red granite running through the craggy rock like veins. To the west is the Elderwood, an old forest filled with large elder trees that twist their trunks around each other, making it hard to pass. In between these two natural walls lie the Castles Longhaven and Meridian, the Silver Knight says dryly, as though stuck together between a rock and a hard place.

If questioned about Longhaven, Meridian, and their history, the Silver Knight intones wearily she is loyal to her Lady, and everything Penelope said back at the castle is true. It's obvious this is not the case, but the Silver Knight seems unwilling to say more as a matter of honor, although she hints her going along on this journey may help the characters with their answers.

If asked why she's called the Silver Knight, she explains it is because she fought in the Battle of the Three Hills to hold the shadowspawn at bay at the Silver River, defending it not only as a strategic point, but also as a beautiful symbol of what made Longhaven great. She believes she had a vision that day from the spirit of the river: that she would always defend this land, and never die or lose honor as long as she did so. Sabeline took the name of the river to represent that loyalty to Longhaven, and to the Hyacanthus family.

GHOULS IN THE HILLS

Along the road to Meridian, a small pack of four **ghouls** attacks the travelers just after sunset (see **Ghoul** in *Blue Rose* **Chapter 12**). They lie in wait alongside the road and attempt to surprise the characters: roll a test of the ghouls' Dexterity (Stealth) total of 4 vs. the characters' Perception (Seeing or Smelling, due to the ghouls' foul stench). If the ghouls win the test, the characters do not get a turn during the first round of combat.

Three rounds into the fight, or before the last ghoul is dispatched, a small pack of six **wolves** appears and attack the ghouls. A majestic, black-furred wolf seems to be their pack-leader. Once the fight is over, the wolves growl at the characters and the Silver Knight warily, then flee off the road and disappear back into the wilderness. Use the **wolf** statistics from **Chapter 12** of *Blue Rose,* if they are needed, but the wolves do not attack the characters, even if provoked.

Efforts to communicate with the wolves are unsuccessful. Any character with the Animism talent senses, with a successful TN 11 Perception (Empathy) test, there is something unusual about them, although it is unclear exactly what. In fact, the wolves do have a spiritual connection to Meridian and its nobles. (For more details, see **Scene 4**, following.)

SCENE 3

CASTLE MERIDIAN

ROLEPLAYING ENCOUNTER

The characters arrive at Castle Meridian, which up close looks like it has most definitely seen better times: the land is not well kept, with wild grasses growing over old stone structures in the grounds and a once manicured garden in a grave state of disrepair. The stained glass windows are darkened and dirty, and there are few people around.

The large, wooden gates into the castle are securely closed, and the guard standing outside questions who the characters are and their reasons for visiting. Use the **Warrior** statistics in *Blue Rose* **Chapter 12**, as required. The guard has a full, brown beard, wears metal armor, and holds a tall spear and is distinctly wary of visitors. He notes the presence of the Silver Knight, and while he gives her a respectful nod, he knows she comes from Castle Longhaven and therefore assumes the whole group does as well.

Given the tense relations between the two castles, the guard needs assurance of the visitors' peaceful intentions before he can permit them to enter. If the characters succeed on a TN 13 Communication (Persuasion) test, they are allowed inside, and directed to the main hall. If they fail, a group of guards equal in number to the party escorts

them into the castle as if they were prisoners. Either way, they're asked to hand over their weapons before they can enter and meet with the Ladies.

A COLD WELCOME

Inside the castle is not much better than outside. Hanging from the walls are old, worn tapestries, beautifully woven but not well cared for. They depict a black wolf, a gray wolf, and a white wolf in various stages of life together. The first is of them lying curled together amidst a beautiful garden of white roses. The second is of them frolicking through hills dotted with trees during the sunset. The third is of them howling at a full moon on the edge of a cliff on a beautiful dark night. Over the hearth are two crossed broadswords with unusual pommels: one shaped like a wolf's head, the other with a crescent moon. The hall is dark, and covered in dust and cobwebs, as though it is rarely used.

Yvayne and Talulah enter the room. They wear gray and white dresses respectively, their long hair loose and flowing. Up close one can distinguish them a little more: Yvayne is taller, Talulah curvier. They walk towards two carved stone seats at the head of the hall. Yvayne holds Talulah's hand, guiding her to sit before taking a seat herself. As they take up their positions, a group of five guards enters the room, stationed at every entrance, though they do not seem hostile, merely protective. The Ladies Meridian gaze upon the group, pensive but stately.

Yvayne asks the characters why they've come, and listens attentively to any response from them, but she needs details before she feels safe enough to give up any information of her own. The two are keen to know what Lady Hyacanthus has told the heroes about them, whether she has sent the characters to kill them, and if they are looking for Vesper. If the heroes ask who Vesper is, other than insisting she is not there, Yvayne and Talulah avoid answering the question until they are satisfied with the heroes' other replies. You can have the players roleplay this conversation with the Ladies, playing their roles yourself, or you can ask for ability tests to convince the Meridian nobles of the characters' good intentions, or a combination of the two, modifying the results of the tests based on the players' roleplaying.

THE LADIES' TALE

Once the Ladies feel they can trust the characters, they ask the guards to leave them before they fill the visitors in on their side of the story. Read or paraphrase the following to the players, adjusting to fit their characters' actions and responses:

"Vesper is…was…our wife. She used to go for long solitary walks, and loved being alone in nature. One night, she didn't return. We were terrified wild beasts had taken her and sent out search parties, but to no avail. We didn't give up hope, but what remained was slim. Then, a month after she vanished, on the night of the full moon, she slid in through our bedroom window, covered in blood and deathly pale. We thought she was dying, but it was worse than that. The blood wasn't hers—it was that of a stable lad from the castle grounds. She seemed to no longer care about life, or love. When we offered to help her she pushed us away. Vesper insisted she didn't want to hurt us, but the pain of being apart from her, knowing she's suffering, is almost worse. We don't have the power to help her. Neither of us is a warrior or adept in the arcane arts, and our guards are no…well, no Silver Knight.

"We never did anything to Penelope. It's some mad tale she's concocted to justify keeping us out of her home. It happened after Vesper vanished. She used to invite the three of us over often. We never really liked how she flirted with Vesper—it seemed oddly possessive. You've met Penelope, you know how charming she can be, but how full of herself she is. We think she wanted Vesper for herself, and she's cursed her because she couldn't have her. That's why we went to the party…we wished to investigate and learn more. That didn't really work out how we'd hoped.

"We just want our wife back, but our forces aren't strong enough to attack Castle Longhaven, and all our efforts to learn about what has happened to Vesper haven't helped us track down where she might be or how to break this terrible curse. Can you help us?"

The Silver Knight listens to all of this, seething with silent anger. If the characters succeed at a TN 13 Perception (Empathy) test they notice her anger isn't directed at Yvayne and Talulah, but at this new information she didn't seem to have before.

If the characters share they were sent to hunt down Vesper and the other vampires with her, the Meridians become furious. They can't believe Lady Hyacanthus would go to such lengths to kill Vesper, or be so cowardly as to send strangers to do the deed. Talulah then becomes sad, hoping her old friend once again finds the light, and worries she's being twisted or used by some dark force. Yvayne wants to retaliate, and feels helpless knowing they cannot.

SCENE 4

DINNER AND CONVERSATION

ROLEPLAYING ENCOUNTER

The heroes are invited to stay at Castle Meridian for the night. There are some beautiful views of the hills from a large, stone balcony circling the upper level. It's easy to extrapolate from the architecture the Meridians care a great deal about the land around them, even if the castle itself has seen better days. There are many open spaces framing the sky, archways designed to let the light in, and balconies to take in the beautiful view of the hills. A simple but delicious dinner is held outside on the main balcony, despite the possible threat of vampire attack. Fresh baked breads, a hearty autumn stew, and red wine are laid out for everyone to share. The ladies make peace that whatever nature wants of them is what will happen.

WHAT THE CHARACTERS LEARN

Sabeline, the Silver Knight, speaks of Yvayne's mother, a hedge witch who aided in the Battle of the Three Hills by whispering to the long grasses and plants by the riverside, and asking them to entangle many of the shadowspawn so the soldiers could destroy them. She remembers walking with her out in the hills and nearby woods while they gathered the ingredients she used for her arcane elixirs and unguents. She wonders aloud if maybe there might be something along those lines that could help with the vampires, and asks if, perhaps, Yvayne might know. Yvayne, in turn, offers to show them her mother's old workroom, if they'd like. Go to **Scene 5** if the characters accept the offer.

Talulah engages the characters in conversation. She's a social creature, and the ladies haven't had many visitors recently. Talulah speaks about her love of the countryside, and asks about the fashions and trends in the city of Aldis, the goings-on at court, and so forth.

They also both tell fond stories of Vesper. They speak sadly of how she used to be a year ago, so full of life and love. She used to tend the gardens, now overgrown. She had names for each of the plants, and Talulah would often catch her talking to them as she pottered about. It was adorable, and speaking of it brings a tear to both women's eyes. Talulah and Yvayne haven't been able to work in the gardens since Vesper left; it's too heart-breaking for them.

The howling of wolves sounds in the hills as dinner comes to a close. Torches have been lit all along the balcony as they've been eating, and the stars and moon glisten in the crisp air. Yvayne and Talulah move to stand in an embrace, leaning on the stone railing of the balcony and looking out into the darkness. They speak of the wolves as though they are kin, fond of their wildness and freedom. The nobles of Meridian supposedly have an old pact with the wolves of this land, that they'll share it and do each other no harm. It might be a legend, or it might be true, they're not really sure. They still honor them in their hall, though.

SCENE 5
THE WITCH'S ROOM
ROLEPLAYING ENCOUNTER

Read or paraphrase the following out loud to the players.

Old dried herbs and spiders' webs hang from the ceiling in this dark, stone room. Aged papers display drawings of internal organs and geometric shapes, and there are pages of notes and letters scattered across the tables and floor. Many colors of yarn, bottles of scented oils, bits of charcoal, and various small animal furs lie strewn about. An entire wall is covered in dusty, dried butterfly wings, meticulously stuck onto the stone with wax.

A successful TN 11 Intelligence (Arcane Lore) test uncovers a small wooden box with roses carved all around it in a pile of arcane detritus. Inside the box is a folded piece of parchment with sketches of some kind of multifaceted glass box, like a large princess-cut diamond with a flattened base, labelled as "The Heart's Blood." According to the marginal notes, it is intended to grant "indestructible life" if a human heart, along with a collection of arcane ingredients, is placed inside while incanting a particular formula. Any adept or character with the Arcane Lore focus knows this is a terrible working of sorcery, and Yvayne can't believe such a thing is even among her mother's effects but, shaking her head, admits her mother was strange and mysterious sometimes. As neither she nor Talulah have any arcane talent, they have largely left this workroom alone, although previous adepts used it before Yvayne's mother.

SCENE 6
NIGHTTIME VISITOR
ROLEPLAYING ENCOUNTER

After dinner, and a visit to Inara's old workroom, Yvayne and Talulah stay up and talk through the night about anything and everything, if anyone is willing to keep them company and listen, although they don't have any more pertinent information to impart to the heroes about the threat they face at this point. The characters are offered guest rooms to spend the night; though comfortable, they are more spartanly decorated than the ones at Castle Longhaven.

THE GHOST

The most psychically-sensitive character has a visitation in the night from the ghost of Inara, Yvayne's mother (see the **Ghost** in **Chapter 12** of *Blue Rose* for the relevant statistics, although conflict is unlikely). Disturbing her workroom has also disturbed her restless spirit, and she has come to them with a message.

An old woman with gray, braided hair in a long, black robe appears in the shadows of the room. Pale, she moves into the light of the window, and frowns. She says, "I think I knew for some time about Sebastian. Our history detailed the murder of his lover and his vengeful spirit. He was a talented adept, and my workplace was his before it was mine.

"I even found those drawings for the arcane device to restore the dead back to life. A hunger-induced, monstrous half-life; a curse passed on through the blood, unable to withstand the true signs of life, love, and light.

"I knew all these things but I was too afraid to admit them. I didn't want Meridian to go down in history as the place where such a great evil arose. I told myself it was nothing but a tale, the worries of a foolish woman. Tell Yvayne...Tell my daughter...Tell her I'm sorry. I could have saved her so much heartache. The heart must be freed and the curse ended. It must."

Then she steps back into the shadows, which swallow her up, and she is gone.

Yvayne can confirm any description the characters give her that the apparition looked like her mother did at the end of her life. An adept or character with the Arcane Lore focus, if they roll a successful TN 11 Intelligence (Arcane Lore) test, concludes the sorcerous device Inara's ghost spoke of, shown in the drawing they found, creates a state almost identical to vampirism, and that those under its curse are vulnerable or repelled by "true signs of life, love, and light," such as things symbolizing those qualities.

PART 3

STALKING SEBASTIAN

In **Part 3**, the characters travel to the Red Cliffs to find the vampire Sebastian and the sorcerous artifact empowering him. They encounter some of Vesper's vampire spawn, which try to intimidate or kill them, only to be saved by Vesper's intervention. She fills them in on more of the story and they have the opportunity to confront Sebastian, only to discover he is not the master vampire, but servant to the creature he created when he raised his dead lover, Ryal. The heroes have the opportunity to overcome the arcane vampires and free their spawn from their blood-curse.

SCENE 1

VAMPIRES ON THE ROAD

COMBAT/ROLEPLAYING ENCOUNTER

The characters must make their way back across the Silver River into Longhaven and strike out north and east for another day to reach the Red Cliffs. On the second day, as the sun is setting and they're nearly at their destination, the heroes are ambushed by Vesper's pack of vampires.

The vampires are there to stop the characters from helping Vesper, because they profess to love her and don't want her to leave them. These are the same vampires that attacked during the party at Castle Longhaven: Vivienne and Ormond. Leading them is a skinny, obnoxious waif named Alek, who talks about Vesper as though they're sweethearts. He serves as the trio's spokesman, and tosses his beautiful hair as he talks, an oddly self-conscious act in one so powerful:

"I know what you are up to. You're going to try and take my Vesper away, aren't you? Well she doesn't want to go back. Just tell her wives she has a new family now—us—and we say they can't have her anymore."

The characters have a choice here: they can try to out-talk the vampires, or outfight them. Convincing them to back off and leave the party alone requires a challenging advanced Communication test, using whatever focuses the Narrator sees fit, with a TN of 14 and a success threshold of 15. Each test takes a minute of interaction and, if the heroes don't meet the threshold within 5 minutes, the vampires attack. If the characters use some means to ward off the vampires (see the **Arcane Vampire** in the **Allies and Adversaries** section), they may buy themselves additional time for the negotiations.

Alternately, the heroes can simply attack the vampires first, engaging them in combat. Handle this conflict normally, but the Narrator may wish to have Vesper intervene before the vampires inflict too much damage on the party.

Either way, Vesper has been watching the exchange from close by. She is, after all, in psychic contact with Alek and Ormond. If the heroes fail to convince the vampires to back off, she intervenes before the fight can become too bloody. She commands Alek and Ormond to leave, and faces down Vivienne, who chooses to flee not far behind the others. If the characters actually manage to get the other vampires to stand down, Vesper waits until they leave before approaching.

Vesper still wears the same torn dress as the night of the party, and a golden locket hangs around her neck. She doesn't intend to attack the characters, but defends herself if attacked. Vesper gives a hollow sounding apology for her fellow vampires.

"I'm sorry for those poor souls. They are corrupted by the curse, by its hunger, but then...so am I. I can no more control them than I can control myself any longer, so I've given up—especially when it comes to that brat, Alek."

The night is cold, and a wind howls up from the nearby cliffs. Vesper goes on, morose.

"I miss life. Everything tastes like dust: love, the air I no longer breathe, people. Nothing satiates me like blood. I remember what it's like to feel remorse, and I can pretend to feel it, but it's really just an echo of what that feeling used to be. I don't want to kill people—I try not to—but they can't possibly understand my need. It was an ancient creature who turned me. His name is Sebastian. I'm certain he was at the party on Gravihain Eve, which is one reason I crashed it. I wanted to kill him for everything he's done to me."

She speaks to the group generally, and even sits with them if they decide to set camp here. Vesper shares three more nuggets of information while conversing with the characters:

- She can't kill Sebastian, because whenever she gets too close to him, he can control her. She was hoping she could get her pack close enough, but she's afraid he might be able to control them, too (she's correct, in fact). She thinks the heroes have a chance because they don't carry his blood inside them.

- She still wears the locket, a gift from Talulah and Yvayne, around her neck. She hasn't stopped loving them but, as with her remorse, it's more like a memory of love rather than the real thing. She has committed so many terrible acts, she feels she can never go back, adding that, if they see Yvayne and Talulah again, they should tell them to forget her. It's better if they consider her dead. A successful TN 13 Communication (Persuasion) test sways her to reconsider her position.

The characters can keep the vampires away from their camp with the garlic and roses Lady Hyacanthus gave them, or similar wards (see the **Arcane Vampire** stats at the end of the adventure for details). Vesper advises them to do it, and to keep her outside as well, as she can't be trusted not to turn on them eventually.

It is quite possible the group decides to bring Vesper along with them to help her enact her vengeance upon Sebastian, despite her warning he can control her.

If the characters do take Vesper with them (an act which certainly promises to enliven their final confrontation with Sebastian), she grows less and less human as they get closer to the cliffs. She doesn't completely lose control, but it helps if she has a little bit of blood before they reach the vampire's lair. If one of the heroes offers Vesper their blood, she becomes less hungry and more manageable. Vesper is also unable to move during the day, so the group has to travel at night.

SCENE 2

RED VEINS

ROLEPLAYING/COMBAT ENCOUNTER

It takes some searching to locate Sebastian's lair since it is nestled among many other cliffs and partially hidden from view. There are dark clouds overhead, and the ocean crashes violently against the rocks beneath them. It's a perilous descent along the cliff side to find the master vampire.

Players need to perform an advanced Strength (Climbing) test, with a TN of 11 and a success threshold of 15, in order for their characters to safely descend the cliffs on the steep rocky paths. Each failure represents a dangerous slip that almost plunges the characters to their deaths, as well as resulting in 1d6 penetrating damage. The number of rolls taken to reach the success threshold determines who finds Sebastian's lair first.

Before the vampire's lair comes into view, the characters spot a waterfall pouring out of the side of the cliffs. It looks like blood rather than water, and is nightmarish to gaze upon. Rounding the corner, they see the water spilling out of a structure carved into the side of the Red Cliffs: a hole like a giant, inhuman mouth with carved, red granite fangs. The rest of the edifice looks like some kind of temple, with gothic buttresses and tall spires. The red veins in the granite here are extremely large.

The path leads to large, wooden double doors; an ominously easy entrance which is not locked or sealed in any way. Within the building is a huge hall, with giant vaulted ceilings and beautiful, luxurious decorations. There is a distinct touch of the macabre about the décor: skulls neatly stacked in piles and painted black; columns decorated with gold leaf and carved with images of broken human bodies twisting around each other; furniture made from giant, dead beasts; and chandeliers of bone. At the end of the hall, atop a dais, is a red granite throne, upon which is draped a beautiful young man: Sebastian. He sits at an angle across the throne, unable to remain entirely still. His movements are reminiscent of a bored cat, and he smiles somewhat threateningly when the heroes come in, baring his fangs.

THE HEART'S BLOOD

The sorcerous artifact near Sebastian's throne holds Ryal's heart, suspended in an unholy mixture as red as blood. Anyone who consumes this "heart's blood," or Ryal's own blood, becomes an arcane vampire like him, suspended eternally between life and unlife, but not truly unliving. See the **arcane vampire** stats at the end of the adventure for further details.

Destroying the artifact or the heart within it breaks its enchantment. The artifact has an effective armor rating of 6 and 40 Health due to its arcane construction. Bringing it to 0 Health smashes it. It can also be opened with a successful TN 15 Intelligence (Arcane Lore) test to access what's inside, although a failed test results in 2d6 penetrating damage in the form of a surge of life-draining energy. Once it is open, the heart can be removed as a major action with no test required, which breaks the enchantment.

If the Heart's Blood enchantment is broken, all of its victims revert to their mortal forms. For Ryal, Sebastian, and Vivienne, this is instantly fatal: Ryal being previously dead, and Sebastian and Vivienne having long outlived their mortal lifespans. Vesper, Alek, and Ormond, however, survive the process and return to being living, mortal people once again.

There's one additional twist to the Heart's Blood that even Sebastian isn't aware of: An adept touching the artifact can use the Heart Shaping and Psychic Domination arcana on any arcane vampire created by it, including Ryal and Sebastian, even if the adept does not know those arcana. Doing so, however, is sorcery and a corrupt act (see **Corruption** in *Blue Rose* **Chapter 2**). An adept touching the artifact is instantly aware of this opportunity, sensing it intuitively.

Sitting on the arm of the throne beside Sebastian is a young man, immensely pale with dark, hollow eyes and long, curly blond hair. His arm drapes possessively around Sebastian in an attempt to hold him despite his near constant fidgeting. An aura of danger and corruption seems to radiate from the saturnine blond figure. He wears simple pants, and a once white silk shirt that has yellowed with age.

Sebastian admits he is disappointed it took the characters this long to find him, since they were all in the same room not so long ago. He even danced with one of them, he points out, holding the fiendishly-horned mask to his face for a moment before lowering it, laughing; a golden yet predatory sound. He, unlike his companion, is dressed like a young rake: a billowing shirt, brocade vest, and tall leather boots. His laughter ceases abruptly when he introduces his lover, Ryal, stating simply it is Ryal's love for him that has made all of this possible, and why they both must kill. "It's us or them," he says. "And that's always the answer—you protect your own, always, even if the cost is blood," he continues, a hint of sadness in his voice.

The diamond-like artifact from Inara's papers sits just beside the throne on a decorative pedestal; a brocade cloth lies crumpled on the floor beneath it, obviously recently discarded there. Sebastian, arrogant and still perversely proud of his cleverness in designing the Hearts' Blood despite all the grief it has caused the pair, insists on keeping it on open display. But Ryal cannot bear to look at it, and uses the cloth to cover over the artifact whenever Sebastian leaves on a "hunting trip."

If any of the characters ask about the arcane device, Sebastian explains he made it to save Ryal after he'd been murdered by a jealous rival. Sebastian didn't expect it to turn Ryal into something akin to a vampire, or that his lover would pass the curse on to him. Sadly, he explains, animal blood isn't enough to sate their thirst; the cost of immortality proved to be human lives. "Humanity is broken anyway," he mutters, obviously trying to justify his actions to himself as much as to those listening. "They're always killing each other. They wanted Ryal dead, so this is no more than they deserve."

Despite the fact Ryal made Sebastian, it seems Sebastian is the one in charge of keeping them both alive. Ryal seems loving and loyal toward Sebastian, but otherwise strangely detached from the events happening around him; his dead eyes seem full of despair, longing, and self-loathing. The heroes get the distinct impression coming back from the dead has left him broken, lethargic, and uninterested in existence apart from his lover.

If the characters permitted Vesper to come along, the meeting doesn't run quite so smoothly. Vesper's first response is to growl at Sebastian, fangs bared. She doesn't care about Ryal, as he had no hand in her conversion. She hisses how she has waited for this moment to come, to see Sebastian's blood spray across the floor and the "life" leave his dead, pathetic eyes. Sebastian is completely nonplussed but amused by her tirade, as he can control any of his vampire "children" easily, although it's obvious he's surprised she thought she could resist him.

Making eye contact with her, Sebastian psychically dominates Vesper and she is drawn back to his side whether she wants to be there or not. She walks up to his throne to stand by him like a guard dog, or a complacent companion. It's an uncomfortable thing to watch. Vesper doesn't attack Sebastian—she can't—but, should the characters attack, she follows Sebastian's orders to deal with them without batting an eyelash.

As long as he is engaged in conversation with the heroes, Sebastian answers any questions honestly; the truth is more frightening than a lie, after all. He is of the opinion there is no point in hiding anything from his "guests" when he and Ryal plan to kill them shortly anyway. He loves sharing the shocking information that it was Lady Hyacanthus who all but gave Vesper into his hands, and that she was also responsible for the deaths on the Longhaven estates.

As they talk, he tries to convince the characters to become vampires in a few different ways:

- Who wouldn't want to live forever? Young, beautiful, powerful—they could have anything they wanted. People die all the time—they're just part of the food chain but there's no reason the heroes have to join them.

- There are still so many things taboo in the world. For Ryal and Sebastian, there are no taboos—not even death can hold them.

- He and Ryal have seen human lifetimes. Nothing really lasts; everything is fleeting. It doesn't matter who is in charge, so long as you can protect your own, and hold on to what is yours—forever.

Hopefully, the characters won't be swayed by Sebastian's arguments and charm, although, if they are, Sebastian does not hesitate in beginning their conversion, offering them his blood to drink. If none of them accept his offer, the Silver Knight attacks first, heading straight for Sebastian. If they do take him up on his offer, the Silver Knight still attacks, in an attempt to prevent any conversion from happening.

Once the fight begins, Sebastian orders his vampire children to "Seize them!" Vesper attacks, along with the hidden Alek, Ormond, and Vivienne, who were lying in wait for their master's command. The vampires attempt to incapacitate their foes (see **Incapacitating** in *Blue Rose* **Chapter 1**), or restrain them so they and their masters can feed on them. The latter involves a regular melee attack but, instead of doing damage, initiates an opposed Strength (Might) test. If the attacker wins, the defender is unable to move or take physical actions other than attempting to break free, which requires another opposed Strength (Might) test as a major action on the restrained character's turn.

Before the end of the fight, Sebastian gains the upper hand in his face off with the Silver Knight, running her through. As she lies bleeding out on the throne room floor,

her final, gasped words are: "Please...Take me back to the river." This may be the final distraction necessary to allow a player character to slip past Sebastian to reach the Heart's Blood.

Destroying the artifact is ultimately the only way to truly overcome the vampires and free Vesper (see **The Heart's Blood** sidebar). Although the heroes might be able to overcome the vampires in combat, perhaps even destroy them, they cannot permanently destroy Ryal, nor can they restore any of the vampires, while the artifact exists.

PART 4
CONCLUSION

After their confrontation at the Red Cliffs, the characters make their way back to Castle Meridian. The Silver Knight is dead, and the heroes must decide whether or not to honor her final request and transport her body back to the Silver River. There is also the matter of dealing with Lady Hyacanthus, now the heroes know the extent of her involvement in recent events, and of what to do with the restored former vampires who survived the final confrontation.

Scenes 2 and **3** can be played in either order. Bear in mind, however, that although the characters pass Castle Longhaven before they reach Meridian, Vesper has absolutely no desire to see Lady Hyacanthus or her precious stronghold and, after her heart to heart with the heroes (**Scene 1**), is keen to return home as quickly as possible.

SCENE 1
THE LONG WALK HOME

ROLEPLAYING ENCOUNTER

If saved from her vampiric existence and restored to life, Vesper is quite a different person. On the trip back, she's quiet, sullen, and depressed, but the anger and darkness in her before is gone. If any of the characters want to talk to her, listen to how she's feeling, and offer her support, it helps her begin the healing process before she returns to Castle Meridian. She speaks in soft tones, indicating the pain she's struggling with as a survivor of all of these horrors.

"I just see their faces, all the time, every time I close my eyes. I can't sleep at night, because I still taste their blood in my mouth and it makes my whole body shudder. You wouldn't believe the horrible things I saw... the horrible things I did. I don't really know how I can go on living, or go home, with all of these terrible deeds I've committed. I was a monster. I should be tried for murder. I'll need to find out who they were and give money or some kind of restitution to their families. Oh, and for all the people my children killed, too. Alek did so much harm; I can't believe I even made him..."

Vesper goes on in a diatribe of painful confession and tears, but talking about it soothes her. It's good to remind her that her vampirism was a curse. Everything she did wasn't really her, but what that curse compelled her to do. It's what Sebastian, and Ryal, compelled her to do. Now she's free, she has the ability to be whoever she wants to be, but she can't go back to exactly who she was. Everybody else goes through this, too, though, to some extent, she admits; nobody remains unchanged in the world.

Alek and Ormond are similarly traumatized by their experience and in even worse shape than Vesper, barely speaking or interacting with anyone. It will take considerable time and healing for them to recover, if at all.

SCENE 2

BACK IN MERIDIAN

ROLEPLAYING ENCOUNTER

Before they enter the Meridians' lands, the heroes must cross the Silver River where, provided they brought the body of the Silver Knight with them, they have a promise to keep.

HEALING WATERS

Although we have put this scene here, it can occur whenever the characters reach an accessible point along the Silver River on their journey back to Longhaven and Meridian.

If the Silver Knight's body is placed in the river, she awakens with a sudden, sharp intake of breath and sits up. Her wound vanishes, and she is, inexplicably, alive and whole again. She struggles to her feet, astounded she has been restored. The vision she had during the Battle of the Three Hills was true, after all! Sabeline kneels in the mud and silently gives thanks to the waters that saved her.

If one of the characters wants to gather up some of the water to take with them, it acts as a healing elixir (*Blue Rose* **Chapter 11**, **Arcane Elixirs**) for them, since they, too, have defended Longhaven and the Silver River. It won't bring someone back from the dead in the way it did the Silver Knight, but it does heal quite effectively. The characters can gather two doses of healing elixir for each of them. Any further river water is just ordinary water.

HOME AT LAST

The wolves of Meridian await the characters' return and howl at them in greeting. The black wolf nods at them, seemingly in approval, before trotting off into the countryside, followed by its pack mates.

The reunion of Talulah, Yvayne, and Vesper is a teary one. Talulah and Yvayne welcome their wife back with open arms and Vesper reluctantly returns to them. They show their gratitude to the heroes with rewards: small, wolf-shaped metal pins that mark them as friends to Meridian's wolves (arcane items the animals recognize in the wild; they won't attack anyone wearing such a pin and may come to their aid, if they are in need). See also *Blue Rose* **Chapter 11: Rewards** for further suggestions.

Before the characters leave, Vesper thanks them for everything they've done for her. She smiles, even, and says they're all amazing people, and that she's so grateful they were there for her and able to bring her back home.

SCENE 3

BACK IN LONGHAVEN

ROLEPLAYING ENCOUNTER

The heroes enjoy a safe and uneventful trip back to Longhaven. When they reach the castle, it is still morning, and the Silver River is gleams in the sunlight. All seems all calm here.

LADY HYACANTHUS' TALE

Castle Longhaven welcomes the characters back and, as they enter through the large, intricately carved doors, they see Lady Hyacanthus framed in a tower window, looking down at them. Her beautiful hair shines in the sunlight as she turns away from them, frowning.

The Castle is quieter than the last time the characters were here. There are vendors' striped tents in the open spaces, set up to sell various metal, clay, and wood crafts. The smell of fire and metal are on the autumn air, wafting in from the blacksmiths' forges and potters' kilns embedded into the castle's framework.

The Silver Knight speaks to a page, insisting on holding counsel with Lady Hyacanthus. The page nods, saying the noble will meet with them over mead this afternoon. First, she insists they clean up and make themselves comfortable. It is clear she is making them wait on purpose, but couching it in terms of etiquette. The characters are escorted back to the rooms they occupied before, and are free to roam about the castle until the afternoon. Penelope has secreted herself away until the proposed meeting time, and refuses to speak to anyone beforehand.

At last, the time of their meeting arrives, and the heroes are escorted to Lady Hyacanthus' study once more. She's sitting behind her desk, upon which lies a pile of neatly stacked papers, pen and ink, a few history books, and a wax seal. Penelope is dressed resplendently in a green robe with long sleeves and a high collar. A turquoise necklace compliments the green of the dress and her eyes perfectly. She smiles thinly when the characters enter the room. When the Silver Knight sees her, it somehow calms the anger she had earlier. As stoic as ever, the Knight waits for her Lady or the characters to speak before uttering a word herself.

Everyone is offered mead in some of the copper goblets made here at the castle. If they haven't already sampled it, the heroes find it to be delicious.

Lady Hyacanthus sets the conversation going by saying:

"I would be grateful if you would tell me all that has transpired since you left."

As Penelope listens to their stories of what happened at the Red Cliffs, a great sadness and shame falls over her. Her whole demeanor seems, for the first time, heavy with a terrible burden, her usual grace and etiquette vanishing.

At some point in the proceedings, the Silver Knight bursts out:

"How did you expect me to protect you if I didn't know about this so-called vampire lord? How could you have kept such a secret from me?"

Angrily, Lady Hyacanthus asks how the knight dares question her authority. She has no idea what it's like to rule over a castle for many years, to shoulder all this responsibility—alone! It's an emotional outburst the characters haven't witnessed from Penelope before and seems quite out of character compared to the demure hostess they're used to. Then, almost as suddenly, her tone becomes conciliatory.

"I was weak. I...I know that now. Years of being alone in this castle, surrounded by beauty, prosperity—even good counsel—all I wanted was for someone to love me and be with me here. I saw what Talulah and Yvayne had and I envied them. When Vesper came, I thought, at last, I, too, could have someone to keep me company through the long nights; someone to share the darkness with during the approaching winter, so we could keep each other warm. That was all that I wanted!

"When Vesper fell in love with Talulah and Yvayne, I could feel the panic deep in my chest. It was a terrible envy, and it grew like a sickness in my heart. They already had each other; why did they get someone else to love them too?

"I don't know what I thought would happen, asking for some kind of miracle from that vampire to keep Vesper all to myself. That we would all live happily ever after once the creature scared Yvayne and Talulah away? That I could trust such a thing, centuries old, that knew only darkness and manipulation? I was foolish, but now I fear I've made my pact, and must accept the consequences."

A single tear falls from Lady Hyacanthus' eye. She seizes a silver letter opener from her desk and moves to plunge it into her own heart. A successful TN 11 Dexterity (Initiative) test allows characters to stop her. If they fail, the Silver Knight intervenes instead. Lady Penelope collapses into her rescuer's arms, sobbing uncontrollably.

Lady Hyacanthus feels she has been cursed as well, but only by the terrible things she's done to the people around her and the woman she desired. Once they prevent her from actually killing herself, Lady Hyacanthus releases the burden that has been in her heart. She weeps, and thanks them for all they've done, saying she hasn't felt herself since Sebastian came to her in her dreams that night. She regrets all the awful things she's done. She needed someone to come and clean up the mess she made, and she's grateful the heroes were able to do what she could not.

It is up to the characters what they do with Lady Hyacanthus after her confession. Depending on their affiliations, they may wish to take her back to Aldis or to a nearby domain to be judged by the law for putting her own people at such dire risk, or they might send a letter with all the information they've learned, including Penelope employing them to rectify the problem, to their superiors asking for advice on how to proceed. The heroes may even decide she has suffered enough, and take no further action, although they will have to convince Penelope not to turn herself over to the authorities in that case. Otherwise, Lady Hyacanthus and the Silver Knight largely defer to whatever decision the characters make.

If, in the end, Longhaven ends up being in need of a new noble to govern it, this may be an excellent opportunity for you to award a noble player character with a permanent domain, or to elevate a character (or characters) to the

nobility and entrust them with Longhaven, starting a new chapter in the series. Certainly, the new noble(s) would have the loyalty and friendship of both the Silver Knight and the neighboring Ladies Meridian.

ALLIES & ADVERSARIES

Here are the statistics for the main NPCs encountered during the events of **The Wanton Curse**.

LADY PENELOPE HYACANTHUS

LADY PENELOPE HYACANTHUS

Penelope Hyacanthus has always had a way with people; a natural social grace that brought her to pursue nobility and to eventually work her way up to governing to domain of Longhaven. Unfortunately, Penelope's skill in handling people made her used to getting what she wants from them, and the prospect of being denied the lovely Vesper gnawed ceaselessly at her mind and conscience. She yielded to the psychic whispers of the vampire Sebastian and now feels trapped by her mistake.

THE LADIES MERIDIAN

TALULAH MERIDIAN

Talulah and Yvayne are a marriage of equals in all regards: Both passionate, devoted to the protection and to the good of Meridian and its people, and both equally in love with the lost Vesper. Talulah and Yvayne come from families with a history of service to Aldis and Meridian: Yvayne's mother was an adept who served the nobles of Castle Meridian, and Talulah's father was a traveling noble. The two women earned noble titles and accepted co-governance of Meridian after their marriage. Now they are torn between their duties to their domain, their people, and each other and their grief from the loss of their beloved wife, allowing the needs of Meridian to languish. They know Lady Hyacanthus dislikes them but have no idea of the depth of her complicity in what happened to Vesper.

YVAYNE MERIDIAN

LADY PENELOPE HYACANTHUS

ABILITIES (FOCUSES)	
1	ACCURACY (LIGHT BLADES)
3	COMMUNICATION (DECEPTION, ETIQUETTE, PERSUASION)
0	CONSTITUTION
1	DEXTERITY (CALLIGRAPHY)
1	FIGHTING
1	INTELLIGENCE
2	PERCEPTION
0	STRENGTH
1	WILLPOWER

SPEED	HEALTH	DEFENSE	ARMOR RATING
11	20	11	0

WEAPON	ATTACK ROLL	DAMAGE
DAGGER	+3	1D6+1

SPECIAL QUALITIES

FAVORED STUNTS: And Another Thing (1 SP), Bon Mot, Sway the Crowd

TALENTS: Intrigue (Journeyman), Oratory (Novice)

WEAPONS GROUPS: Brawling, Light Blades

EQUIPMENT: Dagger

THREAT: MINOR

THE LADIES MERIDIAN

ABILITIES (FOCUSES)	
1	ACCURACY (LIGHT BLADES)
2	COMMUNICATION (ETIQUETTE, PERSUASION, ROMANCE)
1	CONSTITUTION
2	DEXTERITY (ARTISAN)
1	FIGHTING
2	INTELLIGENCE (CULTURAL LORE)
2	PERCEPTION (EMPATHY)
0	STRENGTH
2	WILLPOWER (COURAGE)

SPEED	HEALTH	DEFENSE	ARMOR RATING
12	20	12	0

WEAPON	ATTACK ROLL	DAMAGE
DAGGER	+3	1D6+1

SPECIAL QUALITIES

FAVORED STUNTS: And Another Thing (1 SP), Bon Mot, Sway the Crowd

TALENTS: Armor Training (Novice), Inspire (Novice), Noble (Novice), Observation (Novice)

WEAPONS GROUPS: Brawling, Bows, Light Blades, and Staves

EQUIPMENT: Dagger

THREAT: MINOR

SABELINE THORNTON, THE SILVER KNIGHT

Sabeline Thornton, the Silver Knight, is a local legend in Longhaven, where she has served its nobility and people for decades. In the service of Lady Ilya Hyacanthus, Sabeline fought valiantly against a shadowspawn horde that invaded the Silver River region and helped to hold them off almost single-handedly. Her dedication to her oaths and her duty are paramount, but more recently,

SABELINE THORNTON

Sabeline has become concerned for Lady Penelope, Ilya's daughter and successor as noble of Longhaven. While Penelope has always been the model of the social graces the battle-hardened and practical knight has always lacked, of late her pleasant and winning nature seems to mask a deep pain. and sadness Sabeline does not yet understand. Unfortunately, the Silver Knight's charge refuses to confide in her, and she feels unable to press Penelope to do so.

SABELINE THORNTON

ABILITIES (FOCUSES)	
4	ACCURACY (BOWS, LIGHT BLADES)
1	COMMUNICATION
2	CONSTITUTION
2	DEXTERITY (STEALTH)
4	FIGHTING (HEAVY BLADES)
1	INTELLIGENCE
2	PERCEPTION (SEARCHING)
2	STRENGTH (INTIMIDATION)
3	WILLPOWER (MORALE)

SPEED	HEALTH	DEFENSE	ARMOR RATING
12	45	12	8

WEAPON	ATTACK ROLL	DAMAGE
CROSSBOW	+6	2D6+2
DAGGER	+6	1D6+3
LONGSWORD	+6	2D6+2

SPECIAL QUALITIES

FAVORED STUNTS: Knock Prone, Lethal Blow, Skirmish

TALENTS: Armor Training (Master), Guardian (Journeyman), Single Weapon Style (Journeyman), Weapon and Shield Style (Journeyman)

WEAPONS GROUPS: Bludgeons, Bows, Brawling, Heavy Blades, and Light Blades

EQUIPMENT: Crossbow, Dagger, Heavy Metal Armor, Longsword

THREAT: MODERATE

SEBASTIAN, ARCANE VAMPIRE

Sebastian of Meridian was a promising, brilliant young adept in service to the noble of Castle Meridian, with a burning hunger for arcane lore and skill, which led him to study certain dubious works from the time of the Sorcerer Kings. When his lover Ryal was murdered, Sebastian took terrible vengeance and used sorcery to "restore" Ryal's life, transforming him into a vampire-like creature. Sebastian

SEBASTIAN

was his lover's first victim, and the first to receive his blood-curse, sealing his fate and the path of corruption he embarked upon. Now Sebastian is a saturnine creature of appetite and cruelty, Ryal's eternal caretaker and companion.

Sebastian's Spawn

The servitor arcane vampires, including Vesper, are the spawn (or "children") of Sebastian or Vesper, and relatively recent creations. They include the men Alek and Ormond, turned by Vesper since she became a vampire, and the woman Vivienne, turned by Sebastian decades ago to provide some company and to round out his unnatural "family" with Ryal.

Although Vesper retains some of her human nature, the other three have entirely given in to their unnatural vampiric appetites, which has made their Fate entirely dominant in their personalities (see **Destiny and Fate** in *Blue Rose* **Chapter 2**).

Vesper can exert Psychic Domination over Alek and Ormond, if she chooses, and Sebastian and Ryal can expert Psychic Domination over any of the four, as their "elders."

Use the given stat block for Alek, Ormond, and Vivienne. Vesper has similar traits, but also has the Dexterity (Artisan) focus, the Intelligence (Natural Lore) focus, and has the Self-Discipline focus in place of Morale.

Sebastian, Arcane Vampire

Abilities (Focuses)

3	Accuracy (Bite, Brawling, Light Blades)
5	Communication (Deception, Etiquette, Leadership, Psychic)
4	Constitution
2	Dexterity (Initiative)
3	Fighting
5	Intelligence (Sorcery Lore)
3	Perception (Hearing, Seeing, Smelling)
4	Strength (Climbing, Intimidation)
6	Willpower (Animism)

Speed	Health	Defense	Armor Rating
12	120	12	2

Weapon	Attack Roll	Damage
Bite	+5	2d6+4
Rapier	+5	1d6+5
Unarmed	+5	1d6+6

Special Qualities

Arcana: Animal Summoning, Mind Delving, Mind Reading, Move Object, Psychic Contact, Psychic Shield, Second Sight

Favored Stunts: Disarm, Enrage, Knock Prone (1 SP), Stunned Silence, Skirmish

A Light Snack: Sebastian can feed from someone without killing or infecting them, but the character is anemic for approximately six hours afterwards. This results in the character gaining a level of fatigue. Due to the circumstances through which it is acquired, this fatigue can only be reversed by sleeping for six hours, even if the character is only Winded or Fatigued; all other effects are appropriate to the level of fatigue suffered.

Blood Infection: Anyone who drinks Sebastian's tainted blood becomes an arcane vampire after the next sunset. Sebastian is always in psychic contact with all the arcane vampires he has spawned and can exert Psychic Domination (like the arcanum) over them at will with no fatigue.

Cunning Evasion: Sebastian can evade harm with unnatural swiftness, granting him an armor rating equal to his Dexterity while unarmored, so long as he remains mobile. The Pierce Armor combat stunt overcomes all of this armor, rather than reducing it by half.

Impaling: A wooden or silver weapon driven through Sebastian's chest where his heart is paralyzes, but does not kill, him. Staking Sebastian is a special combat stunt, costing 4 SP. Removing the weapon restores his mobility immediately.

Nocturnal Predator: A creature of darkness, Sebastian suffers no penalties from acting in darkness, natural or arcane. He can exert Psychic Domination (like the arcanum) over any predatory beast summoned with his Animal Summoning arcanum, without the need for psychic contact.

Undying: The sorcerous power sustaining Sebastian's unnatural life means he cannot truly die unless his body is entirely destroyed. Sebastian does not need to eat, drink, sleep, or breathe, and does not age. He can also regenerate Health equal to his Constitution as a special stunt, costing 2 SP.

Unnaturally Swift: When taking the Run action, Sebastian moves at ten times his Speed, able to cover distances with unnatural swiftness, either to attack or escape.

Warding: Certain signs of life, love, and purity are anathema to Sebastian. These include certain plants (particularly garlic, lily, rose, and wolfsbane), either fresh or dried; salt; sunlight; and any of the icons of the Primordials or the gods of Light. Sebastian cannot touch these things or affect them directly using arcana, and this protection extends to any creature carrying, holding, or presenting a warding item.

Weakness to Sunlight: Sunlight burns Sebastian, causing 3d6 penetrating damage per round for partial exposure and 6d6 penetrating damage per round in full sunlight. If reduced to 0 Health by sunlight or fire damage, Sebastian is destroyed.

Talents: Animism (Novice), Psychic (Master), Shaping (Novice)

Weapons Groups: Brawling, Light Blades, Natural Weapons

Equipment: Rapier

Threat: Dire

Ryal, Arcane Master Vampire

Ryal of Meridian never asked to live forever, but he loved the handsome, ambitious, and brilliant adept Sebastian, in service to the nobles of the domain, and that meant Ryal's days were numbered. Murdered by a jealous rival, Ryal awoke to a nightmare existence of incessant hunger. His first victim was his beloved Sebastian, and Ryal "saved" him by passing his curse along. Watching Sebastian become increasingly

RYAL

cruel and vicious as the long nights and years passed has shattered the bright and loving young man Ryal once was, and he spends his endless existence in a stupor, unable to acknowledge or accept what he and Sebastian have become. Ryal rarely acts other than to sigh and cling to his beloved, although when threatened, his feral instincts take over and he fights viciously. Otherwise, he relies almost entirely on Sebastian to care for him and make decisions.

Arcane Vampire Spawn

ABILITIES (FOCUSES)	
3	ACCURACY (BITE, BRAWLING)
1	COMMUNICATION (DECEPTION)
4	CONSTITUTION
4	DEXTERITY (STEALTH)
3	FIGHTING (CLAWS)
2	INTELLIGENCE
3	PERCEPTION (HEARING, SEEING, SMELLING)
4	STRENGTH (CLIMBING, INTIMIDATION)
4	WILLPOWER (MORALE)

SPEED	HEALTH	DEFENSE	ARMOR RATING
14	75	14	4

WEAPON	ATTACK ROLL	DAMAGE
BITE	+5	2D6+4
UNARMED	+5	1D6+4

SPECIAL QUALITIES

Favored Stunts: Knock Prone (1 SP), Seize the Initiative, Set Up, Skirmish

A Light Snack: As Sebastian's Special Quality.

Blood Infection: As Sebastian's Special Quality.

Cunning Evasion: As Sebastian's Special Quality.

Impaling: As Sebastian's Special Quality.

Nocturnal Predator: As Sebastian's Special Quality, except these vampires cannot Dominate animals.

Undying: As Sebastian's Special Quality.

Unnaturally Swift: As Sebastian's Special Quality.

Warding: As Sebastian's Special Quality.

Weakness to Sunlight: As Sebastian's Special Quality.

Talents: Scouting (Novice), Unarmed Style (Master)

Weapon Groups: Brawling, Natural Weapons

THREAT: MAJOR

Ryal, Arcane Master Vampire

ABILITIES (FOCUSES)	
3	ACCURACY (BITE, BRAWLING)
2	COMMUNICATION
4	CONSTITUTION
2	DEXTERITY (INITIATIVE)
2	FIGHTING
2	INTELLIGENCE
3	PERCEPTION (HEARING, SEEING, SMELLING)
4	STRENGTH
6	WILLPOWER

SPEED	HEALTH	DEFENSE	ARMOR RATING
12	120	12	2

WEAPON	ATTACK ROLL	DAMAGE
BITE	+5	2D6+4
UNARMED	+5	1D6+4

SPECIAL QUALITIES

A Light Snack: As Sebastian's Special Quality.

Blood Infection: As Sebastian's Special Quality.

Unnaturally Swift: As Sebastian's Special Quality.

Cunning Evasion: As Sebastian's Special Quality.

Heart-Bound: Ryal is arcanely bound to the Heart's Blood artifact containing his living heart; he cannot move more than 100 feet away from it without becoming paralyzed and incapacitated (much like when he is impaled, following). If the artifact's enchantment is ever broken, Ryal is destroyed, his unnatural existence ended.

Impaling: As Sebastian's Special Quality of the same name-except Ryal is capable of purely mental actions, including using psychic arcana, while paralyzed.

Nocturnal Predator: As Sebastian's Special Quality of the same name, except he cannot Dominate animals.

Undying: As Sebastian's Special Quality, except Ryal automatically regenerates 1 Health per round. Even if his body is completely destroyed, such as by fire or arcane means, Ryal will reincorporate at the next sunset and begin regaining Health, so long as his arcane heart still exists.

Warding: As Sebastian's Special Quality.

Weapon Groups: Brawling, Natural Weapons

THREAT: MAJOR

HANDOUT: CHILDHOOD FEARS

To make a random selection, roll 1d6 to select the column (1 or 2 for Column 1, 3 or 4 for Column 2, 5 or 6 for Column 3). Roll another 1d6 to select a result from that column.

ROLL	COLUMN 1	COLUMN 2	COLUMN 3
1	Spiders/insects	Darkness	Being buried alive
2	Fire	Water	Knives/sharp objects
3	Heights	Flying/floating	Cramped spaces
4	Wild/loud animals*	Loud noises	Thunderstorms
5	Strangers	Death	Separation**
6	Masks	Blood	Snakes

*Can apply to a specific species, such as dogs or bears, or more generally to any particularly loud or uncontrolled animal.

**Separation from a loved one or specific object, such as special blanket or doll.

HANDOUT: THE POEM

By ⬛⬛ rs ⬛⬛ and ⬛⬛⬛⬛ on
in ⬛⬛⬛⬛⬛ on an ⬛⬛⬛⬛.
⬛⬛ trap ⬛⬛⬛, y hope ⬛⬛ h,
he ⬛⬛ er of good ⬛⬛⬛ ab⬛.
⬛⬛⬛⬛ mar s ⬛⬛ bove my ⬛,
May ⬛⬛⬛⬛ wa⬛ me ⬛⬛ bed

HANDOUT: MEAL DIARY

Met Lycon Byrhill. Diagnosed with imbalance of the humors and began treatment as follows:

Day 1: filtered asparagus juice breakfast; mashed soup supper; one orange dinner

Day 2: strained tomato soup breakfast; one orange supper; mashed soup dinner

Day 3: one orange breakfast; filtered asparagus juice supper; strained tomato soup dinner

Day 4: one orange breakfast; one orange supper; mashed soup dinner with orange rind

Day 5: one orange breakfast; no supper due to poor behavior; filtered asparagus juice dinner

Day 6: orange rind breakfast; strained tomato soup supper; mashed soup dinner

Day 7: orange rind breakfast; mashed soup supper; one orange dinner

Note: Daily complaints of headaches and pain in right side just below ribs. Imbalance of humors seems to be worsening. Three meals per day seem too much for the poor boy. Reducing to two and cancelling outdoor exercise.

HANDOUT: ERILA QINREL

Erila met Jaymes Gloamhale when she was a Jarzoni orphan and he a young healer who visited the orphanage where she lived. When she was old enough to leave, he offered her a job at his sanatorium. She helped tend the sick children there, acting as nurse and teacher. Grieving families brought more sick children to their door, desperate for help.

Despite their best efforts, tombstones bloomed like flowers in the backyard. Erila gradually realized Jaymes was not healing, but hurting. Sick children arrived, then only got worse. She snuck them food and medicine; Gloamhale didn't know. He fell in love with her; she didn't know. Cradling another dying child, she decided to leave. Jaymes didn't want her to go; he wanted to marry her, but she was engaged to a Jarzoni man in the village.

Gloamhale flew into a rage. He lost all control. He lost physical form. It was as though he became a being made of pure fury and possessiveness. He melted into the very floor. Erila tried to flee. Doors flew shut in front of her, and furniture moved to block her path. The house itself turned against her. He had become the house.

He imagined her to have transformed into some kind of beast. He tracked her down like one of the animals in the parlor. He slaughtered her. He slaughtered the remaining children. The house was discovered. There was horror. The house was flooded. It lay dormant, but not dead.

The water receded. The ghosts grew restless. They cried out. They cried out for love, for companionship. They cried out to be remembered. They cried out, and other children came. They wasted away among the dead. The cycle continues, and there is no peace.

Other facts:

- Erila despises being a ghost and being trapped in this house. The casual use of something as dangerous as arcana goes against everything she believes in as a Jarzoni, and it is torturous to feel condemned to spending an eternity trapped in a house so full of wild, unrestrained forces. She hates even having to use it for the purpose of this communication.

- Whenever a party member uses arcana, Erila forces the possessed hero to say something to the effect of, "May Leonoth have mercy on our souls," "Leonoth forgive me/him/her," "May Leonoth smite the Shadow lurking in our hearts," or similar.

- When alive, Erila possessed some natural arcane talent, although she tried to hide it and stifle it. She (incorrectly) blames her lack of control as a child for the accident that led to the death of her parents.

- If the possessed hero enters the playroom, Erila can explain Jaymes' thoughts on playtime. It was considered dangerously stimulating for sick children (though useful as a motivator) and severely restricted. Toys were kept under lock and key most of the time for the children's safety. Erila may admit she saw logic in this at first and regrets being so blinded by Jaymes' authority and charm.

- Erila knows the haints are responsible for the symbol on the floor of the playroom. It was created in a time when the haints retained more of their former selves. Some of the children at the sanatorium were "corrupted" by "sorcery" and had hoped to accomplish something by creating the symbol. She does not know what their intent was and tried to distance herself from this activity.

- She does not know how her spirit can be freed from this place.

STORM OVER KAMALA
HANDOUT: THE NOTICE

Wanted: Skilled adventurers with shadowspawn experience to reclaim site of Rezean heritage. Must bring own weapons. Military experience preferred, knowledge of Rezean territory and dangers suggested. Compensation: based on experience.

Ask for Jessari

Inquire at The Blue Bee

A WANTON CURSE
HANDOUT: THE INVITATION

Dearest Friends of the Realm,

You are hereby invited to a celebration of Gravihain Eve is to be held at Castle Longhaven. Your presence is requested on this occasion by Lady Penelope Hyacanthus, the right appointed noble of Longhaven.

Please wear suitable Gravihain costumes and masks to celebrate this darkening time of the year.

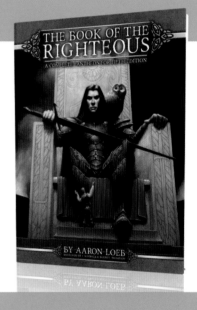
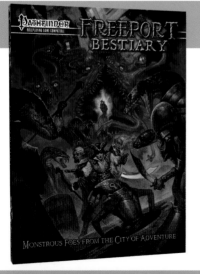

FANTASY AGE BESTIARY

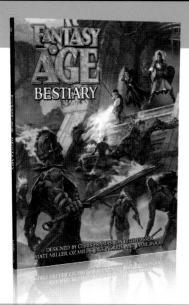

A SOURCEBOOK FOR THE FANTASY AGE RPG

What does every fantasy RPG campaign need? Monsters! Monsters! Monsters! The Fantasy AGE Bestiary gives Game Masters a plethora of new foes to challenge their players, from classics like the basilisk and minotaur to new monsters like the eldritch crown and shard lord. Each creature is fully detailed, with background information, adventure hooks, game stats, and variants. This beautiful full-color hardback is the first sourcebook for the Fantasy AGE RPG and an indispensable resource for Game Masters. Unleash the creatures within these pages on your Fantasy AGE players at your peril!

144 PAGE HARDBACK BOOK. MSRP: $32.95, GRR6004

CINEMA AND SORCERY

THE COMPREHENSIVE GUIDE TO FANTASY FILM

From the dawn of feature films, fans—be they artists, gamers, visionaries, writers, or dreamers—have drawn inspiration from the big screen. Now, between the covers of Cinema & Sorcery, embark on a decades-long journey through time from the earliest days of sword and sorcery films up to the present day. Learn the who, the what, the where, and the how of your favorite fantasy movies (and perhaps a few you may have never even heard of until now). Fifty films are covered in great detail, followed by shorter entries for every fantasy film we could find. So turn up your Krull soundtrack, slip into your Labyrinth t-shirt, and brush up on your Princess Bride quotes—this is Cinema & Sorcery: The Comprehensive Guide to Fantasy Film!

496 PAGE SOFTBACK. MSRP: $29.95, GRR4003

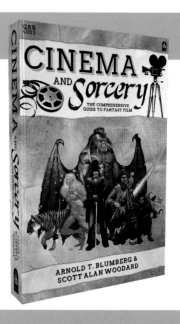

ATLAS OF EARTH-PRIME

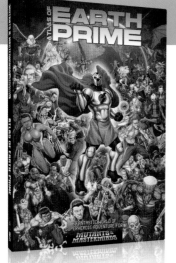

A CAMPAIGN SETTING FOR MUTANTS & MASTERMINDS

Visit a world not our own, but strangely familiar—a world of heroes and villains, of wonders and dangers, and limitless adventure! The Atlas of Earth-Prime is a trip around the world of the Freedom City and Emerald City settings for the Mutants & Masterminds RPG. Your heroes can explore the sites and perils of all seven continents, as well as fabled Atlantis, the Lost World, and the strange realms of Sub-Terra that lie at the center of the earth. Packed with locations, heroes, villains, and worldwide agencies, the Atlas of Earth-Prime is the campaign setting book Mutants & Masterminds fans have been waiting for!

264 PAGE FULL COLOR HARDBACK. MSRP $44.95, GRR5514

ROLL INITIATIVE!

Welcome to *Dragon Age*, a pen & paper roleplaying game of dark fantasy adventure. In *Dragon Age* you and your friends take on the personas of warriors, mages, and rogues in the world of Thedas and try to make your names by overcoming sinister foes and deadly challenges. Based on the hit video game franchise, the *Dragon Age RPG* brings the excitement of BioWare's rich fantasy world to the tabletop. This is classic roleplaying, where the story is yours to create and the action takes place in your imagination.

This comprehensive Core Rulebook includes the full rules for the *Dragon Age RPG* under one cover for the first time. The game features:

- The *Adventure Game Engine*, a rules system that is easy to learn and fun to play.

- An innovative stunt system that keeps the action cinematic and exciting.

- Complete level 1-20 advancement rules for mages, rogues, and warriors, plus specializations for each class such as the arcane warrior, assassin, berserker, force mage, marksman, and spirit warrior.

- Advice for both players and Game Masters, plus rules options for creating organizations, narrative mass combat, and rune magic.

- Adversaries for your heroes, from the lowly genlock to the mighty Archdemon!

- Extensive background information on the nations, peoples, and organizations of the world of Thedas.

- Three complete adventures, including a brand new introductory adventure.

- A variety of campaign frameworks for GMs to choose from. You can run a campaign during such events as the Fifth Blight, the Mage-Templar War, or the rise of the Inquisition.

The Dragon Age RPG was featured on Wil Wheaton's *Tabletop* show and it is a perfect portal to pen & paper roleplaying. So gather your friends, grab some dice, and get ready to enter a world of heroes and villains, of Grey Wardens and darkspawn, of gods and demons…the world of…

Dragon Age RPG Core Rulebook
440 pages, full color, hardback
MSRP: $59.95
Product Code: GRR2808
ISBN-13: 978-1-934547-62-5